MYSTERY FESTIVAL

Teacher's Guide

Elementary, my dear Watson (and middle school too)

Grades 2–8
(with modifications for Grade 1)

Skills

Observing, Comparing, Relating, Sorting, Classifying, Analyzing and Evaluating Evidence, Making Inferences, Distinguishing Evidence from Inference, Problem Solving, Drawing Conclusions, Communicating, Describing, Working in Teams, Logical Thinking, Organizing Data, Role-Playing, Debating, Drawing & Mapping

Concepts

Forensic Science, Evidence, Fingerprints, Footprints, Chromatography, Acids, Bases, Neutrals, pH Testing, Powder Testing, Thread Comparison Testing, Crystals, Dissolving, DNA

Science Themes

Systems & Interactions, Matter, Patterns of Change, Models and Simulations, Stability, Scale, Structure, Diversity and Unity

Mathematics Strands

Number, Pattern, Logic, Measurement

Nature of Science and Mathematics

Scientific Community, Changing Nature of Facts and Theories, Creativity and Constraints, Theory-Based and Testable, Cooperative Efforts, Objectivity and Ethics, Real-Life Applications, Interdisciplinary

Time

Five sessions, varying in length depending on options chosen

by
Kevin Beals
with
Carolyn Willard

LHS GEMS

Great Explorations in Math and Science (GEMS)
Lawrence Hall of Science
University of California at Berkeley

Cover Design
Lisa Haderlie Baker

Photographs
Richard Hoyt

Illustrations
Lisa Haderlie Baker
Carol Bevilacqua
Rose Craig
Lisa Klofkorn

Lawrence Hall of Science, University of California,
Berkeley, CA 94720

Chairman: Glenn T. Seaborg
Director: Marian C. Diamond

Publication of *Mystery Festival* was made possible by a grant from the Hewlett Packard Company. The GEMS Project and the Lawrence Hall of Science greatly appreciate this support.

Initial support for the origination and publication of the GEMS series was provided by the A.W. Mellon Foundation and the Carnegie Corporation of New York. Under a grant from the National Science , GEMS Leader's Workshops have been held across the country. GEMS has also received support from the McDonnell-Douglas Foundation and the McDonnell-Douglas Employees Community Fund, the Hewlett Packard Company, and the people at Chevron USA. GEMS also gratefully acknowledges the contribution of word processing equipment from Apple Computer, Inc. This support does not imply responsibility for statements or views expressed in publications of the GEMS program. For further information on GEMS leadership opportunities, or to receive a publication brochure and the *GEMS Network News*, please contact GEMS at the address and phone number below.

Reprinted 1995, 1996.

International Standard Book Number: 0-912511-89-3

COMMENTS WELCOME !

Great Explorations in Math and Science (GEMS) is an ongoing curriculum development project. GEMS guides are revised periodically, to incorporate teacher comments and new approaches. We welcome your criticisms, suggestions, helpful hints, and any anecdotes about your experience presenting GEMS activities. Your suggestions will be reviewed each time a GEMS guide is revised.
Please send your comments to:
GEMS Revisions, c/o Lawrence Hall of Science,
University of California, Berkeley, CA 94720.
The phone number is (510) 642-7771.

Great Explorations in Math and Science (GEMS) Program

The Lawrence Hall of Science (LHS) is a public science center on the University of California at Berkeley campus. LHS offers a full program of activities for the public, including workshops and classes, exhibits, films, lectures, and special events. LHS is also a center for teacher education and curriculum research and development.

Over the years, LHS staff have developed a multitude of activities, assembly programs, classes, and interactive exhibits. These programs have proven to be successful at the Hall and should be useful to schools, other science centers, museums, and community groups. A number of these guided-discovery activities have been published under the Great Explorations in Math and Science (GEMS) title, after an extensive refinement process that includes classroom testing of trial versions, modifications to ensure the use of easy-to-obtain materials, and carefully written and edited step-by-step instructions and background information to allow presentation by teachers without special background in mathematics or science.

Staff

Glenn T. Seaborg, **Principal Investigator**
Jacqueline Barber, **Director**
Kimi Hosoume, **Assistant Director**
Cary Sneider, **Curriculum Specialist**
Carolyn Willard, **GEMS Centers Coordinator**
Laura Tucker, **GEMS Workshop Coordinator**
Katharine Barrett, Kevin Beals, Ellen Blinderman, Beatrice Boffen, Gigi Dornfest, John Erickson, Jaine Kopp, Laura Lowell, Linda Lipner, Debra Sutter, Rebecca Tilley, **Staff Development Specialists**
Jan M. Goodman, **Mathematics Consultant**
Cynthia Eaton, **Administrative Coordinator**
Karen Milligan, **Distribution Coordinator**
Lisa Haderlie Baker, **Art Director**
Carol Bevilacqua and Lisa Klofkorn, **Designers**
Lincoln Bergman, **Principal Editor**
Carl Babcock, **Senior Editor**
Kay Fairwell, **Principal Publications Coordinator**
Erica De Cuir, Nancy Kedzierski, Felicia Roston, Vivian Tong, Stephanie Van Meter, Mary Yang, **Staff Assistants**

Contributing Authors

Jacqueline Barber
Katharine Barrett
Kevin Beals
Lincoln Bergman
Celia Cuomo
Gigi Dornfest
Philip Gonsalves
Jaine Kopp
Linda Lipner
Laura Lowell
Linda De Lucchi
Jean Echols
Jan M. Goodman
Alan Gould
Kimi Hosoume
Susan Jagoda
Larry Malone
Cary I. Sneider
Debra Sutter
Jennifer Meux White
Carolyn Willard

Reviewers

We would like to thank the following educators who reviewed, tested, or coordinated the reviewing of *this series* of GEMS materials in manuscript and draft form. Their critical comments and recommendations, **based on classroom presentation of these activities nationwide**, contributed significantly to these GEMS publications. Their participation in the review process does not necessarily imply endorsement of the GEMS program or responsibility for statements or views expressed. Their role in an invaluable one, and their feedback is carefully recorded and integrated as appropriate into the publications. **THANK YOU!**

ALASKA

Wasilla, Alaska

Iditarod Elementary School
- Cynthia Dolmas Curran
- Tacy M. Carr
- Carol Lowery
- Ruth Felberg

ARKANSAS

Jonesboro, Arkansas

Coordinator: Mark McJunkin

Valley View Elementary School
- Karen Rogers
- Jane Ryals
- Virginia Moore
- Faye Fowler

CALIFORNIA

Huntington Beach, California

Coordinator: Susan Spoeneman

Daniel Webster Elementary School
- Kathryn Donley
- Joan Prater
- Ruthie H. Mendoza
- Doris P. Lipiz

San Francisco Bay Area

Coordinators: Cynthia Ashley
Cynthia Eaton

Downer School, Berkeley
- Lina Prairie
- Kathleen Smallfield
- Laura Olson
- Emily Vogler
- Douglas Wheeler

Lafayette School, Lafayette
- Michael Meneghetti
- Linda Marsden
- Terese Atallah

Longfellow School, Berkeley
- Cris Barrere
- Hillary Hoppock

Malcolm X School, Berkeley
- Gloria Thornton
- Angela Archie
- DeEtte LaRue
- Jessie Shohara

John Marshall School, Oakland
- Lew Williams

Carl Munck School, Oakland
- Judy Finch
- Marka Carson
- Dorothy Hamilton
- Steven Miyamoto

Marie Murphy School, Richmond
- Mary Neuman
- Debby Callahan
- Patsy Christner
- Sandra Petzoldtt

Oxford School, Berkeley
- Barbara Edwards
- Carolyn Dobson
- Jessica Vaughan

Park Day School, Oakland
- Karen Corzan
- Michelle Krueger
- Harriet Cohen

Sequoia School, Oakland
- Lisa Taymuree
- Cindy Cathey
- Jeannie Kohl
- Barbara Schmidt
- Laurie Wingate

St. Augustine School, Oakland

Patricia Schmitz,
Diane Dias
Helen Raphael
Rita Samper

Steffan Manor School, Vallejo

Don Baer
Annie Howard
Bridget Winkley

COLORADO

Fort Collins, Colorado

Barton Elementary Sc

Ted P. Stoeck
Valeria A. Lin
Alice Atencio
Judith Viola

GEORGIA

Harlem, Georgia

North Harlem Elemen

Julie Sibilsky
Roberta A. Gr
Linda M. Barr
Barbara M. W

IDAHO

Sagle, Idaho

Sagle Elementary Sch

Betty Collins
Steve Guthrie
Susan E. Stev
Tim Hanna

KENTUCKY

Louisville, Kentucky

Fern Creek Elementary School

Charlotte Nedros
Ginny Gilliland
Donna J. Stevenson
Carol Porter

MICHIGAN

Grand Blanc, Michigan

Indian Hill Elementary School

Mary Ann Schloegl

TEXAS

Decatur, Texas

Coordinator: Shirley Watson

Decatur Elementary School

Shirley Watson
Carmen Antoine
Carol Hale
Agnes Burnett
Lori Clark

WASHINGTON

Forks, Washington

Coordinators: David Kennedy,
State Superintendent of Schools
Sherry Schaaf

Forks Elementary School

Mary Anne McClaire
Campbell Crawford
David N. McIrvin
Laurie Turner

Contents

Acknowledgments

GEMS Director Jacqueline Barber stands accused of being the source of the original inspiration that led to the creation of the *Mystery Festival*. Jacquey also reviewed the manuscript of this guide at key stages.

Very special thanks to our informant Ferdinand G. Rios, Ph.D., a forensic scientist who has taught classes in the subject on the University of California at Berkeley campus and elsewhere, and whose experience and friendly advice were of great assistance.

Many staff members of the Chemistry Department past and present have engaged in a conspiracy to play extremely helpful roles in the development of *Mystery Festival*. Special thanks to Sylvia Carol Velasquez and Grace Alba for their help during early stages of this project. Peri Ann Wood and Hernan Espinoza assisted with information on DNA. Lynn Barakos, Laura Lowell, and Rebecca Tilley took part in meetings to help transform the outreach festival into a GEMS guide. They made suggestions, sometimes over–ruled, but often sustained, on successive drafts based on their own extensive teaching and presentation experience. Special thanks to Lynn as well for researching background information on iodine and for carefully checking the "What You Need" and "Getting Ready" sections to help prepare the "Preparation Checklist" portions of the Summary Outlines. Thanks as well to Cynthia Ashley and Cynthia Eaton for coordination of the local and national testing process, and to Stephanie Van Meter of the GEMS staff for the assembly of the trial test kits.

Colin Hocking aided and abetted in early brainstorming of one of the mystery plots. Lincoln Bergman pleads guilty to being the author of the "What Is A Mystery?" poem, begs for lenience from the court, and justifies all lapses in meter or rhyme on the basis of "poetic license." Thanks also to Kayton C. Carter, Bernadette Lauraya, Margey Race, and John Michael Seltzer, present or former LHS staff members who allowed us to use their "mugs" to depict the imaginary suspects in the "Felix" mystery. As for Felix himself, there are reports that, for mysterious reasons, he never allowed himself to be photographed. Special canine thanks to unofficial Lawrence Hall of Science mascot, Samantha, the dog, whose footprints adorn the crime scene, and who was patient enough to allow her paws to be dipped in paint on at least three separate occasions.

Last but far from least, we wish to express our thanks to the students and teachers who have a long record of taking part in the hundreds of Mystery Festivals we've presented at California schools, in our summer "Crime Camps" and in other related Lawrence Hall of Science classes. Thanks as well to all students and teachers who helped us test these activities for publication as a GEMS guide. Selections from some of their writings are included in the guide. Trial-test teachers are acknowledged in the front of this guide. Very special GEMS appreciation to Mike Meneghetti and his class at Lafayette School in Lafayette California and to Judy Finch and Dorothy Hamilton and their classes at Carl Munck School in Oakland for allowing us to take the classroom photographs of students conducting the crime lab science tests that appear in this guide. The "crime scene" photos were taken at the Lawrence Hall of Science Summer Crime Camp, 1993.

WHAT IS A MYSTERY?

A mystery's a magnet
Attracting eager minds
We gather clues and evidence
And ponder what we find.

A mystery's a puzzle
Of pieces all askew
Putting it together
Is what detectives do.

A mystery's a winding maze
With choices we can make
We follow lines of evidence
To find which path to take.

A mystery's a questioning
A who, where, what, when, why
We reconstruct what happened
To distinguish truth from lie.

A mystery's the great unknown
Just waiting to be found
A speck of dust, a strand of hair,
Did someone hear a sound?

A mystery's the sudden shout
Clock ticking, creaking door,
Suspense and thrill and scariness
"Quoth the Raven—nevermore."

A mystery's exciting book
Or you can write your own
Create a plot and characters
Jessica Fletcher, Sherlock Holmes

A mystery gets curiouser
And curiouser, they say
Clues pile up inside our heads
Until, at last, one day

We see a way to solve it
A light begins to shine
It starts to fit together
In a logical design.

Then something else might happen
Another clue pops up
It's back then to the drawing board
To figure out what's up.

Solutions are elusive
It's wise to bide your time
It isn't always obvious
Who perpetrates a crime.

Elementary my dear Watson
Aha! Eureka! too
The moment of discovery
Jumps out at me and you

A mystery's a Festival
Of stations to explore
Whose fingerprints are left behind?
Whose tracks are on the floor?

A mystery's a Festival
It's yours to sleuth and share
In the *Mystery Festival* Hall of Fame
We're sure to find you there!

by L.B

For the past two years, Lawrence Hall of Science has presented Mystery Festivals as large group events, for up to 150 people at a time. During these Festivals, participants examine a make-believe "crime scene," and then conduct a variety of tests on the "evidence" at different learning stations around the room. This teacher's guide adapts the Mystery Festival for use in the classroom.

GEMS Festival guides differ from other GEMS guides in that they present students with a variety of different challenges at learning stations set up around the classroom, rather than a more structured presentation. ***A "learning station" is a classroom table, cluster of desks, or counter-top set up with equipment or materials designed to encourage students to make their own discoveries.*** **The class participates in exploration and investigation in an informal, student-centered way. Sessions 3 and 4 of both mysteries in this guide use this learning station format, as students conduct tests on the evidence at "crime lab" stations.**

Mystery Festival is one of several GEMS guides that adapt the large group festival format to learning stations in the classroom. We highly recommend the other GEMS Festival guides, including *Bubble Festival* and *Build It! Festival.*

●

Introduction

Using Science to Solve a Mystery/ Using a Mystery to Draw Students into Science

Everybody loves a mystery. Although some students might tell you that they don't like science, you'd be hard pressed to find one who doesn't like to investigate, explore, and do experiments. The *Mystery Festival* unit combines mystery and investigation in a highly exciting, engaging and educational experience. Your student-detectives will conduct many hands-on forensic science tests on evidence found at a "crime scene." Any one of these tests is interesting and educational in itself— together they add up to a powerful and motivating experience that your students will remember for years.

Because these mysteries (like all mysteries) are layered in complexity, some students (depending on grade level and experience) may arrive at fairly simple solutions. Other students may see through the superficial, misleading evidence and come up with more complicated solutions, even involving conspiracies, deceptions, and other conniving schemes. Throughout the entire *Mystery Festival*, from start to finish, you'll watch the gears turn in student-sleuth heads as they struggle to sort through the evidence. You'll see them perhaps change their minds many times, use a multitude of critical thinking skills, and directly experience both real-life applications of science and the joys of scientific exploration.

Session-by-Session

Forensic science is the application of science to issues of civil and criminal law, including using scientific tests and methods to help solve crimes. See "Behind the Scenes" on page 233 for more on forensic science.

Session 1: For the first class session of the unit, you set up the make-believe "crime scene" that will launch an entire five day festival of exciting investigations. Your students enter the classroom to find a roped-off area full of curious clues. Working in teams of two, students examine the evidence and record their observations very carefully, just like real forensic scientists.

Session 2: In this session, you help the class use a "Clue Board" to organize their observations of the evidence they gathered at the crime scene, which has by now been dismantled. Students listen eagerly to hear more about the suspects and what is known about the case. As excitement grows and accusations fly, you'll need to ask the class to resist the temptation to theorize about "who done it," until they've examined all the evidence. You'll introduce the distinction between what the students know for sure ("hard evidence") and their guesses or ideas ("inferences") about what must have happened. For scientists and detectives alike, making the distinction between evidence and inference is an important skill.

Sessions 3 and 4: Your classroom is transformed into a forensic laboratory. During each of the two sessions, students circulate to five different activity stations and perform tests on the various clues found at the scene of the crime in Session 1. They do thread comparison tests, chromatography, pH tests, and powder tests, to name a few. Signs at each learning station explain the procedures.

At the end of each of the forensic station sessions, the class pools results and revises their evidence charts from Session 2. Which clues are most helpful in solving the crime? Could any of the evidence be there just by coincidence, or maybe even "planted" by the culprit to make someone else look guilty?

In **Session 5,** after all their observations, experiments and discussions, the class attempts to solve the mystery. By the end of the unit, students feel energized and empowered, having experienced the value of science as a tool for investigation.

Who Really Did It?

At the conclusion of any Mystery Festival, the teacher is hounded by students eager to know, "Who really did it?" Of course, no one *really* did it, since these are made-up mysteries, but we did have specific scenarios in mind when designing them, so they would appear realistic. The *Bear* mystery has a clear solution. To date, however, only one author knows the "answer" to the more complex *Felix* mystery, and he doesn't respond to bribes! There are several reasons why we prefer that this "answer" remain undisclosed:

1) To drive kids crazy (not really!).

2) If the "answer" were to get out and be passed around, the mystery would lose its appeal. Who would want to try to figure out a mystery to which they already knew the answer?

3) Students who come up with a different answer would feel like they had failed. We have heard many very creative and plausible solutions that did not match the "correct" answer.

4) Students who came up with the "right" answer would feel great, but they would also stop thinking about it. Without having been told a "correct" answer, they continue to think about it for a long time, searching for verification of their current "theory," or piecing together new theories that they believe better explain what happened.

5) It would not be representative of a real-life situation, in which a jury is never told whether or not their verdict is "right" at the end of a trial. Indeed, scientists are not told the "answer" to their investigations either, and most novel ideas in science come from the questioning of other scientists' "right answers."

Why Are There Two Mysteries In This Guide?

The *Mystery Festival* concept is appropriate for grades two through eight and can be adapted for first grade. (See page 96 for modifications for first grade.) The guide provides two different mysteries, one for Grades 2–3, and one for Grades 4–8.

The *Mr. Bear* mystery for more primary students has a simpler story and activity stations, and a solution that will be fairly obvious when your class looks at the results of their tests.

The *Felix* mystery for older students, on the other hand, is *not* simple, and there is no obvious culprit. There is evidence pointing to each of the four suspects. The lack of a simple answer is intentional, both to make it more realistic, and to allow students to be creative and exercise critical thinking skills in formulating their own theories. There is no right or wrong answer. Your students may decide that the evidence is not clear enough to convict anyone. This is one of many good conclusions. All answers are considered successes. Such uncertainty and/or ambiguity is also true of many actual crime-solving situations.

Although it is not necessary and we don't recommend that you read both sections, some teachers of advanced third grade students may wish to look over the *Felix* version in case it is preferable for their classes. In the same way, some fourth grade teachers may want to check out the *Mr. Bear* version, or use it early in the year, then present *Felix* later on.

This introductory portion of the guide applies to **both** versions of the mystery, but the rest of the text is two distinct and separate sets of teacher instructions: **one for *Mr. Bear* (pages 19–106) and one for *Felix* (pages 107–210). A background "Behind the Scenes" section and a brief section on materials needed for presentation in a large group format are included at the end.**

Please note that the Introduction is on plain white paper. The Mr. Bear mystery is printed on light yellow paper, and the Felix mystery on light blue. The "Behind the Scenes" and "Large Group Festival" sections are again printed on plain white paper. Student data sheets, signs, and other pages that need to be duplicated are included immediately following the session for which they are needed. The one exception is the footprints that appear on pages 211–231. These same footprints are needed for both mysteries and are printed on white paper. Preparation Checklist/Summary Outlines for Mr. Bear begin on page 98 and for the Felix mystery on page 201. These are intended to help you guide your students through these activities in an organized fashion. Given the large amount of preparation involved, the "Getting Ready" portions of the Summary Outlines have been designed to serve as a helpful **Preparation Checklist** for you. The entire guide has been spiral bound for your copying convenience.

Is Mystery Festival Gruesome?

We have occasionally been asked by concerned adults if *Mystery Festival* might offend their students or in any way condone violence and crime. Of course, these were also concerns of ours while designing the program. In the many hundreds of presentations of *Mystery Festival* to date, we have not received any comments expressing this concern from teachers, parents, or children who have taken part in the program. Certainly the *Mr. Bear* mystery is exceedingly gentle. The characters involved belong to a "Stuffed Animal Adventure Club." The "heinous" crime involves one of the stuffed animals having been borrowed without permission.

For the *Felix* mystery, we did choose to draw on the classic "who-done-it" tradition of fictional mysteries, such as the Sherlock Holmes stories or Agatha Christie thrillers, in which a complex and often surprising process of elimination points the evidence toward one or more crime suspects. We've found that older students become most involved when faced with a more compelling scenario, more typical of the standard murder mystery. However, while it may be true that *The Mystery of Felix* does involve his supposed untimely death, there is no body involved, only a body outline, and the body has disappeared. A poisoning seems a strong likelihood, but there is no direct evidence of other violence. Is it possible that Felix, a not-very-likable fellow, simulated his own demise for ulterior motives of his own? There are even unconfirmed

Note: Some teachers have chosen not to include a body outline in the crime scene in order to further de-emphasize the possibility of murder in the mystery.

reports that Felix has been spotted nearby. The mystery is clearly fictional; the characters imaginary caricatures with humorous names. The main goal, like that of all popular mystery novels for young and old alike, is for students to become wrapped up in the excitement generated by the search for clues that can then be strung together in intricate and logical thought processes. In turn, their examination of the evidence can convey a strong sense of the value and usefulness of scientific investigation.

It is also worth noting that both classic and modern mystery tales are in fact basic morality plays, in which good and truth triumph over evil and falsehood. Almost always, Justice prevails and the evildoer is apprehended. Depending on your own point of view and the levels of understanding of your students, you may also wish to have discussions on the ethical and moral issues raised by criminal behavior, and/or on any other related issues you or your students might raise.

Is the Preparation Reasonable?

The amount of preparation for *Mystery Festival* is extraordinary, but so are the benefits! After presenting Session 1: The Crime Scene, one teacher told us, "The preparation seemed unreasonable, but now that I know what the crime scene is like, it will take a reasonable amount of time." She goes on to say, "I cannot begin to tell you how enthusiastic the students were when involved in *Mystery Festival*. You know it's fantastic when students stop you during P.E. and lunch to tell you their theory of 'who done it!'"

The enthusiastic energy we've seen so quickly generated in students of all backgrounds and levels (including adults!) has convinced us that this unique combination of fun, storytelling, problem-solving, science, mathematics, and mystery is of great educational benefit, and worth the extra effort. Once you are familiar with the unit and have gathered the materials, preparing for future Mystery Festivals will be much easier. But even the first time, you can benefit from the experience of teachers who have presented Mystery Festivals. Here are the two strongest pieces of advice teachers have for you:

• GET PARENTS OR OTHER VOLUNTEERS TO HELP YOU GATHER AND ASSEMBLE THE MATERIALS.

• SHARE THE CRIME SCENE AND THE LEARNING STATION ACTIVITIES WITH AT LEAST ONE OTHER TEACHER.

Although it is fine to present a Mystery Festival for just one class, we recommend that you invite one or more

The crime scene will be dismantled after the first class session. Since observing and recording the evidence takes about an hour per class, the crime scene area will be needed for only about as many hours as there are classes using it. Of course, other scheduling considerations may mean that the crime scene will need to be kept available for several days.

If your school library has space for the crime scene, perhaps you can get the librarian involved in the Mystery Festival. She could use the excitement it generates to kick off a school-wide extravaganza of reading and writing mystery fiction! Please see pages 241–246 for a list of literature connections for your Mystery Festival.

colleagues to teach the unit concurrently. If there is a common space available somewhere in the school, several teachers can work together to set up the crime scene and schedule all their classes to observe the scene at different times. The same "economy of scale" works for the learning station activities in Sessions 3 and 4. Many more students will benefit from the activities, and each teacher will have **much less preparation** to do!

You'll find helpful suggestions below and in the "Getting Ready" sections of each session to make preparation as easy as possible, whether you share the festival or present it on your own. **We have also included sample letters to parents requesting materials for both mysteries. In addition, to assist you in obtaining materials we have listed all materials needed for both mysteries starting on pages 16–18.** GEMS guides are revised frequently—send us your ideas, shortcuts, and creative adaptations so we can consider them for inclusion in future editions.

Finally, it's worth noting that while Sessions 1, 3, and 4 do require much special preparation, the other two sessions, Sessions 2 and 5, require much less.

Planning Your Festival

Where to Have Your Mystery Festival

Making Space for the Crime Scene

For the crime scene in Session 1, you will need at least 7 x 10 feet of floor space, preferably not against a wall. A class should be able to gather around the scene to observe all at once, if possible. If space is limited, you could have one row of students kneel and the other stand, so all can see, or have students file by the scene slowly.

You'll also need an area for the students to sit in small groups **away from the scene** to record their observations and hold a class discussion. Because students will need to return to the scene to reexamine evidence, the crime scene and the discussion area really should be in the same room. A good-sized classroom, library, cafeteria or any large room with tables is best.

Space Considerations in the Learning Station Sessions

For Sessions 3 and 4, in which the students circulate around the room to five learning stations, you'll need to have five large, flat surfaces for stations. You can use tables, counters or desks pushed together. Provide as much distance as possible between stations, both to avoid congestion and to make it less likely that students will see and overhear the discoveries being made at other stations. You'll also need a place away from the stations to gather the whole class when you introduce and conclude the session. If your classroom is too small and/or does not have enough flat surfaces to comfortably accommodate all the students at stations, plan to use the cafeteria or another spacious room with tables for these sessions.

If possible, each station should accommodate **eight** students, for a total of 40 workspaces at stations. This way there will be more "parking spaces" than you have students, and "traffic congestion" is less likely! If your tables aren't big enough for eight students, plan instead for only six students at each station, and make an extra station by having one of the five activities available in two places. This way you'll have six spaces at each of six stations, for a total of 36 spaces. In Session 3, the best activity to use for a duplicate station is the "Brown Stain" activity, because it takes longer to do than the other activities and students tend to "pile up" if there is only one "Brown Stain" station. In Session 4, the best activity to use for a duplicate station is the "Powders" station.

Although you assign students, in teams of two, to their first stations, from then on, they will go with their partners to any station that has space available. One of the advantages of the learning station format is that it allows students to work at their own pace. This is why we do not recommend a "timed rotation" in which students would move to a new station at your signal. Instead, we suggest that students should just move to a new station when they have finished conducting that test. Usually, they'll find room at a new learning station, and, if you ask them to try to avoid more crowded stations, there should be little waiting.

In case there is no room at a station they need to visit, you may want to plan for a place students can go while they wait. Some teachers have students study the class Map of the Crime Scene and the Clue Board they created in previous sessions. Others teachers have students sit and analyze the evidence from the tests they have done so far.

One teacher did not have enough space at stations for all of her students, so she placed half the group at a time at stations. While waiting, the other half of the class used the time to draw a small clue board of their own for their portfolios by reviewing the Clue Board the class had made in the last session.

If two classes are sharing the festival, you might set up the five learning stations in one room, and exchange students after an hour. To share with more classes, you could set up all 10 learning stations in one big room, or two small ones, and cycle several classes through. Someone will need to replenish consumable items and tidy up after each class uses the learning station activities, but getting the stations ready in the first place will not take extra time. (Note: If you use stations from both Session 3 and Session 4 on the same day, you'll need extra pH color keys and cut up pH paper.)

Finally, a note about wall space. You'll need to have room to display several large butcher paper charts. For the *Mr. Bear* version, you will create three charts: a Map of the Crime Scene in Session 1, a Clue Board in Session 2 and an Evidence Chart to record the results of the learning station activities in Sessions 3 and 4. For the *Felix* version, there are two charts: a Map of the Crime Scene (Session 1) and a Clue Board (Sessions 2–5). These charts will need to be left up for the students' reference throughout the unit.

Using the Signs

At the end of Sessions 3 and 4 in both the *Mr. Bear* and *Felix* sections of the guide are signs explaining the procedures for each station in those sessions. The signs are numbered to correspond with the numbers of the station activities on the student data sheets.

The signs are illustrated and have a minimum of words, but in the excitement of the festival, your students may find it hard to read them carefully. As you introduce the session, read the signs aloud to the students as a whole class and demonstrate each procedure **briefly, and without completing the procedure or giving too much away.** This will help non-readers, who then have the pictures to remind them later. For primary students, you may decide simply not to use the signs for the students at the stations, especially if you have adult volunteers to help with the more complex activities.

Having Adult Volunteers Help at Learning Stations

Most teachers strongly recommend having an adult volunteer to help for the Brown Stain and for the Fingerprint stations in Session 3 of the *Mr. Bear* Mystery. It's nice to have an extra pair of hands for Session 4, too.

In Session 3 of the *Felix* mystery, a volunteer is helpful at the "Brown Stain" station, and necessary for safety at the "Threads" station because of the candle flame. In Session 4 of the *Felix* mystery, the "Powders" station is also a "likely suspect" for adult help. It is important to emphasize to volunteers that their role is to help explain to students how to conduct the tests, **to enable students to conduct the tests themselves, and make their own discoveries and conclu-**

sions, rather than doing the tests for the students or influencing their thinking processes. What if students disagree about the results of their experiments? That's OK! The class can discuss how to evaluate differing results and discuss reasons why different groups may obtain different results. It's worth remembering that scientists disagree all the time—controversy often leads to new discoveries!

Getting Ready

Gathering and preparing materials **before** the day of the festival is the hardest part of presenting *Mystery Festival*. For the crime scene, certain fingerprints need to be put on a plastic cup, a secret note needs to be written, and a special brown stain put on pieces of paper towel, just to name a few examples. Each task is straightforward, but there are lots of them! Once the materials are gathered and prepared, however, setting them all up on the day of the *Mystery Festival* is not too difficult, and storing them in labeled ziplock bags or boxes will make future presentations much easier! This is also true of the materials and preparation for the stations in Sessions 3 and 4.

Once again, we strongly recommend having parents or other volunteers help gather and prepare the materials before beginning the unit.

The instructions for both mysteries include a complete list of materials and steps in their preparation. The "What You Need" and "Getting Ready" sections of each session provide detailed listings and preparation directions for both mysteries. (The materials and preparation are different for the *Mr. Bear* and *Felix* mystery festivals.) For a more shorthand checklist that may be helpful, the "Getting Ready" portions of the Summary Outlines (starting on page 98 for Mr. Bear and page 201 for Felix) can also be used as a **"Preparation Checklist."** For a full listing of materials needed, see page 16. These lists are intended to give you a sense of what is involved overall and to help you keep track of all the details.

Teachers who have presented *Mystery Festival* strongly recommend getting an overview of the unit first. **Give yourself time to read through all five sessions of the unit you are presenting once before beginning to prepare.** Start planning your *Mystery Festival* weeks ahead of time. A sample "Letter to Parents" is provided at the beginning of each version of the mystery to use in asking for donations of materials.

Making Connections

Mystery Festival can stand alone, and has great value even when it's not connected formally to other areas of your curriculum. You and your students will no doubt make many natural connections to your science curriculum, as well as to language arts, writing, literature, mathematics and social sciences. In fact, integrating the Festival into your curriculum will probably be irresistible, whether it's by having students read or write mysteries, letting them act out a courtroom drama, or a variety of other possibilities. The excitement and motivation generated by the festival can be channeled into a variety of subject areas. Please see the *Going Further* sections on pages 94 and 198 for more ideas.

Several other units in the GEMS series relate very well to the activities in *Mystery Festival*. *Crime Lab Chemistry* involves the technique of chromatography; *Fingerprinting* uses simplified fingerprinting techniques; these techniques are used at the Festival's "Brown Stain" and "Fingerprints" learning stations, respectively. In *Of Cabbages and Chemistry,* students discover acids, neutrals, and bases—related to the "Cola" and "Melted Ice Cube" Mystery Festival stations. In the *Involving Dissolving* GEMS unit, young students learn that a powder stirred into a liquid is still there, even though it seems to disappear, a handy concept to have at the "Powders" and "Melted Ice Cube" stations. In *Involving Dissolving* students watch crystals form as a salt solution evaporates, which is a perfect introduction to the Crystals activity in *Mystery Festival*.

Presenting one or more of these other GEMS units **before** the Festival allows younger students to gain experience with the skills and concepts they will encounter when they approach the *Mystery Festival* learning stations. (See also "A Note about Pre-Teaching" on page 12.) On the other hand, for upper elementary students, the informal, student-centered format of the *Mystery Festival* can serve as an excellent introduction to some of these more structured GEMS units. *Mystery Festival* does not replace or subsume any of these other units— while any one or more of these GEMS units connects well to *Mystery Festival*—each can also be presented as a highly effective stand-alone unit.

Evidence and Inference

In addition to the many scientific and mathematical skills, processes, and themes that weave mysteriously throughout *Mystery Festival*, students also gain stimulating and valuable experiences in making the important distinction between ***evidence*** (things/facts/data they observe/experience directly and thus can know for sure) from ***inference*** (deriving possible guesses, hunches, theories, conclusions, or explanations from the evidence and based on logic and reasoning). As students evaluate how much weight to place on a particular piece of evidence, and continue testing, they are also learning to refine and adjust their initial inferences based on their further investigations. At every turn in the unfolding of the possible plots, they learn anew lessons about "not jumping to conclusions," the need for careful and thorough experimentation, and the unending questioning process that is the essence of science.

Another GEMS guide that explores evidence and inference in a compelling way is Investigating Artifacts: Making Masks, Creating Myths, Exploring Middens. This interdisciplinary guide for Grades K-6 focuses on Native American cultures, maskmaking and mathematics, and the evidential/inferential art of archaeological investigation.

There is absolutely no necessity with younger students to inject confusing vocabulary to describe thinking processes. Although the process of making at least simple inferences is appropriate for students of all ages, it is not at all necessary or advisable to use the word "inference" itself. You will probably want to use a more common word, such as "explanation" or "best guess." Or you can simply focus on looking for "clues" to help find out and explain more. The central philosophy of the entire GEMS series has to do with "learning through doing," and there is plenty to *do* in this series of activities. Your students' guesses, thoughts, ideas, *inferences* and conclusions will blossom through their hands-on involvement and creativity.

For older students, the theme of evidence leading to inference that runs throughout these activities can be a very important and conscious area of intellectual development. This theme is intimately related to science and mathematics, but it is also important in the social sciences, and is a central part of problem-solving and lifelong thinking skills. Many teachers have remarked that after engaging in this series of activities, they can see striking growth in ways that their students analyze and evaluate physical evidence, debate possible inferences and make conclusions.

"Mystery Festival sets the stage for future science investigations. My students learned to observe, process information, and draw conclusions. I intend to use it to start off and set up my whole science curriculum for next year."

Mike Meneghetti

(One of the teachers who tested these activities)

Throughout the five sessions of the unit, students will eagerly share not only facts about the case, but also their guesses and "theories" about what happened. Don't worry if they have difficulty distinguishing hard facts from more speculative ideas, especially at first. Thinking skills will improve gradually as the sessions progress. And even if the identity of the culprit(s) remains a mystery—one thing is for sure—a fun, memorable, and unique learning experience will be had by all!

■

A Note About Pre-Teaching

Using any of the other GEMS units mentioned above in "Making Connections" will give students experience with concepts and skills that will enhance their learning in *Mystery Festival.*

Many teachers have found it useful to have their students practice using their observation skills **before** approaching the crime scene in Session 1. Following are four observation activities you may want to consider. The composite drawing activity offers students an opportunity not only to practice careful observation, but also to distinguish between evidence and inference.

1. Sharp Eyes: Have your students stand in two lines facing each other. Tell them that the person opposite them in the other line is their partner, and that their job is to carefully study and memorize every detail of their partner from head to toe. Explain that in a minute, their partner will change some small detail on themselves, and it will be up to them to see if they can identify it. After about a minute, instruct your students to all turn to face the opposite direction, and to make a subtle but visible change on themselves. (The partner might unbutton a button on a shirt, put their hair behind their ear, etc.) When everyone is ready, have them all turn back around to face each other and look for the changes in silence. Give them each an opportunity to guess at the change their partner made. If they can't figure it out, have their partner reveal what they changed. (Your students will probably want to repeat this activity!)

2. Find the Change: Change something about yourself or the classroom each day or each class period, and challenge your students to sleuth out what it is.

3. Mystery Stories: Read a mystery with your class or else read just a section in which the author or detective describes or analyzes the scene of a crime.

4. Composite Drawing: Have a visitor dressed in a distinctive outfit or costume come into your classroom very briefly, and draw attention to herself (perhaps squirt you with a water bottle?). After the visitor has left, challenge your students to remember as many details as possible about the person and draw them, either in teams or as individuals. You may wish to assign different portions (pants, shoes, shirt, face, etc.) to different teams to be assembled later as a composite. (If you choose this option, have someone lie down on a piece of butcher paper. Trace their outline. Then cut it up into the sections to be assigned to each group. When the drawings are done you can re-assemble the figure to make the composite drawing.) When all the drawings are finished, have the visitor return, so that your students can compare their drawings with the "real thing." (You could also bring in a newspaper picture of an actual composite drawing.)

Ask for volunteers to hold up their pictures and describe what happened. A student may say, for instance, "You got angry when she squirted you." To help students see the distinction between evidence and inference, ask frequently now and throughout the Mystery Festival, "Do we know that for sure, or is it a guess?" It is not necessary to introduce the words "evidence" and "inference" to the students, although teachers of older students may wish to do so.

5. Footprint Activities:

Classifying Shoeprints

Have each student in your class paint the bottom of one shoe with tempera paint to make a footprint on half of a manila folder, or on some other non-transparent paper. You may wish to make this voluntary, since some students are very reluctant to get paint or anything else on their shoes, even on the bottoms. Be sure to have a cleaning procedure worked out *in advance*. Another option might be to have students bring in one of their old shoes.

Instruct students to make the same number of copies of their shoeprints as the number of groups you plan to divide the class into for the activity. When the prints are dry, make up sets, so that each group has one copy of every footprint in the class. Tell each group to first go through the prints one by one, describe them carefully, sort them into groups, then name the groups. You may wish to save these sets for use in future years.

Find that Print

Have each student take a copy of his or her footprint and sit in a circle. Tell the students that you have a footprint that matches one of theirs. You'd like them to guess which print it is—but you aren't going to show it to them! Instead, they can ask you as many questions as they want, and you will only answer "yes" or "no."
Can they "find that print?"

Footprint Concentration

Gather two sets of 10 different footprints from the "Classifying Shoeprints" activity described above. This will give you two copies of each footprint, making a total of 20 cards in all. (Depending on the level of your class, you could choose to use more than 10 footprints.) Randomly mix the footprints you've chosen and number the back of each card from 1 to 20. Place the cards in order, face down, on a floor surface, and have your class gather around. When their turn comes, students name two numbers of cards to be turned over. If the two footprints match, they get to hold those cards. If they do not match, the cards are turned back over, face down. You may choose to have your students play individually, or in teams. If they play in teams, each student still gets her own turn to make a final decision, but other team members may help each other out. Play until all cards have been matched.

Footprint Mysteries

On a long piece of butcher paper, make footprints of yourself performing various distinctive activities (skipping, running, jumping, tiptoeing, walking forward then backward on the same prints, jumping rope, cartwheels, etc.). Wash and repaint your feet a different color for each activity. Barefoot prints work best. With the whole class, examine one set of the footprints and model how to make detailed observations and inferences about what the person was doing. Pair up students and give them a recording sheet to describe what activity they think made each colored set of prints. Reassemble the group and have students take turns acting out what they think the maker of each set of colored prints was doing before you reveal what they were actually doing. Be sure to save your butcher paper prints for future years!

Student Footprint Mysteries

Divide the class into small groups, and have each group decide secretly among themselves an activity to perform and record with painted feet on butcher paper (skipping, playing hopscotch, etc.) You may want to have the groups get your approval of their idea first, as there is a tendency for student ideas to become overly complicated and difficult to decipher. Have the groups work together to make their mystery footprints. When all groups are finished making the prints, hand out recording sheets, and rotate the groups through all the other stations to try to figure out which activities made the prints. When each group has been to all the stations, elicit their ideas, then have the creators of the prints reveal what they were really doing.

Time Frame (for both mysteries)

Both classroom versions of the *Mystery Festival* include five sessions, three of them at least an hour in length. Times given here are approximate, and will vary depending on your class size/level and your own needs and preferences.

Please note that the amount of time required to gather and prepare materials **before the day of the activity** is not listed below. The first time you present a Mystery Festival, the advance preparation is substantial. The time needed to gather, prepare, and organize the materials will vary depending on how much help you have. Allow a few weeks, if possible. A team-teaching, well-organized group effort is highly recommended.

Some junior high school teachers have class periods of only 45 minutes or so. If this is your situation, try to make special arrangements, if possible, to allow 60-minute class periods for Sessions 1, 3 and 4.

Session 1: Scene of the Crime —Students discover the scene of the crime, then look for, and record clues.

- teacher preparation on the day of the activity........... Mr. Bear: 1 hour
Felix : 2 hours
- class presentation.. 45–60 minutes

Session 2: The Story —The suspects are introduced, and their alibis heard. This information is used to re-examine the crime scene clues.

- teacher preparation .... 30 minutes
- class presentation.. Mr. Bear: 30–45 minutes
Felix: 45–60 minutes

Session 3: Crime Lab Stations A —Students, in teams of two, conduct tests on five pieces of evidence at separate stations, then take a new look at the suspects in light of each piece of evidence.

- teacher preparation on the day of the activity........... Mr. Bear: 45 minutes
Felix: 60 minutes
- class presentation.. 60 minutes

Session 4: Crime Lab Stations B —Students conduct tests on five more pieces of evidence at five additional stations, then take another look at the suspects in light of each piece of evidence.

- teacher preparation on the day of the activity........... Mr. Bear: 40 minutes
Felix: 45 minutes
- class presentation.. 45–60 minutes

Session 5: Solving the Mystery —The teacher and her class use one of the options presented to attempt to solve the crime.

- teacher preparation .... 10 minutes
- class presentation.. 30–60 minutes

Mr. Bear Mystery

• Shopping & Gathering List for all five Mr. Bear Sessions •

(for a class size of about 32)

See page 97 for a sample letter asking parents to contribute materials.

- ❒ five stuffed animals (one of which must be a bear)
- ❒ ~ 6 feet of white cotton yarn
- ❒ ~ 6 feet of colored cotton yarn
- ❒ ~ 6 feet of colored wool yarn (best if the yarn looks "woolly.")
- ❒ 1 long piece of string or rope to barricade crime scene (~50 feet)
- ❒ 16 pencils
- ❒ 1 brown felt water-base marker
- ❒ at least 1 marking pen (variety of colors is ideal)
- ❒ 1 package white paper towels
- ❒ 3 white sheets of 8 1/2" x 11" paper
- ❒ 40 feet butcher paper
- ❒ 1 roll of Universal pH paper (the exact brand is not important)
- ❒ 1 roll of tranparent adhesive tape
- ❒ 1 roll of masking tape
- ❒ 1 pair of scissors
- ❒ 16 clear plastic cups
- ❒ 3 empty film canisters
- ❒ 1 ice cube tray
- ❒ 2 white test trays ("styrofoam" egg cartons cut in half work well, if these are not available, use white plastic paint trays from an art store or white ice cube trays.)
- ❒ 1–4 small dropper bottles (empty medicine dropper bottles, saline bottles or similar small bottles are fine)
- ❒ 2 empty cola cans
- ❒ ~ 1/4 cup cola
- ❒ ~ 1/2 ounce of iodine
- ❒ 2 tablespoons of red food coloring
- ❒ 1 tablespoon of green food coloring
- ❒ ~ 1/4 cup of baking soda
- ❒ ~ 5 tablespoons of corn starch
- ❒ 1/2 teaspoon salt
- ❒ 11/2 teaspoons sugar
- ❒ 1/4 teaspoon
- ❒ 1/8 teaspoon
- ❒ a yardstick
- ❒ stir stick
- ❒ 1 paintbrush (any kind)
- ❒ 1 paint container (a plate or cup is fine)
- ❒ 2 colognes or perfumes, as different from each other as possible. (get samples from department stores, bathroom cabinet, magazines, etc.)
- ❒ 1 wastebasket
- ❒ 4 small mirrors, preferably with stands (clay works as a makeshift stand)
- ❒ 1 large plastic trash bag
- ❒ 1 sponge
- ❒ ~ 30 strands of pet hair (dog or cat hair is fine)
- ❒ ~ 1 handful of grass

Optional for Session 1:

- ❒ a Polaroid or video camera to record pictures of the crime scene

Pages to be copied from this guide:

- ❒ footprints for scene of the crime (page 25)
- ❒ pictures of suspects (pages 40–44)
- ❒ Clue Board illustrations (page 39)
- ❒ 4 copies of the "Suspect Fingerprints" sheet (page 63)
- ❒ 4 copies of the "Cup Fingerprints" sheet (page 62)
- ❒ 8 copies of the "Mr. Bear Footprints"sheet (page 31)
- ❒ 4 copies of each of the station signs
- ❒ For every two students: 1 copy of the "Mr. Bear Mystery Data Sheet" (pages 64–65)

Depending on the option you choose in Session 5, you may also need:

- ❒ paper
- ❒ crayons or colored markers
- ❒ a chalkboard and chalk

Felix Mystery

• Shopping & Gathering List for all five Felix Mystery Sessions •

(for a class size of about 32)

See page 200 for a sample letter asking parents to contribute materials.

- ❒ ~ 6 feet of white cotton yarn
- ❒ ~ 6 feet of colored cotton yarn
- ❒ ~ 6 feet of colored wool yarn
- ❒ a long piece of rope or string to barricade crime scene (~ 50 feet)
- ❒ 21 pencils
- ❒ 2 marking pens (1 permanent)
- ❒ 1 brown felt water-base marker
- ❒ 1 package of white paper towels
- ❒ ~ 40 feet white butcher paper
- ❒ 12 sheets of 8 1/2"x11" white paper.
- ❒ ~ 50 lined 3" x 5" index cards
- ❒ 1 pad of 100 3" x 5" Post-it® notes (not needed if you make a chalkboard Clue Board—see #2 in Getting Ready)
- ❒ 1 roll of Universal pH paper with color chart (the exact brand is not important)
- ❒ 1 piece of tag board ~8 1/2" x 11" (the cardboard back of a notepad is fine)
- ❒ 1 roll of 3/4" clear adhesive tape
- ❒ 1 roll of masking tape
- ❒ 1 pair of scissors
- ❒ 18 clear plastic cups
- ❒ 2 one-gallon zip lock plastic bags
- ❒ 6 empty film canisters
- ❒ 2 white test trays (Styrofoam egg cartons cut in half work well. If these are not available, use white plastic paint trays from an art store or white ice cube trays.)
- ❒ 2–5 dropper bottles (empty medicine dropper bottles, saline bottles or similar small bottles are fine)
- ❒ 2 empty cola cans
- ❒ 1 meter or yardstick
- ❒ 1 metric ruler
- ❒ five 1/8 teaspoons (or use 1/4 teaspoons &have students estimate half)
- ❒ ~ 1/2 ounce of iodine
- ❒ ~ 2 cups baking soda
- ❒ ~ 2 cups corn starch
- ❒ ~ 1/4 cup cola
- ❒ 1 ice cube tray
- ❒ 1 paintbrush (any kind)
- ❒ 1 paint container (a plate or cup is fine)
- ❒ 1 wastebasket
- ❒ 1 chocolate candy wrapper
- ❒ 1 white cotton towel
- ❒ 1 comb with several strands of human hair
- ❒ 3 tablespoons of red food coloring
- ❒ 1 tablespoon of green food coloring
- ❒ 1 "broken" alarm clock
- ❒ 4 colognes or perfumes, as different from each other as possible (get samples from department stores, your bathroom cabinet, friends, magazines etc.).
- ❒ 1 small container of Krazy Glue®
- ❒ 1 pair plastic gloves
- ❒ 2 sheets of aluminum foil about 12" x 16"
- ❒ 2 votive candles
- ❒ 1 book of matches
- ❒ At least 1 pair of safety goggles (4 pairs would be ideal, swimming, snorkeling or ski goggles are all fine).
- ❒ 4 pairs of metal tweezers, tongs or equivalent
- ❒ 4 small mirrors, preferably with stands (clay works as a make-shift stand)
- ❒ 2 "eggs" of Silly Putty™
- ❒ 1 large plastic trash bag
- ❒ 1 sponge
- ❒ 4 old sweaters or t-shirts
- ❒ 4 bags (brown paper shopping bags or plastic bags are fine)
- ❒ ~ 30 strands of pet hair (dog or cat hair is fine)
- ❒ pinch of human hair, grass, threads, yarn, for tape lift examples sheet.

Pages to be copied from this guide:

- ❒ footprints for scene of the crime (page 116)
- ❒ pictures of suspects (pages 141–144)
- ❒ 4 copies of the "DNA Fingerprints" sheet (page 178)
- ❒ 4 copies of the "Suspect Fingerprints" sheet (page 130)

continued ▶

- ❐ 4 copies of the "Suspect Handwriting Samples" sheet (page 185)
- ❐ 4 copies of the "Tape lift Examples" sheet (page 178)
- ❐ 8 copies of the "Suspect Footprints" sheet (page 129)
- ❐ 4 copies of each station sign
- ❐ for every two students: one copy of the "Felix Mystery Data Sheet"

Optional for Session 1:

- ❐ a Polaroid or video camera to record pictures of the crime scene

The following items are optional, but are great for "spicing up" the crime scene:

- ❐ 1 guitar pick
- ❐ 1 pair of sunglasses
- ❐ 1 clip-on earring
- ❐ 1 package carpet tacks

Depending on the option you choose in Session 5, you may also need:

- ❐ paper
- ❐ a chalkboard and chalk

WHO BORROWED MR. BEAR?

(A mystery for younger detectives: Grades 2-3)

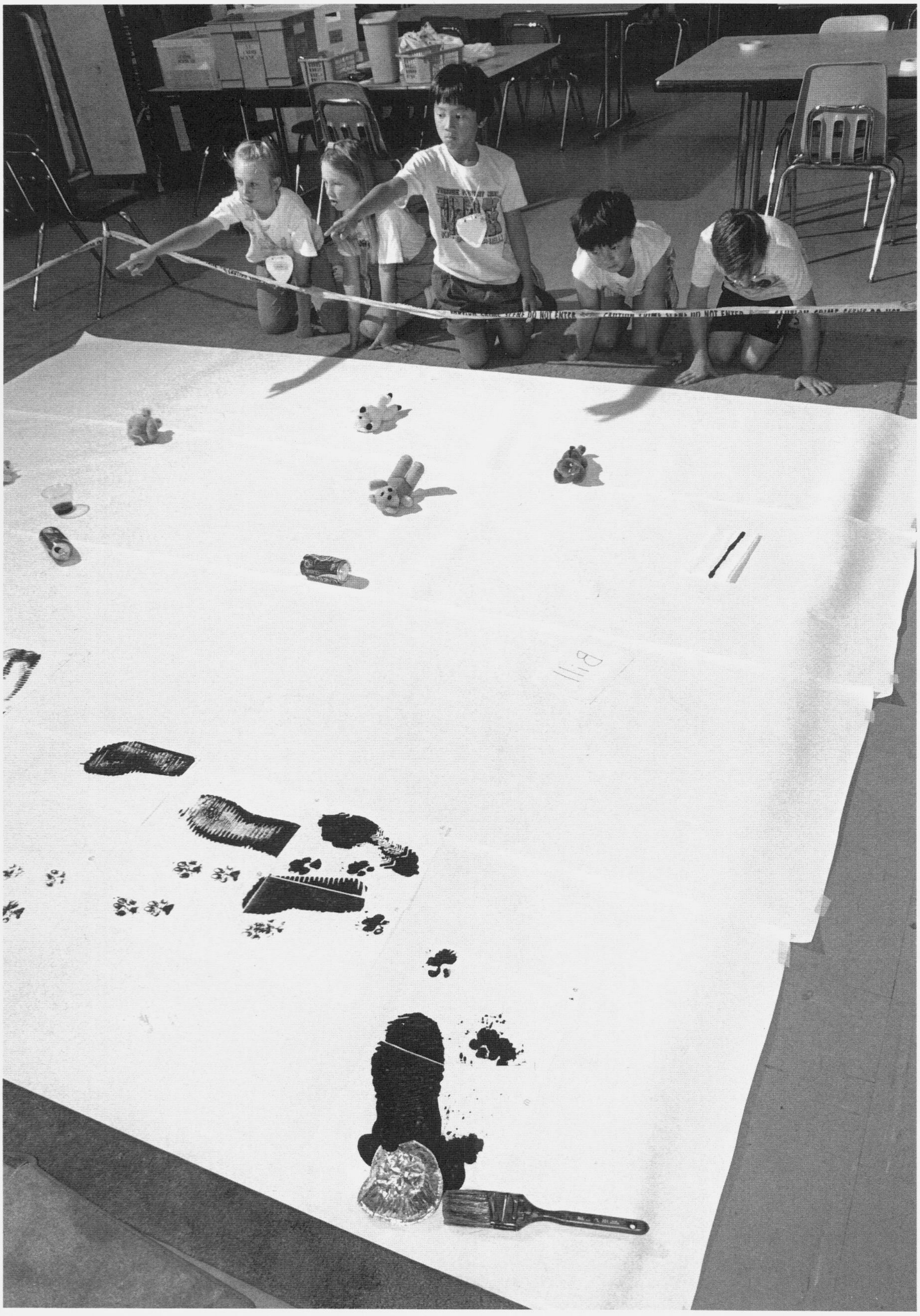
DO NOT ENTER
Bill

Session 1: Scene of the Crime

Overview

As your students enter the room they are intrigued to discover a roped-off "crime scene" full of curious items. Students have a chance to fully exercise their powers of observation, as they get their first look at the evidence left behind.

After a brief introduction, the students search the crime scene for clues. When the class reassembles, the students describe each of the clues they found as the teacher draws them on a large piece of posted butcher paper. This "map" of the crime scene will be used as a reference throughout the rest of the unit.

What You Need (for a class size of about 32)

See page 97 for a sample letter asking parents to contribute materials.

For the Crime Scene:

- ❐ five stuffed animals (one of which must be a bear)
- ❐ 1 paintbrush (any kind)
- ❐ 1 paint container (a plate or cup is fine)
- ❐ 1 clear plastic cup
- ❐ 3 plastic cups (for making crystals)
- ❐ 1 box of baking soda
- ❐ 1 cup for mixing baking soda and water
- ❐ 2 empty cola cans
- ❐ about 1/4 cup cola
- ❐ 1 ice cube tray

- ❒ 2 white paper towels
- ❒ red and green food coloring (small squeeze bottles are fine)
- ❒ 1 small container with a lid, such as a film canister (or jar), in which to save some food coloring
- ❒ ~10 inches of white cotton yarn
- ❒ 1 blank piece of paper
- ❒ 1 long piece of string or rope to barricade crime scene
- ❒ 1/2 teaspoon salt
- ❒ 1 1/2 teaspoons sugar
- ❒ stir stick
- ❒ 1/4 teaspoon
- ❒ a sprinkle of cornstarch (to put on Mr. Bear)
- ❒ 2 colognes or perfumes, as different from each other as possible. (get samples from department stores, your bathroom cabinet, magazines, etc.)
- ❒ 3 or 4 seven foot lengths of white butcher paper to cover the floor under the crime scene
- ❒ 1 roll clear tape to attach footprints to the butcher paper

For the Class Crime Scene Map:

- ❒ 1 piece of butcher paper about 3 x 5 feet
- ❒ copies of 21 pages of footprints (from pages 211–231)
- ❒ at least 1 marking pen for drawing crime scene on the crime scene map (A variety of colors is ideal.)
- ❒ Optional: a Polaroid or video camera to record pictures of the crime scene

Getting Ready

To help you keep track of the preparation tasks below, we have included a Preparation Checklist at the start of the Summary Outlines. The Summary Outlines for Mr. Bear begin on page 98. The checklist contains all the tasks in this Getting Ready section, but in a more condensed style. You might want to make a copy of the Preparation Checklist and use it to check off tasks as you or a volunteer complete them.

Before the Day of the Activity:

1. Decide where the scene of the crime will be:

Choose a rectangular floor area, at least 7 x 10 feet, preferably not against a wall, around which your whole class can gather to observe.

2. Prepare the footprints:

- Make one copy of each of the 21 pages of footprints on pages 211-231.

- Make 16 copies of the students' Suspect Footprint Sheet, page 31.

3. Prepare the "brown stain" paper towel

Note: Although you will put only one brown stain paper towel at the crime scene, you need to make two. This is so your students will have enough pieces of towel to test in Session 3. Set aside the second paper towel until Session 3.

- Make brown food coloring by mixing 1/2 teaspoon of red food coloring with 1/4 teaspoon green.

- Cut two pieces of white paper towel about 3 inches by 10 inches.

- Use the brown food coloring to make a stain across the middle of each strip of paper towel, using a stir stick, straw, or cotton swab dipped in brown food coloring (see diagram). Save what you don't use now in a sealed container labeled "brown food coloring" for use in Session 3.

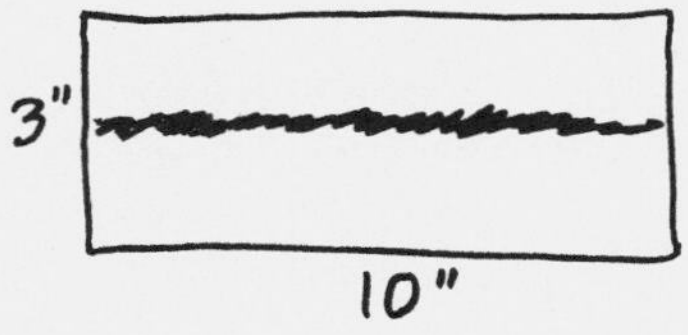

- Allow the stain to dry.

4. Prepare the cotton threads:

Cut five 2" pieces of white cotton yarn.

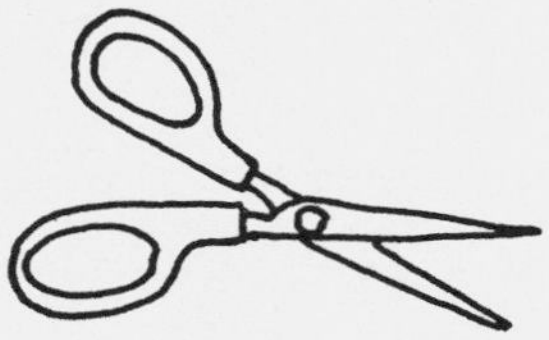

5. Prepare Mr. Bear's scent:

Put a few drops of one of the perfumes on Mr. Bear. Make a note of which perfume you chose, since this will be Jan's perfume in Session 3. The other perfume will be Bill's, but will not be used until Session 3. Set aside both perfumes for Session 3.

6. Make the Secret Note:

Write the name "Bill" backwards in large letters on the blank piece of paper. In a later lesson, the students will use a mirror to read this note. If you think that just the name Bill will be too easy for your students, you may want to write, "William" or a longer backwards note, such as: "Bill borrowed Mr. Bear."

7. Prepare the Crystals for Session 4:

Note: Since the crystals may take about two to four days to form, this step is included here. **The crystals are not used until Session 4.**

1. Measure 1/4 teaspoon of salt into each of 2 cups.
2. Measure 1 1/2 teaspoons of sugar into another cup.
3. Add 1 tablespoon of hot water to all three. Very hot tap water will work. Boiling water might warp the plastic cup.
4. Stir until mostly dissolved. Set in a warm, dry spot until crystals form (in several days).

MR. BEAR CRIME SCENE SET-UP

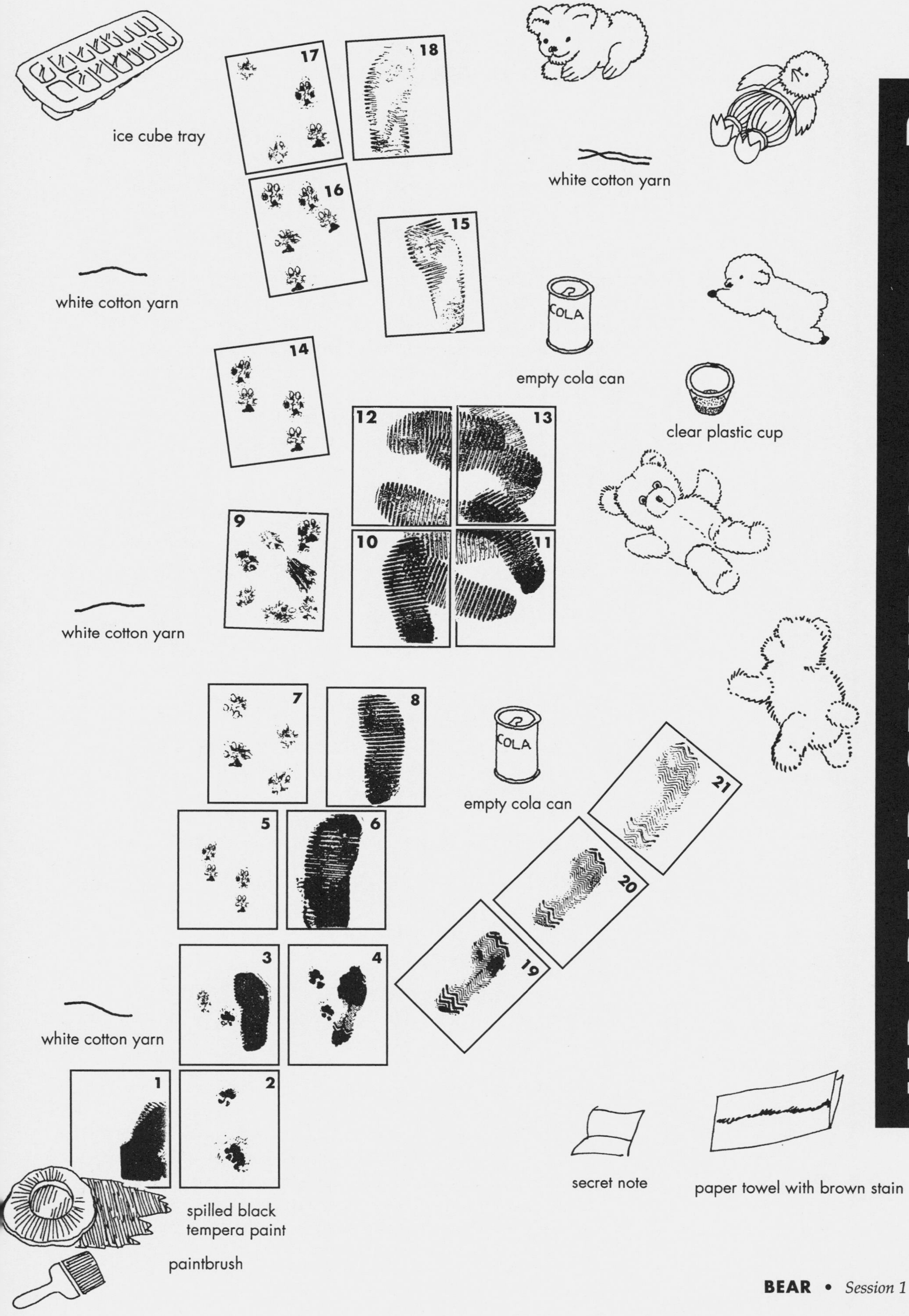
ice cube tray
17
18
white cotton yarn
16
15
white cotton yarn
empty cola can
clear plastic cup
14
12
13
9
10
11
white cotton yarn
7
8
empty cola can
21
5
6
20
3
4
19
white cotton yarn
1
2
secret note
paper towel with brown stain
spilled black tempera paint
paintbrush

The Day of the Activity:

Setting up the crime scene will probably take you about an hour (less if you have help). If possible, set it up after school the day before the activity and start the activity first thing in the morning. If you are sharing the set-up with another teacher or volunteers, you may have time to set it up at lunch time and begin the activity right after lunch. Use the diagram on the previous page as a guide to place all the clues. **Although it is important that the footprints and the spilled paint/brush be placed as shown on the diagram, *the location of the other items does not need to be exactly as shown.* Don't worry if your placement of the other clues isn't *precisely* like the diagram.**

1. Spread butcher paper on the floor:

Clear the space you have chosen for the crime scene, and cover the floor with lengths of butcher paper. Use string or rope to "rope-off" the crime scene. Chairs make good corner supports around which to wind the string.

2. Add the footprints:

- The 21 pages of footprints you duplicated earlier need to be set out in the pattern shown by the numbered rectangles on the previous page.

- Tape the footprints to the butcher paper. (After the festival, roll up the butcher paper with the footprints, and save it for future festivals.)

3. Place all the clues on the crime scene:

- Use the diagram on the previous page to place each item on the scene. Three of the items need some last-minute preparation. These three are:

1. Mr. Bear
Sprinkle a little cornstarch and a few of the white cotton threads on Mr. Bear. Get him slightly damp with water in a few spots.

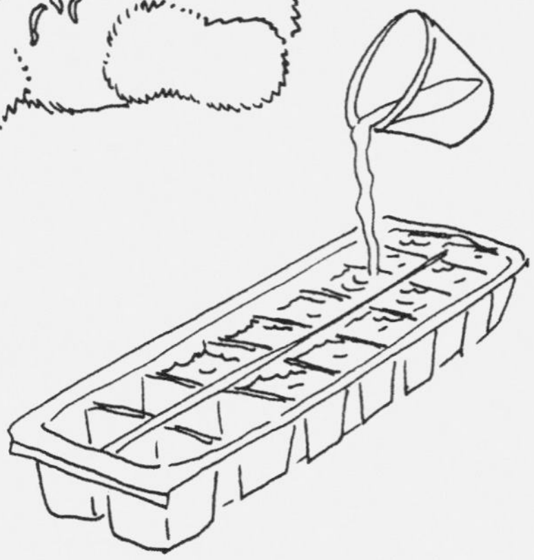

2. Ice Cube Tray
Place the tray right side up. Leave four compartments empty. Fill the other compartments with a baking soda solution. To make the baking soda solution: stir approximately 1 tablespoon of baking soda into 1 cup of water until dissolved. **When you dismantle the crime scene, save the ice cube tray and baking soda water for later use in Session 4.**

3. The Clear Plastic Cup
Add about 1/2 inch of cola to the cup before setting it out at the crime scene. Stir in about 1/8 of a teaspoon of baking soda into the cola until it's dissolved.

4. Set up the Crime Scene Map:

- Tape a rectangular piece of butcher paper, about 2 feet by 3 feet, on the wall. It should be in a place where the whole class is able to see it when you discuss and record their observations.

- Have a marking pen or pens on hand for you to draw the crime scene map. A variety of colors is ideal.

- Have handy the 16 copies of the "Suspect Footprints" sheet.

GO!

Introducing the Challenge

1. Gather your students away from the crime scene and tell them that they are going to have the chance to solve a make-believe mystery. Ask them, "What is a mystery?" [Something that we wonder about; something that has not been explained. Often a mystery is about something that has happened or been done by someone, such as something that is against the rules or against the law, a **crime**, and we don't know who did it or why.] Tell them that the people that we think *might* have done it are called "**suspects**."

2. Ask, "How can we *solve* a mystery (figure out what happened) ?" [By observing, thinking, testing our ideas until we come up with an answer that fits.] You may want to ask, "Can we tell who did it just by the way people look?" or "Should we just guess who did it?" Ask, "Who solves mysteries?" [Detectives, scientists, and many other people.] Tell them that they're going to become crime lab scientists and solve a make-believe mystery.

3. Mention that today they will get to observe a "scene" where something happened. Someone borrowed a stuffed animal that did not belong to them, without asking permission. Explain that that's all you can tell them about what happened at the "crime scene" at this time, but they will find out more facts in the next few days.

4. Emphasize that their first job is to look carefully at the scene of the crime., to observe all the details. Ask them why they think the crime scene has a rope around it. [to keep someone from walking there and messing up the clues.]

5. Have them gather outside the rope to observe the crime scene for a few minutes. (Some teachers prefer to have this first visit to the crime scene be a silent activity, so students are focused on looking at the scene themselves, rather than talking and listening to each other.)

One teacher placed large loops of colored yarn on the crime scene during the observation to highlight certain areas. For some students, it was easier to focus on the items within one area of the scene.

Recording Their Observations

1. Regroup your students near the blank butcher paper "Crime Scene Map."

2. Tell them that after today the crime scene will be taken down. In order to remember everything, they need to record what they observed. Explain that their next job will be to go back to the scene, and find at least five things to study and remember. Explain that when they gather again, they'll tell you all about those things, so that you can draw them on the butcher paper. Explain that the paper on the wall will become a "crime scene map" that will help the class remember all the clues and where they were.

Throughout Mystery Festival you are asked to help students make "inferences," that is, to derive possible explanations or conclusions based on evidence and reasoning, and also to distinguish evidence from inference. As they become more and more involved in solving the mystery, students also gauge the strength and validity of various pieces of evidence, while refining and adjusting their earlier inferences. Although the process of making at least simple inferences is appropriate for students of all ages, it is not at all necessary to use the word "inference" itself, especially not with younger students. You will probably want to use a more common word, such as "explanation" or "good guess." The very process your students are so involved in—looking for and analyzing "clues" to find out more about what happened—provides them with great practical and direct experience differentiating evidence from inference!

3. To give the students practice in careful observation, hold up and have them describe an object, such as a tape dispenser or stapler, or even a mini-crime scene, such as a mug that has been knocked over. Ask for details, allowing some students to examine it up close. If students come up with ideas or conclusions (inferences) that are not direct observations, you may want to discuss the distinction briefly.

4. Let the students go to observe the crime scene again for about five minutes, then re-group them to share their findings. As each item is described, draw a labeled, rough outline of it on the butcher paper map. If your students have difficulty deciding where you should record the clues, you might add points of reference to the map. For instance, on one edge of the map, you might write, "near the sink" or draw a picture of windows or other fixed objects.

5. Record the location of the footprints. To make this go faster, you might just record the human footprints as arrows and the dog's prints as circles.

6. If students have difficulty remembering details, let individuals go back to check and report them to you. If no one has noticed certain clues, you can have them all return to look in a specific area to scout them out.

Some teachers recommend taking Polaroid photos of the crime scene, either to supplement or replace the Crime Scene Map. One group of students suggested using a video camera to record the scene.

Using the Suspect Footprint Sheet

1. Ask what kinds of patterns there might be on the bottom of a shoe. [Circles, squiggly lines, zig-zag lines, words or letters, bumps] Have each student look at the bottom of one of her shoes and notice any patterns.

2. Have everyone find a partner to compare shoe types. Then have each team of two team up with another to make a team of four, and compare all four different kinds of patterns. Ask them to notice any unusual patterns, or shoes that were hard to tell apart.

3. Have your students return to their teams of two.

4. Hand out a copy of the Suspect Footprint sheet to each pair of students. Mention that later on they will find out more about the people (and the dog!) whose names are on the paper. For now, all they need to know is that these are the footprints of the suspects that may have been at the scene of the crime.

5. Ask questions to focus the students on the patterns, such as, " Which footprints have squiggly (or straight) lines? Which prints have thick lines? Thin lines?" After they have observed and described these footprint patterns and their differences, send the students back to attempt to identify the footprints at the crime scene.

6. Regroup, and ask whose footprints are at the scene. [Jan's, Bill's and Puppy's]. If there is disagreement, discuss further, and send one or two students back to the scene. With the students' help, identify which prints on the class Crime Scene Map are Jan's or Bill's by quickly writing the initials "J" or "B" near the footprints.

7. Explain that during the next session they will hear a story that will help them learn more about what happened to Mr. Bear, and who might have borrowed him.

Breaking Down the Crime Scene

By the end of Session 1, the evidence has been recorded by the class on the Crime Scene Map, so the crime scene can be dismantled. Most of the materials can be put away and stored for a future Mystery Festival. **However, keep the following items handy for use in later sessions of this Festival:**

Keep on hand these items you prepared, but didn't place on the crime scene:

____ the extra brown stain paper towel

____ the two perfumes or colognes

____ the two cups with crystals

Keep on hand these items from the Crime Scene:

____ the brown stain paper towel from the scene

____ the stuffed animal Mr. Bear

____ baking soda and cola mixture

____ ice cube tray with baking soda water

____ the backwards "Bill" note

Going Further

Invite a member of the local police department as a guest to your classroom. The guest could talk about a crime scene she investigated and/or how important careful observation is in police work. She could also explain the kind of work police officers, detectives, and forensic scientists do. You could help focus the discussion on the gathering of evidence and point out how the way students make observations of the "crime scene" in Session 1 is similar to police detective work.

Mr. Bear FOOTPRINTS

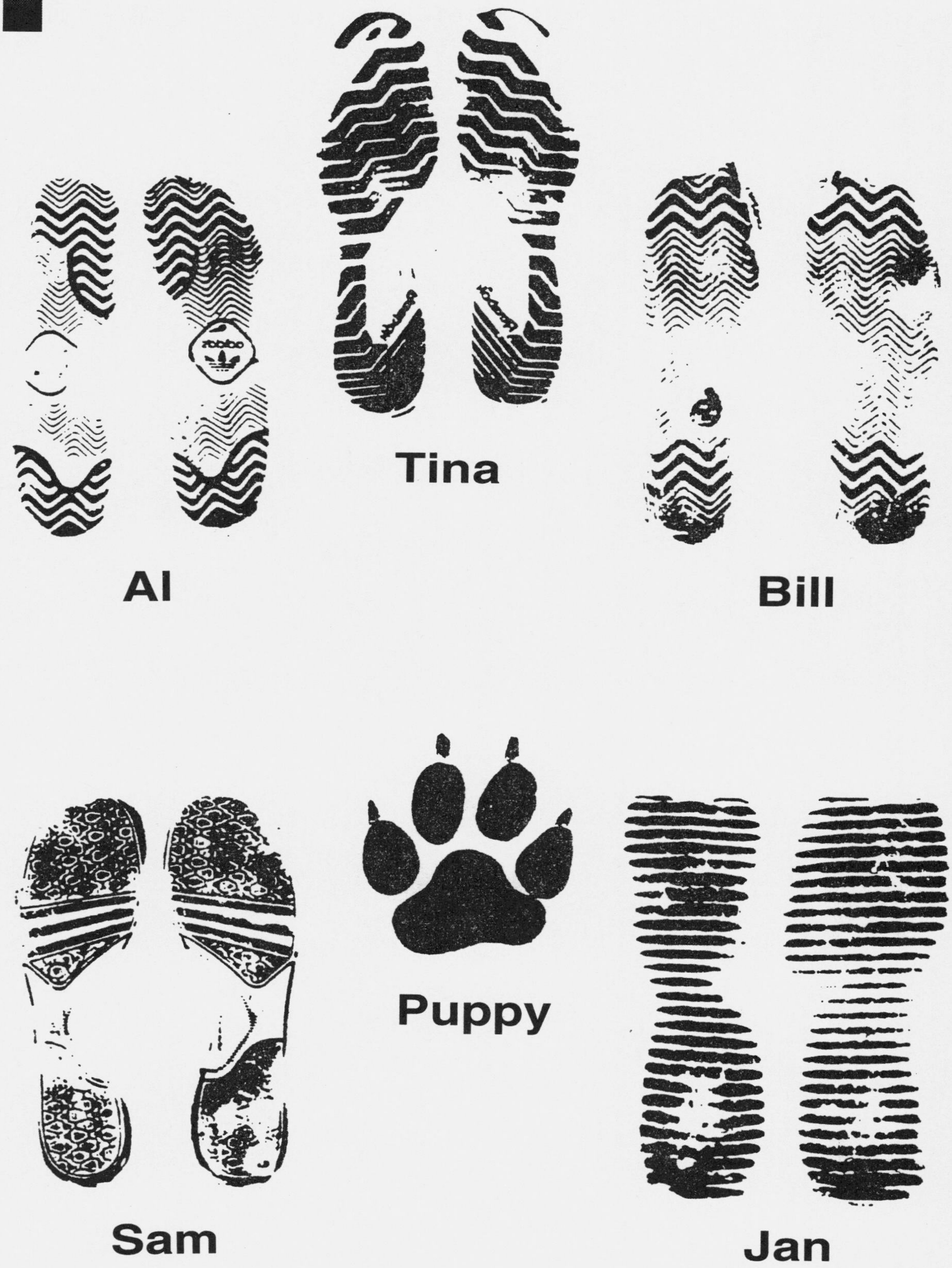

Clue Board
NAME
Sam
Bill
Jan
Tina
Al
Hopscotch
Beach
Grass
Pool
Pool
Blue T-shirt
White cotton sweater
White wool sweater
Red T-shirt
White cotton sweater
Cookies
Pie
Pie
Cookies
Cookies
BILLS
JANS
DYE
Dye
Pen
Pen
Puppy

Session 2: The Story

Overview

During this session, students first review what was found at the scene of the crime during Session 1. The mystery story and the characters involved are then introduced to the students. The teacher tapes or tacks the character pictures and clues on a "Clue Board" at the appropriate points in the story.

What You Need

- ❐ the Crime Scene Map from Session 1
- ❐ 1 roll masking tape
- ❐ 1 piece of butcher paper, about 4 feet by 4 feet
- ❐ a yardstick and felt-tipped marking pen to make lines on Clue Board
- ❐ pictures of suspects (masters on pages 40–44)
- ❐ Clue Board illustrations (masters on pages 45–47)

Getting Ready

1. Assign a stuffed animal to each of the suspects (Sam owns Mr. Bear). Jot down the animals next to the suspects' names in the story, page 36.

2. Duplicate the suspect pictures on pages 40–44 and the Clue Board illustrations on pages 45–47 and cut them out. (They can be colored, if desired.)

3. Tape the five suspect pictures along the top edge of the butcher paper.

4. Use a yardstick and marking pen to draw the grid on the Clue Board (see illustration below). The grid should have boxes at least six inches square, so that the clues will fit into them. (Don't add the clues yet!) Tape the Clue Board on the wall where the whole class can see it.

You can use a chalkboard or bulletin board for the Clue Board instead of butcher paper, as long as it can remain visible during all the following sessions.

Here's how the Clue Board will look at the end of the session, after you and the students have recorded the clues. At the beginning of the activity, only the suspect pictures and names will be on the chart, with the boxes below them empty.

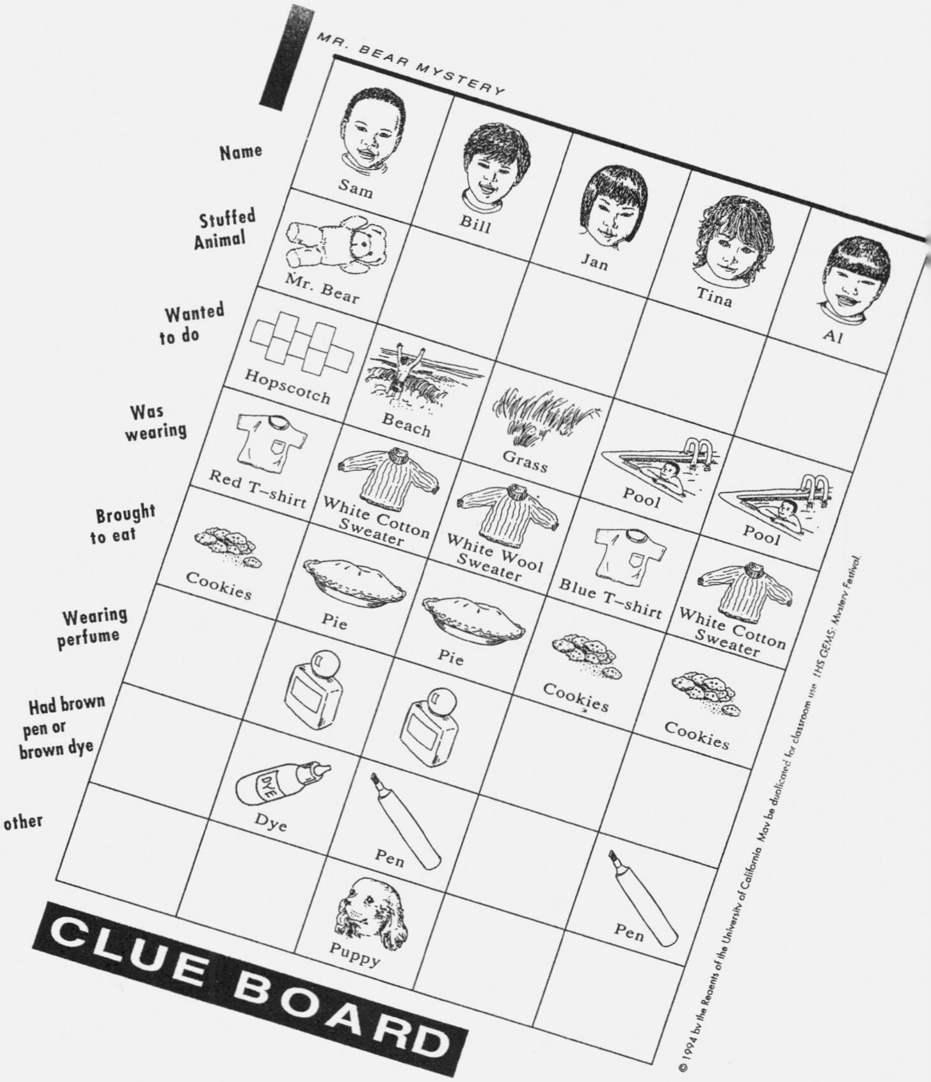

5. Lay out the clues in the order that they are mentioned in the story on page 36. Have them handy, along with some loops of masking tape so that you can quickly stick them on the Clue Board as you read the story to the class. Decide whether you will stick on the clues at the appropriate points, or have student volunteers do it.

Introduce the Session

1. Ask the students to tell you what they remember about what they did during Session 1. As they look at the Crime Scene Map, have them describe in general what they observed.

2. Tell the class that today they'll learn more facts about the suspects and what happened at the scene of the crime.

As appropriate, introduce the terms "clue," as a fact that might help solve the mystery, "suspect" as someone who MIGHT have borrowed Mr. Bear without permission, and "evidence" as anything that might help solve the crime, such as a fingerprint, a note, what a "suspect" or witness says, etc.

Present the Story

1. Explain that the chart on the wall will be a place for the class to record clues that they learn today about "The Case of the Borrowed Bear."

2. Tell the story that appears at the end of this session, on page 36. Then read it a second time, asking students to raise their hands every time they hear a clue that they think should be put on the Clue Board. Help them discriminate between clues and non-clues.

Be aware that the class may have trouble sitting for a long enough time to finish the story ***if too much discussion is allowed.*** *For younger students, it's important to keep the group discussion short, and to read the story more than once.*

3. Read the story again, sticking clues to the Clue Board at the appropriate points in the story. You may even want to read the story one more time, this time leaving out crucial words, and having the students fill them in orally.

The Case of the Borrowed Bear

There is a group of friends named Sam, Bill, Jan, Tina and Al, who all love stuffed animals. They have a club, called "The Stuffed Animal Adventure Club." Here is some information about the friends and some of the things that happened on the day Mr. Bear was borrowed:

Each friend has a favorite stuffed animal. (Beginning with Sam's Mr. Bear, identify the stuffed animals each suspect owned, and set them up near the Clue Board under their owners' pictures.)

1. Sam: Mr. Bear

2. Bill: ____________

3. Jan: ____________

4. Tina: ____________

5. Al: ____________

The five friends got together one afternoon to build a clubhouse for their stuffed animals, and to have a picnic. They all brought their stuffed animals. They also brought paint and wood. After working on their clubhouse for a while, they got tired of building and decided to do something else.

1. Sam wanted to play hopscotch.

2. Bill wanted to take the stuffed animals to go swimming in the salt water at the ocean.

3. Jan wanted to play in the grass.

4. Tina and Al both wanted to swim in a swimming pool, because they don't like salt water.

It's important to know what each of these suspects was wearing:

1. **Sam was wearing a red T-shirt.**

2. **Bill and Al were both wearing white *cotton* sweaters.**

3. **Jan was wearing a white *wool* sweater.**

4. **Tina was wearing a blue T-shirt.**

Everyone brought some treats to the picnic.

1. **Bill and Jan both brought pie.**

2. **Sam, Tina and Al all brought cookies to share.**

Bill and Jan were also both wearing their own favorite kinds of perfume or cologne. Jan and Al both had brown pens with them. Bill had a bottle of brown dye. Aside from her stuffed animal, Jan also has a real puppy that she left at her house. Her house is nearby.

The group couldn't figure out what to do, and soon got tired of arguing, so they decided to share the two cans of cola Sam had brought. They poured some of the cola into a cup with ice. Some of them wanted cold cola, and they passed around and shared the cup with ice and cola in it. The others drank straight from the can, with no ice. Some of them started to get very sleepy, so they all decided to take a nap.

When they woke up, it was two hours later, and Sam was upset. Mr. Bear was soaking wet! It seems that *someone* had not taken a nap. They all figured that someone must have stayed awake and played with Mr. Bear.

It's your job as crime lab scientists to try to solve the mystery by figuring out who stayed awake and played with Mr. Bear without asking permission.

Introducing the Next Two Sessions

1. After all the clues are on the Clue Board, remind your students that if they think they've solved the mystery already, they may have been tricked. Just like real crime scientists, they will need to look carefully at all the clues, all the evidence, and then try to solve the mystery.

2. Explain that in the next two class sessions, they'll be using science to test the evidence they found at the scene of the crime during Session 1 for things like fingerprints.

3. Stress that they will need to complete their tests on the evidence during the next two sessions before they attempt to solve the crime.

Going Further

One teacher said, "This activity helped my kids understand charts and how they are constructed. This would be a good time to have students make additional charts."

1. Have students write stories about the characters in the story or write their ideas so far about the mystery.

2. As a review of the story, you may want to have your students act it out, leaving out what happened while the characters were asleep, since that is the mystery. Tell your students that this is the part they will try to figure out and fill in during the next sessions.

3. Instead of duplicating the drawings of suspects and clues included in this guide, you may choose to take advantage of the art skills of your students and have them do the illustrations themselves.

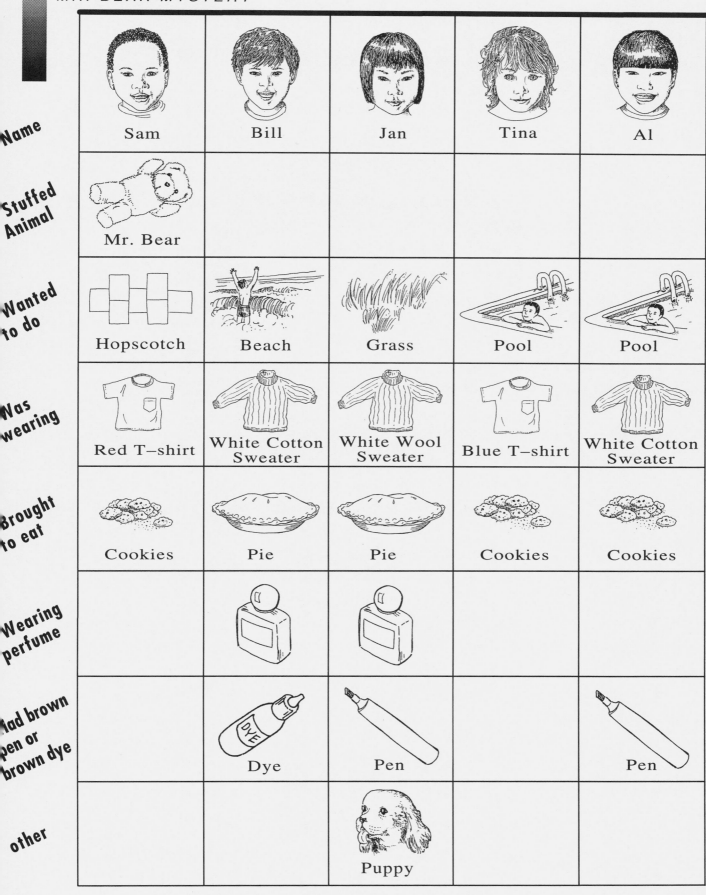

Name	Sam	Bill	Jan	Tina	Al
Stuffed Animal	Mr. Bear				
Wanted to do	Hopscotch	Beach	Grass	Pool	Pool
Was wearing	Red T–shirt	White Cotton Sweater	White Wool Sweater	Blue T–shirt	White Cotton Sweater
Brought to eat	Cookies	Pie	Pie	Cookies	Cookies
Wearing perfume					
Had brown pen or brown dye		Dye	Pen		Pen
other			Puppy		

CLUE BOARD

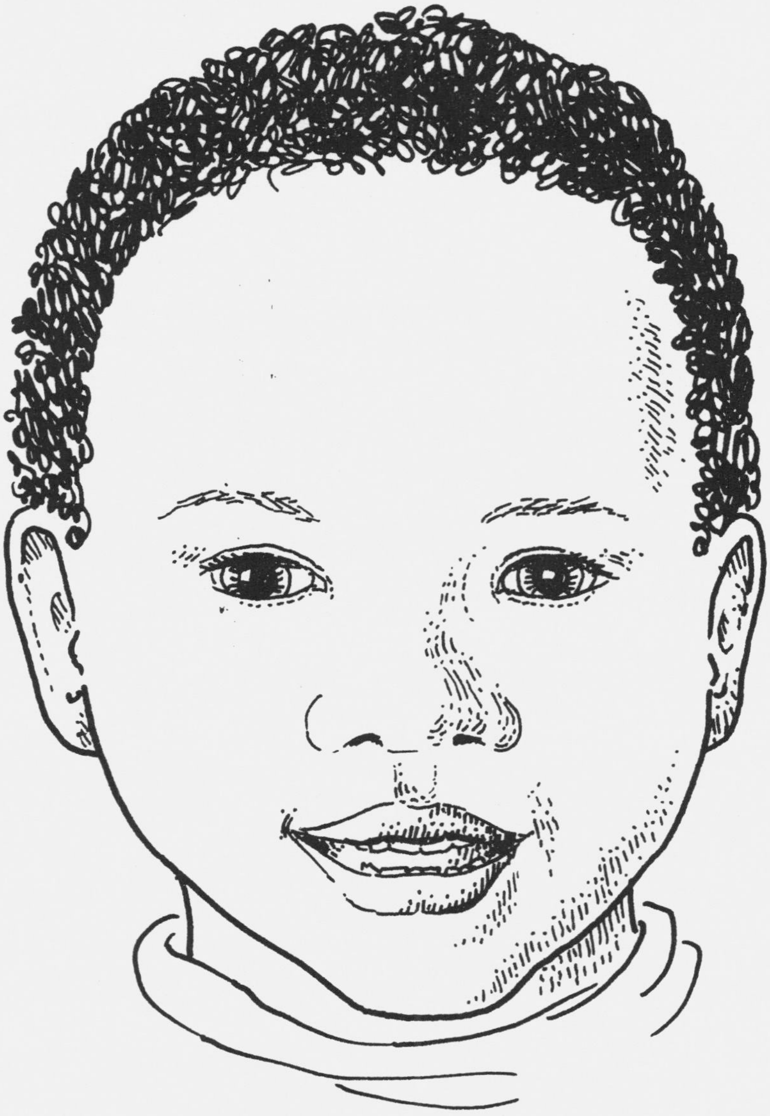

Sam

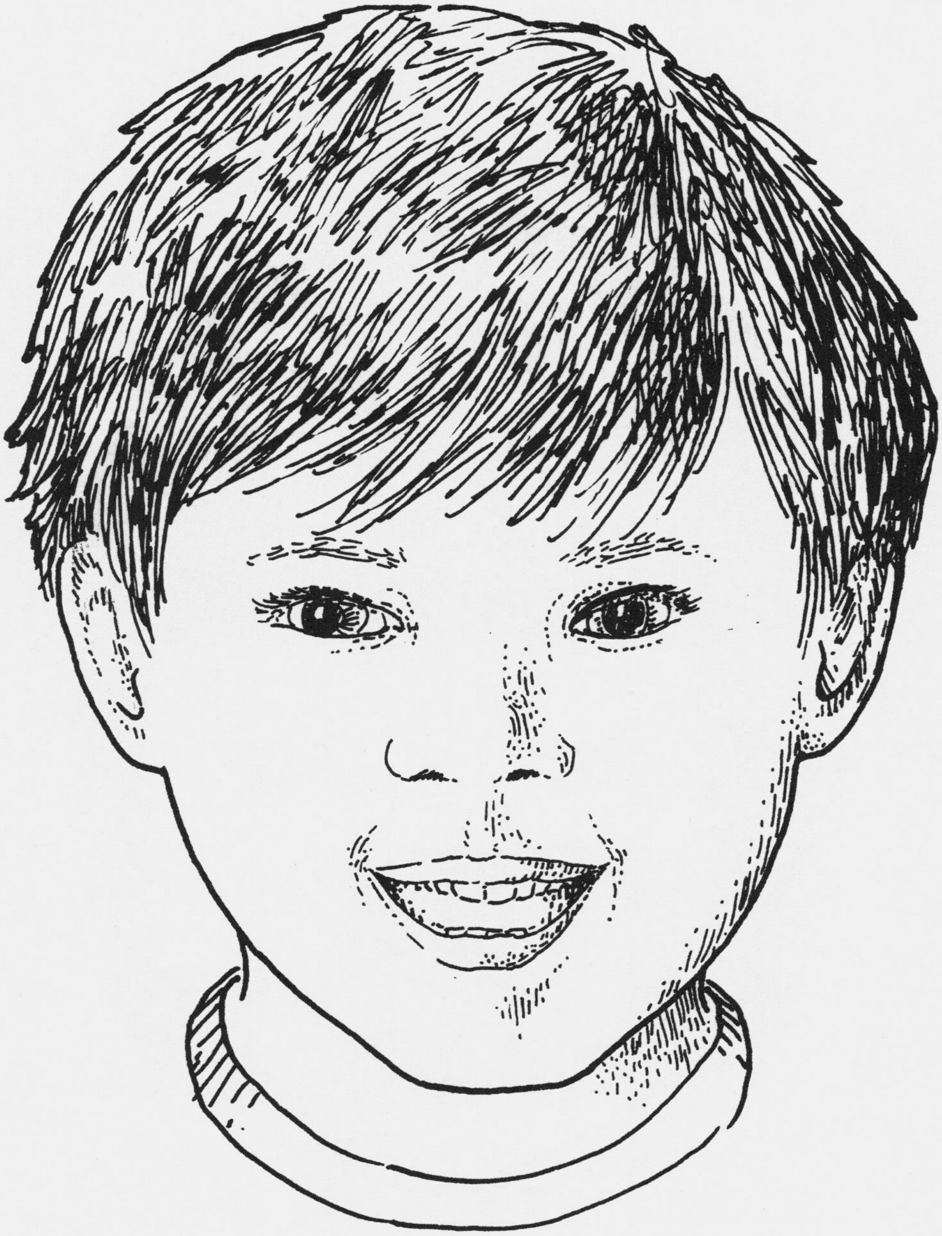

Bill

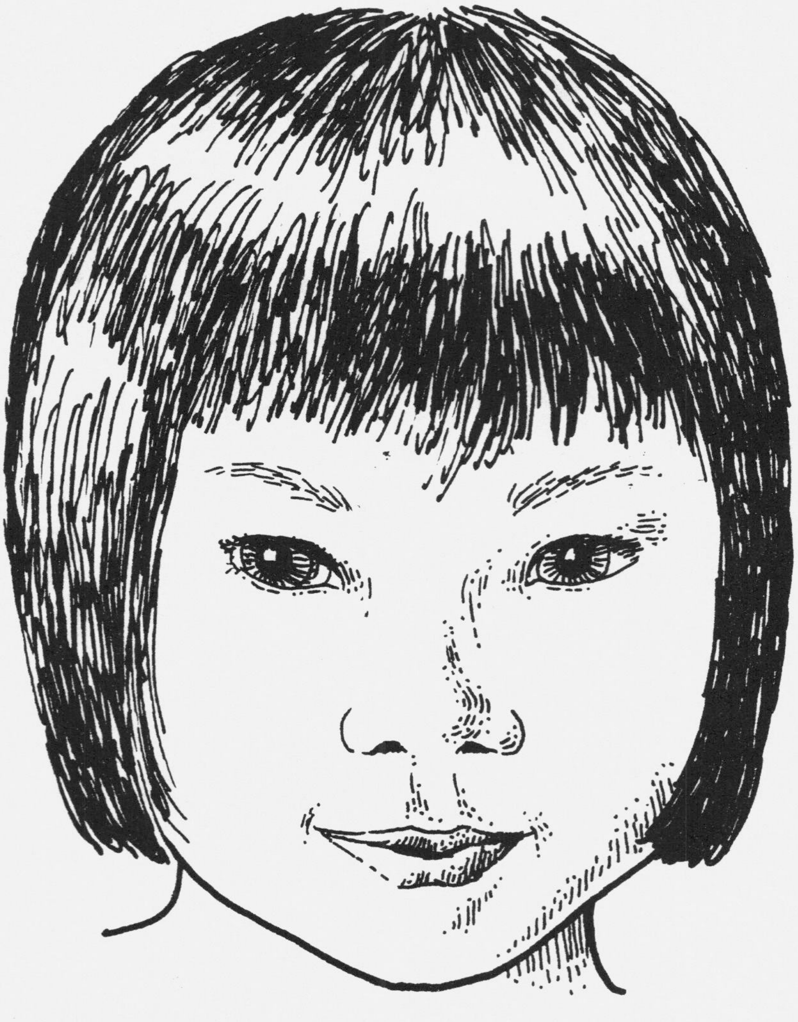

Jan

Tina

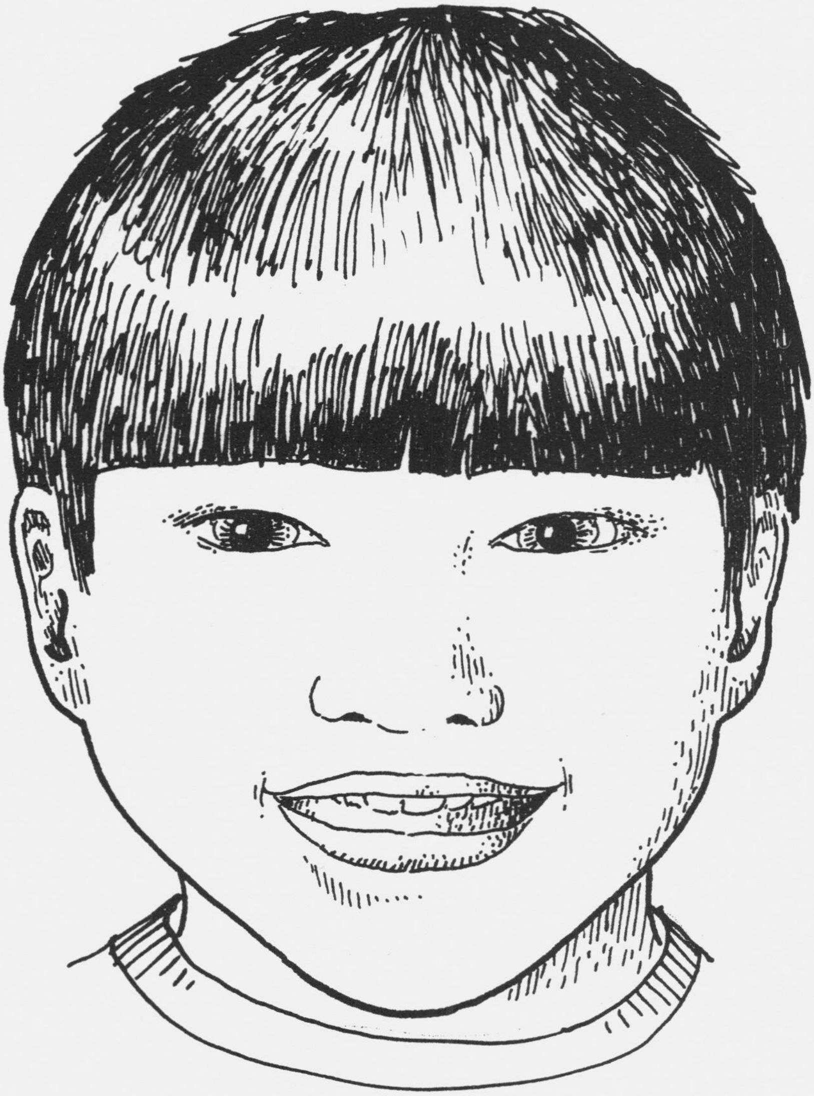

AI

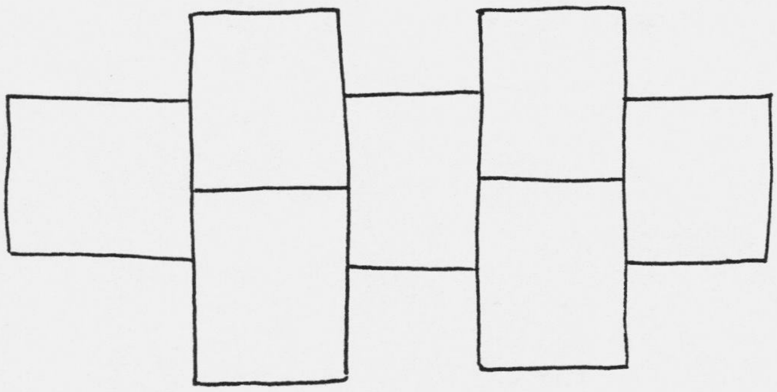

Hopscotch

Beach

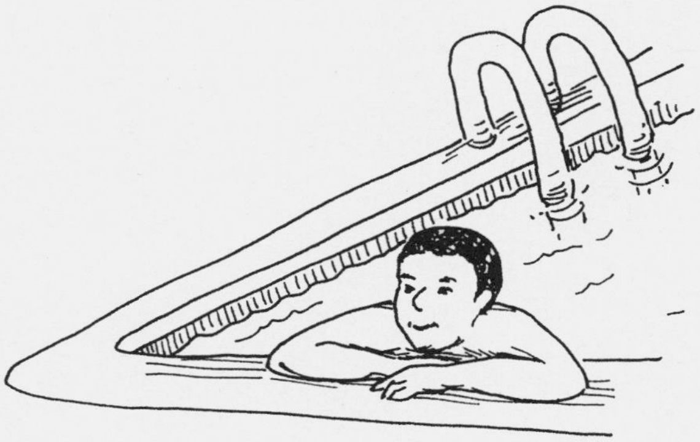

Pool

Pool

Grass

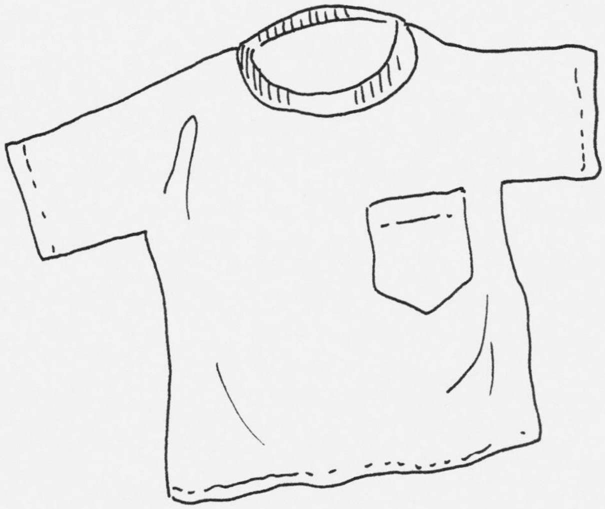

Red T–shirt

White Cotton Sweater

White Wool Sweater

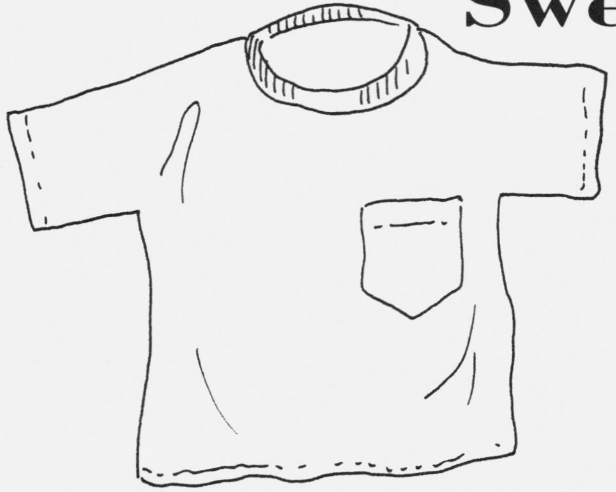

Blue T–shirt

White Cotton Sweater

Cookies

Cookies

Cookies

Pie

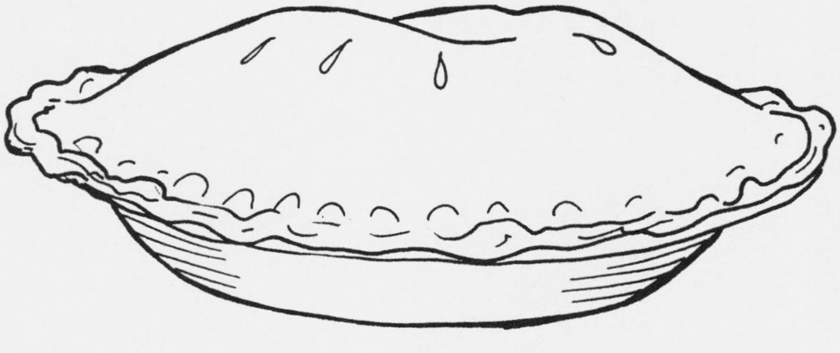

Pie

Bill's

Jan's

Dye

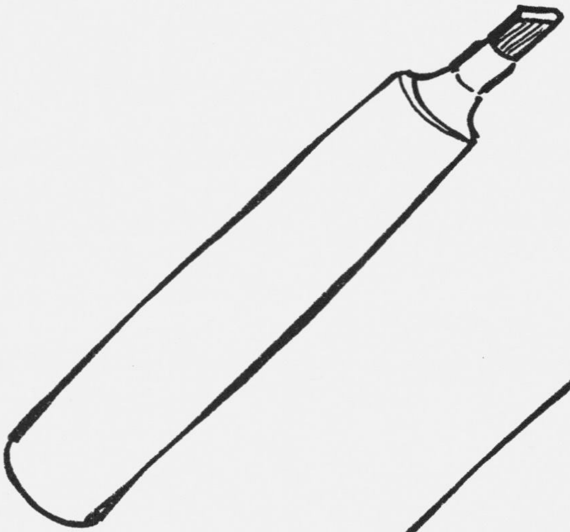

Pen

Pen

Puppy

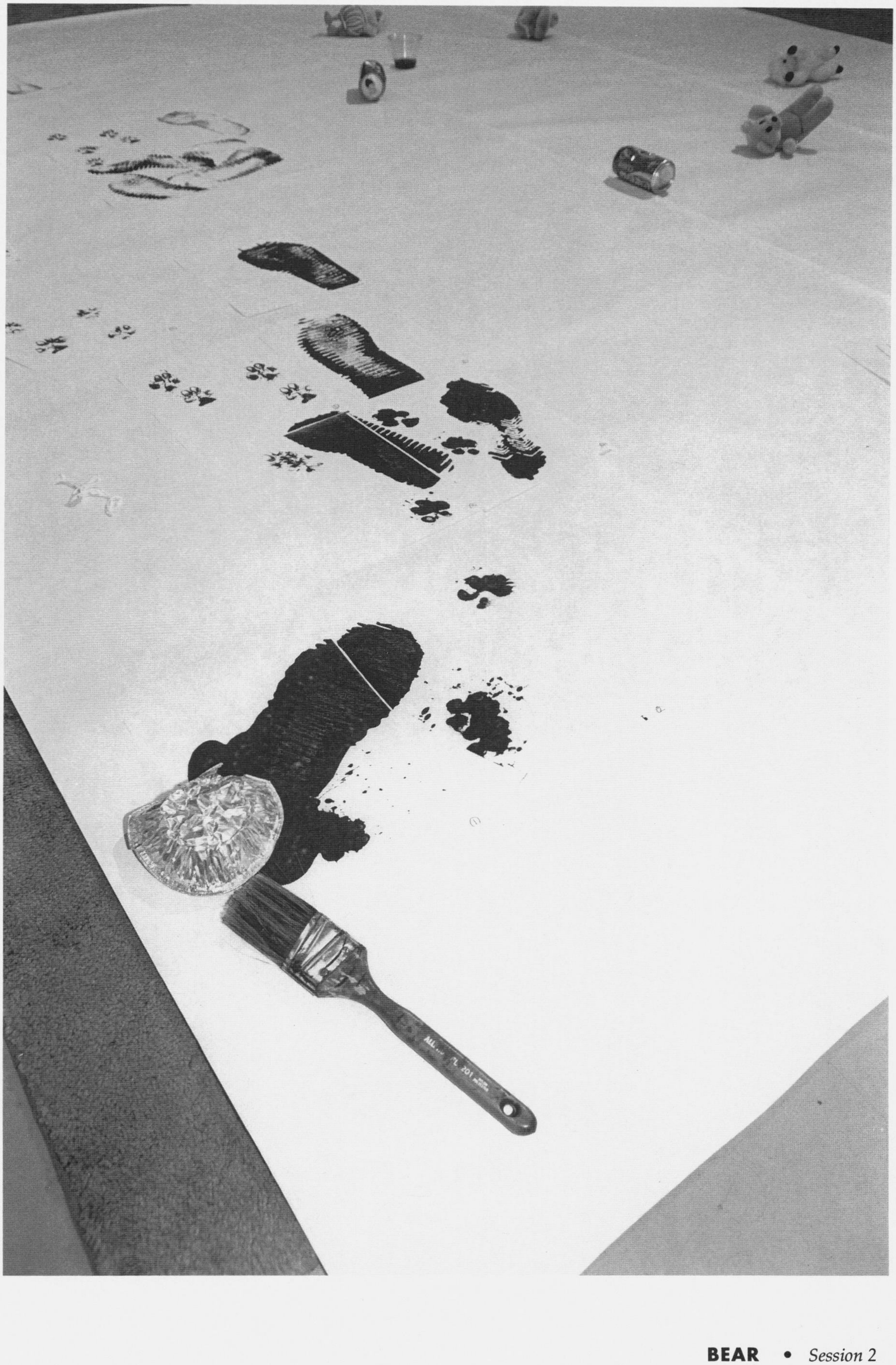

Session 3: Crime Lab Stations (Part 1)

Overview

During this and the following session, your classroom will be transformed into a forensic lab. In all, there are ten basic "crime lab" test stations, five of which are used during this session, and the other five during the next. During this session, the students conduct tests at the following five stations:

Brown Stain
Cola Test
Fingerprints
Smells
Threads

At each of these stations, students conduct tests on the evidence found at the scene of the crime during Session 1, and record their results on data sheets. Illustrated signs explain what to do at each station. At the end of each of the crime lab station days, the class pools their results on an Evidence Chart.

What You Need

- ❐ 1 piece white butcher paper (about 3 feet x 3 feet) for the Evidence Chart
- ❐ a felt-tipped marking pen to record on Evidence Chart
- ❐ masking tape and a permanent pen to label cups

For every two students:

- ❐ 1 copy of the "Mr. Bear Mystery Data Sheet" (master on pages 64–65) (This will also be used in Session 4.)

For the Brown Stain Test Station:

- ❐ four cups (any kind)
- ❐ brown food coloring from Session 1
- ❐ the two brown stain pieces of paper towel you prepared in Session 1
- ❐ 1 brown felt water-base marker
- ❐ 1 roll of clear tape
- ❐ five pencils
- ❐ white paper towels

For the Cola Test Station:

Scientific supply companies are a good source for pH paper. Flinn Scientific, Inc., for example, carries Hydrion 1–14 pH paper, sold by the roll (a roll is 15 feet).

- ❐ 2 cups
- ❐ cola and baking soda sample from Session 1
- ❐ 1 roll of Universal pH paper (this can also be used in the "Melted Ice Cube Test" in Session 4). The exact brand of the pH paper is not important.
- ❐ wastebasket

For the Fingerprint Station:

- ❐ Suspect Fingerprint Chart from page 63
- ❐ Cup Fingerprints illustration from page 62

You may want to use cabbage juice pH paper instead of the commercial type paper. Boil a red cabbage in water in a non-aluminum pan till the water is deep purple. Paint the cabbage juice on white paper with a paintbrush, set it out to dry, then do another coat and let it dry. Cut up into strips. Your simplified pH chart could then simply be pink = acidic, purple = neutral, green = basic. You could even avoid the need to boil the cabbage by using a blender and straining out the cabbage juice.

For the Smells Station:

- ❐ Mr. Bear stuffed animal from Session 1 crime scene
- ❐ 2 empty film canisters
- ❐ 2 colognes or perfumes from Session 1
- ❐ masking tape, for making labels

For the Thread Test Station:

- ❐ 3 cups
- ❐ ~ 6 feet of white cotton yarn
- ❐ ~ 6 feet of colored cotton yarn
- ❐ ~ 6 feet of colored wool yarn (It's best if the yarn looks "woolly.")

Getting Ready

To help you keep track of the preparation tasks below, there is a **Preparation Checklist on page 98**. The list contains all the tasks in this Getting Ready section, but listed more briefly. You might want to make a copy of the Preparation Checklist and use it to check off tasks as you or a volunteer complete the tasks.

Before the Day of the Activity:

1. Make four copies of each station sign.

Having four copies of the sign spread out on the surface of each station allows eight students to use the directions without crowding. If you will have fewer than eight students at each station, or if you prefer to mount signs on the wall or on manila folders to stand, just make as many copies of each sign as you need.

2. For the Fingerprint station, make four copies of the "Whose fingerprints are on the cup?" page (master on page 62), and make four copies of the Suspect Fingerprint Chart (page 63). It is important to make as high-quality a copy as possible, so the fingerprints can be clearly seen.

3. Make one copy of the data sheet for every two students in your class. (pages 64–65) Have a pencil handy for every pair of students.

4. If your students have not had previous experience with the Brown Stain activity (chromatography), we recommend having an adult volunteer at this station. If possible, arrange for a volunteer for this class session. The volunteer could supervise two Brown Stain stations if they are placed close together.

5. Decide if you will make two stations of the Brown Stain activity. If you want two Brown Stain stations, you'll need to double the materials under *Brown Stain,* What You Need, above, and set up two identical stations like the one detailed just below and in "On the Day of the Activity." The only items you will not have to duplicate for the second station are the brown stain paper towels you prepared in Session 1; when you cut them into strips, just put half the strips at the second station.

6. To save time on the day of the activity, you can prepare the materials for the "Brown Stain" and "Cola Test" stations before the day of the activity, as detailed below:

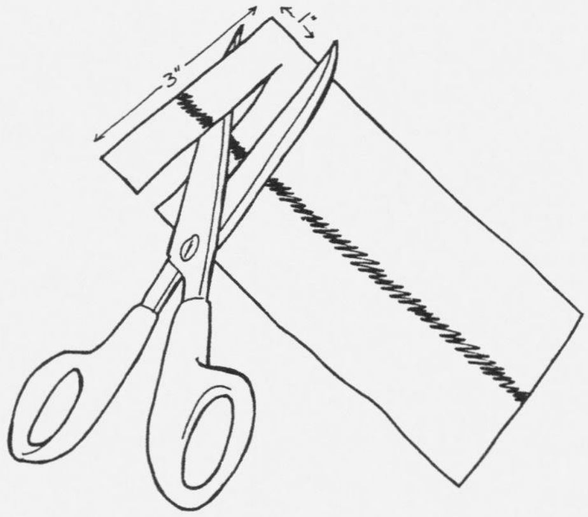

- **Brown Stain Station:**

Prepare the Materials:

1. Cut the brown stain paper towels that you prepared in Session 1 into 1" by 3" strips, one for each pair of students, plus at least one extra.

2. Make the sample **PEN and DYE Sheet** (students will use this sheet for reference at the station). Make two of these sheets if you will have two Brown Stain stations:

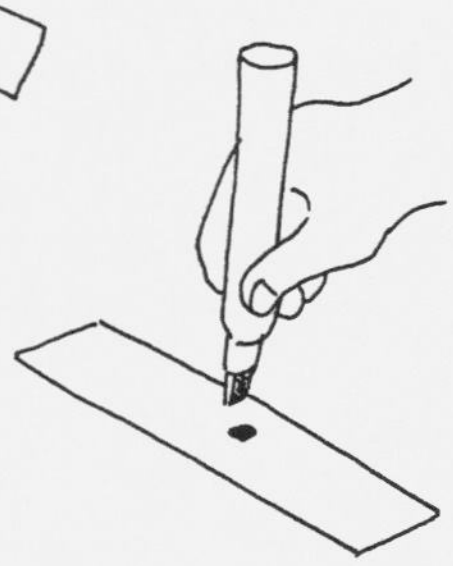

a. Cut one blank strip of a white paper towel, just like the strips in #1 above, but without the brown stain.

b. Make a mark in the middle of the blank strip with the brown felt pen.

c. Tape the strip to a pencil, and do the same with one of the brown stain strips from #1 above. Tape each paper strip to the pencil so that when you set the pencil on top of the cup, **the other end of the strip will hang into the water, but the brown spot will be above the level of the water.**

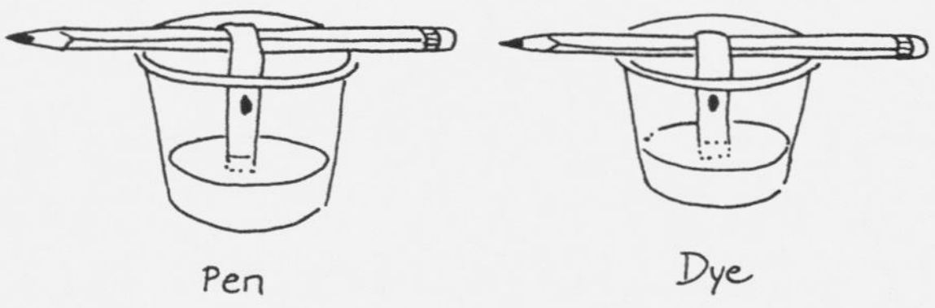

d. Set each pencil, with the paper towel strip taped to it, on top of one of the cups. Let the water crawl up until the paper is wet up to about an inch above the mark.

e. Take the strips out and let them dry.

f. Tape both strips onto one piece of white paper and label them, "PEN" and "DYE."

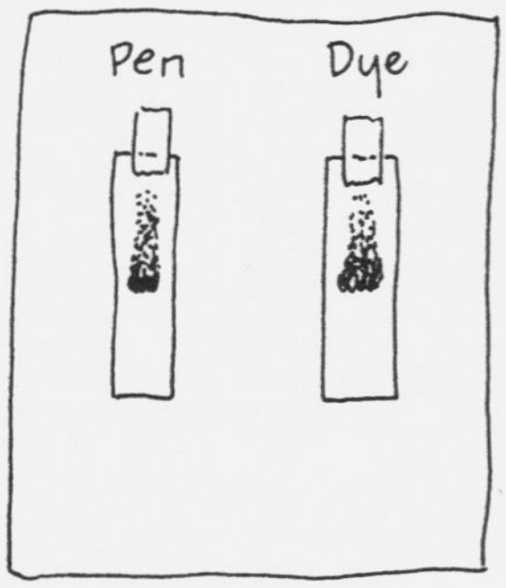

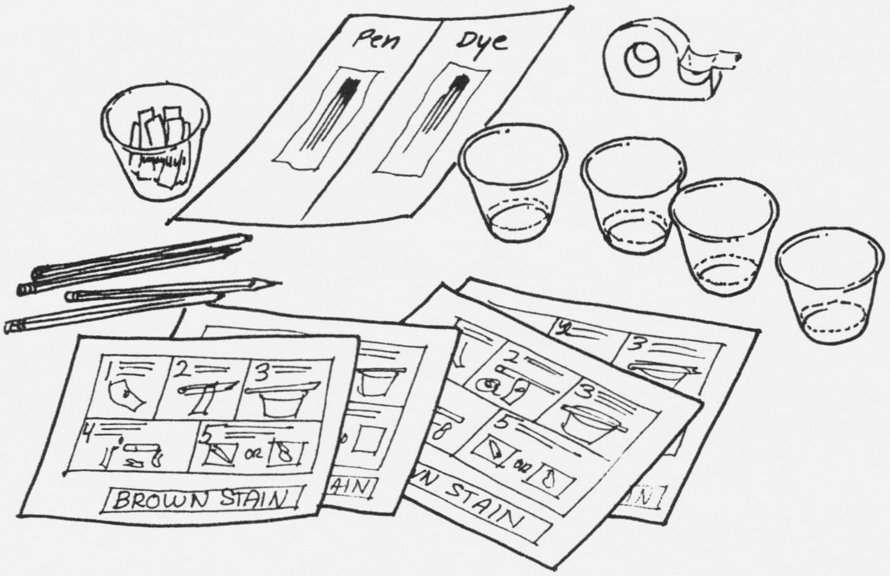

7. Make advance preparations for the Cola Test Station as detailed below:

• Cola Test Station:

Prepare the Materials:

1. Label a cup: "Cola from the cup."

2. Fill it with about 1/2" of the cola and baking soda mixture from the Session 1 crime scene.

3. Cut the pH paper up into strips about 1" long, 1 for each pair of students. Put these into the other cup. (Note: If you have enough pH paper, you might like to provide enough pH strips so that each student can have one. Students will also need the same amount of these pH strips during the next session for the ice cube station.)

4. Optional: Color code the words "Green" and "Yellow" on the sign.

8. If you have adult volunteer(s), briefly explain the station activity they will be helping with, and make sure the volunteer understands the central importance of allowing the students to make their own discoveries and conduct the experiments themselves.

• Set up the Evidence Chart:

1. Post butcher paper on the wall, or set aside chalkboard or bulletin board space of about three by five feet. **This chart will be used during the remaining sessions. It is best to keep it posted in an accessible spot all through the Festival.**

2. Copy the **bold lettered portion only** of the "MR. BEAR" EVIDENCE CHART SHEET (see page 61) onto the chalkboard or butcher paper.

On the Day of the Activity:

1. **Brown Stain**

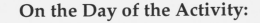

At this station, students will do a test in which they hang a strip of paper towel from a pencil into a cup of water, so that the bottom end of the strip gets wet. Water moves up the paper, causing a stain on the middle of the strip to separate into different colors. This kind of test is called "paper chromatography."

1. Gather the paper strips and PEN and DYE sheet prepared previously (as described under "Brown Stain" in "Before the Day of the Activity," above).
2. Pour about 1/2" of water into each of four cups, or enough so that the 3 inch paper strip will just touch the water when suspended from a pencil.

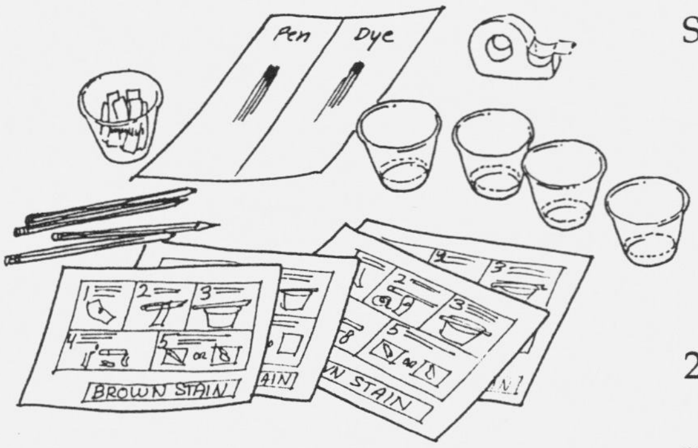

Set out these materials at the station:

1. The brown stain paper towel strips described above.
2. The PEN and DYE sheet described above.
3. 1 roll of transparent adhesive tape
4. At least five pencils
5. The Brown Stain signs
6. Cups with water in them

2. **Cola Test**

At this station, students test a cup of cola for acidity, using pH paper.

Gather the cola cup with cola and baking soda mixture, and pH paper strips, as previously prepared under "Cola Test Station" in "Before the Day of the Activity."

Set out these materials at the station:

1. The cup with cola and the pH strips
2. The Cola Test sign
3. Wastebasket

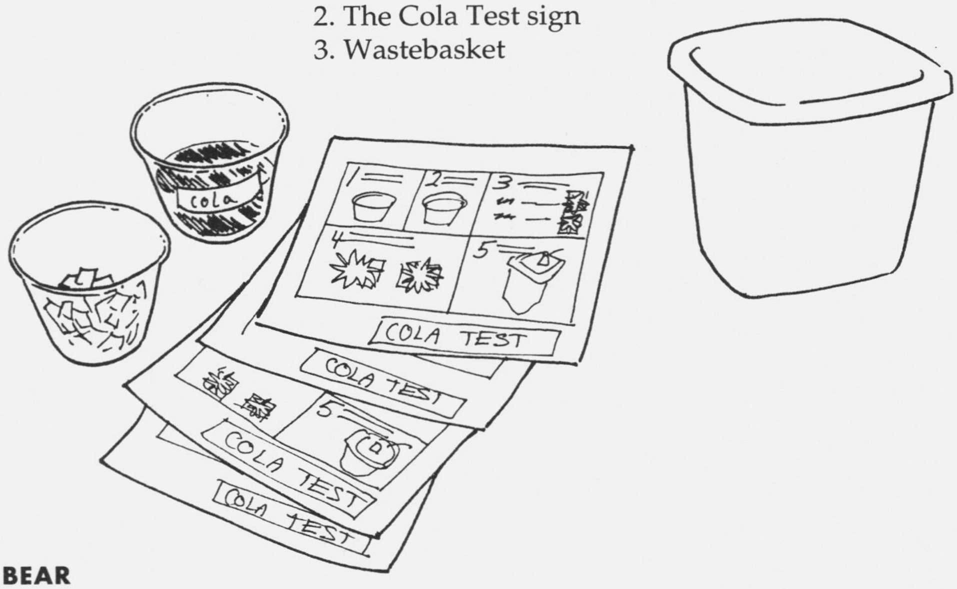

3. **Fingerprints**

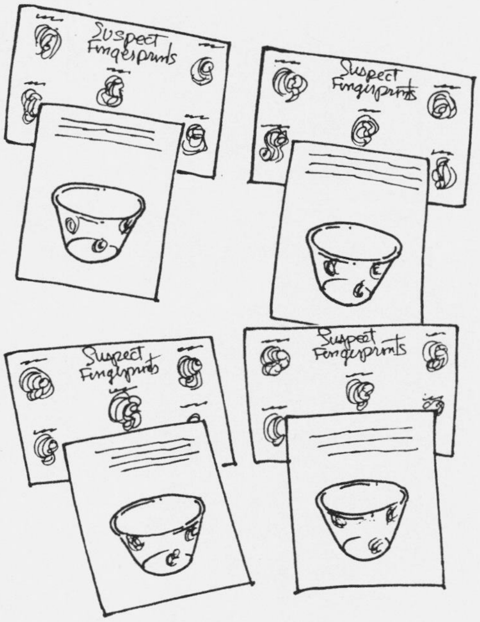

At this station, students compare fingerprints on a cup to those on the Suspect Fingerprint Chart.

Set out these materials at the station:

1. The four copies of the "Cups with Fingerprints" page.
2. The four copies of the Suspect Fingerprint Chart.
3. The Fingerprints sign.

4. **Smells**

At this station, students compare the scents in two film canisters with the smell on Mr. Bear.

Prepare the materials:

1. Label the two film canisters with Jan and Bill's names.
2. Put about one drop of the same perfume as you put on Mr. Bear into the container labeled "Jan." Close the container.
3. Put about a drop of a *distinctly different-smelling* cologne or perfume into the container labeled "Bill." Close the container.

Set out these materials at the station:

1. Scented stuffed animal "Mr. Bear" from Session 1 crime scene.
2. The two scented film canisters.
3. The Smells sign

5. **Threads**

At this station, students compare three types of thread.

Prepare the materials:

1. Cut the three types of yarn (white cotton, colored cotton, and colored wool) into 2" pieces, 25 of each.
2. Label the 3 cups, "Mystery Thread," "Cotton Thread" and "Wool Thread."
3. Put the white cotton yarn into the cup labeled, "Mystery Thread."
4. Put the colored cotton yarn and the colored wool yarn into the other two cups.

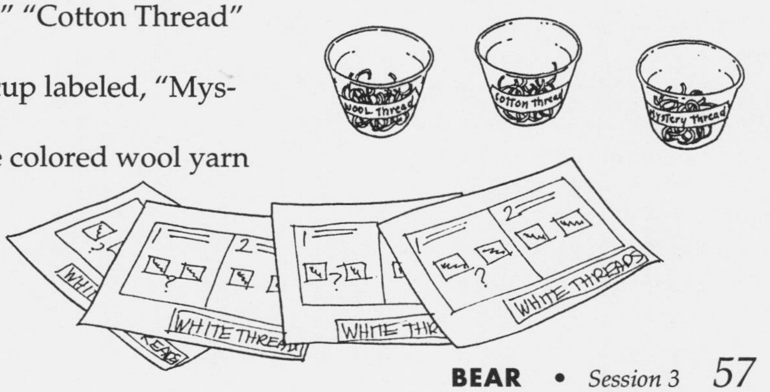

Set out these materials at the station:

1. The Thread Test sign
2. The cups with yarn in them

Introduce the Stations

1. Explain to the students that today they will perform scientific tests on the evidence found at the scene of the crime in order to find out more about who borrowed Mr. Bear.

2. Tell the students they will work with a partner to do the tests at each station. Hold up a sign and tell them they'll need to look at the pictures and/or read each step on the signs to understand how to do each test.

3. Demonstrate the procedures for each station **without actually doing the tests or giving away the results**. Read the appropriate steps on the station sign before each demonstration.

4. Explain **very briefly** how each test ties in with the mystery, as in the following:

> **Brown stain station:** "We found a brown stain on a piece of paper at the crime scene. Some suspects had brown pens, some had brown dye. Was it pen or dye that made the brown stain?"
>
> **Cola station:** "Was there sleeping potion in the cola ? We'll do a test to find out."
>
> **Fingerprints on plastic station:** "Who drank cola from the cup? We'll find out by checking whose fingerprints are on the plastic cup." Be sure to mention to the class that more than one person's fingerprints may be on the plastic cup.
>
> **Smell station:** "On Mr. Bear we also found the smell of perfume or cologne. Bill wears cologne and Jan wears perfume. Which scent is on Mr. Bear?"
>
> **Threads station:** "We found threads at the crime scene. We know that some suspects wore white wool sweaters and some wore white cotton sweaters. Which kind of threads are the ones we found at the crime scene?"

*Please note: At this station, it will not be important that your students understand **why** the paper changes color when dipped in the cola solution. For primary students, the discovery that they can identify different substances with this process is wonderful enough. Your students' experiences here will serve as a solid foundation of experience on which to build future concepts of pH and acid-base chemistry. The GEMS units **Of Cabbages and Chemistry** and **Acid Rain**, for upper elementary and middle school students, explore these concepts further.*

Many teachers find it helpful to do a pre-teaching activity on fingerprints before students go to the fingerprinting station, so that students know what to look for. Consider teaching the GEMS unit Fingerprinting or presenting an activity on Footprints (page 13) in the weeks before your Mystery Festival. For a shorter introduction, make the "Suspect Fingerprint Sheet" for this session into an overhead transparency. Take a few minutes before the day of Session 3 to focus students on the lines and patterns, asking "What do the lines remind you of?" [bulls-eyes, hills, swirls...] Tell them that each person has different fingerprints from everyone else's, and they are going to look carefully at the prints on the cup of cola left at the scene of the crime to see if they match any of the suspect's prints.

Some students will probably have difficulty distinguishing between the scents at this station. That's to be expected! Let them know that smells are hard to tell apart and that scientists and detectives might have the same kind of difficulty. Have students do their best, and perhaps together the group will be able to reach a conclusion.

Crime Lab Testing and Recording Results

1. Tell the students that each team will carry with them a data sheet and pencil to record their results. Explain that the numbers on their data sheets correspond to the numbers on the station signs. Show them how to record their results by circling their answer on their data sheet.

2. Explain to the class that when they finish their first station, they may go to any other available station they like, until they have completed all five. Remind them not to run, and to try to go to less crowded stations. (If you have two Brown Stain stations, explain that they are identical.)

3. Mention that when they are between stations, or if they finish early, they may return to the Crime Scene Map and Clue Board to attempt to piece together the evidence.

4. Caution students not to jump to conclusions after doing only one or two stations. Solving a mystery is like putting together a big puzzle—it is very hard to see the whole picture if you have only one or two pieces.

5. When the students understand what they are to do, have them choose partners, hand out data sheets and pencils, and assign each team to its first station.

Pooling Class Data

1. When all, or at least most, of your students have completed the stations, gather the partners with their data sheets in front of them near the blank Evidence Chart. Give pairs or teams a few minutes to discuss among themselves, to make sure that they agree on the results they recorded on their data sheet. This helps to avoid arguments between partners in front of the class.

2. Refocus the group to gather the results from each of the five station activities. In each case, ask first for a volunteer to report their results. Ask the rest of the class to raise their hands if they agree. Ask those who disagree to raise their hands. Find out the results of those who disagree.

3. Make sure students feel comfortable reporting results that differ from those of their classmates. There may be a lot of disagreement. If there is, ask the students how they think that different students conducting the same test could come up with completely different results. They may suggest: Impurities in the substances, procedure not performed identically,

faulty equipment, students observing the same thing but describing it differently, errors in recording data etc.

4. Make sure the students realize that scientists often disagree, and they shouldn't feel like they have failed if their results are different from other people's. Below are three different strategies to deal with a variety of results.

- Write down all results on the board, but record only the results of the majority on the Evidence Chart.

- If the students disagree completely, you may want to declare that particular piece of evidence inconclusive, and not use it with your class. Or, you may want to have your students, or a small team of students, return and redo this experiment with particular care.

- Simply record how many groups in your class came up with different results, and move on.

3. Once the class has agreed on a set of results for each station, record them on the Evidence Chart in the results column.

4. Compare these results with the information on the Clue Board, and ask your students which of the suspects each piece of evidence points to. Record this under the "Who Looks Guilty?" column. A list of probable results is also included for the teacher, and is written in italics on page 61.

5. Tell your students that during the next session they will conduct five more tests on the remaining evidence.

6. Collect their data sheets so they will have them for the next session.

"Mr. Bear" EVIDENCE CHART

Session 3

Station	Results	Who Looks Guilty?
1) Brown Stain	*Dye (He had a bottle of brown dye)*	*Bill*
2) Cola test	*Yes — sleeping potion (They were the only two who didn't drink the cola with sleeping potion in the cups)*	*Jan and Bill*
3) Fingerprints	*Al, Tina, and Sam (Jan and Bill must have drunk straight from the cans—without ice cubes)*	*Jan and Bill*
4) Smells	*Jan's perfume*	*Jan*
5) Threads	*Cotton (both were wearing cotton sweaters)*	*Al and Bill*

Session 4

Station	Results	Who Looks Guilty?
6) Crystals		
7) Melted Ice Cube Test		
8) Secret Note		
9) Powder Study		
10) Tape Lift		
	<u>Other Results</u>	
11) Footprints	*Bill, Jan & Puppy*	*Bill, Jan & Puppy*
Going Further:		

Whose fingerprints are on the cup?

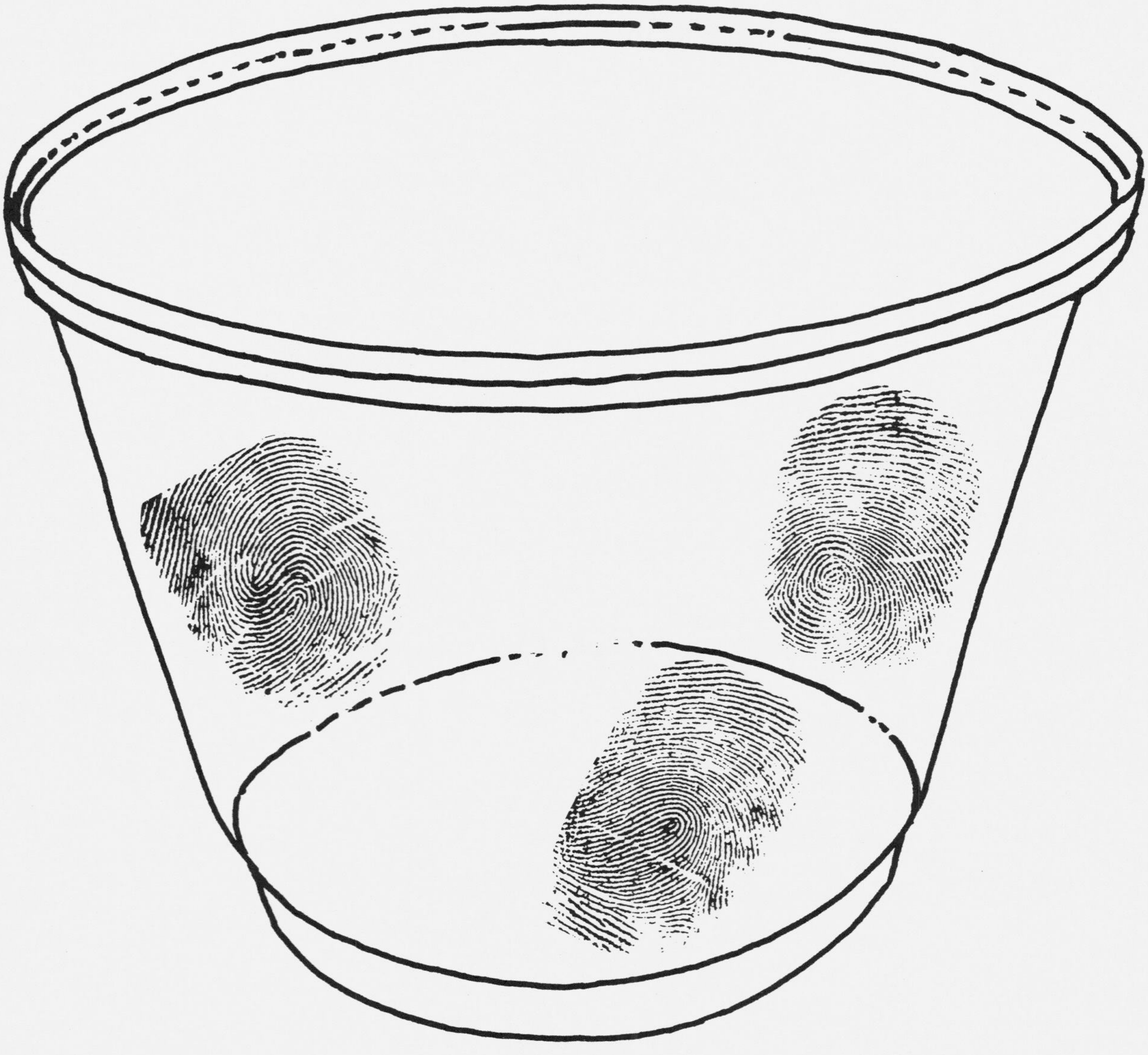

SUSPECT FINGERPRINTS

TINA

JAN

AL

SAM

BILL

NAMES ______________________________

____

CIRCLE YOUR ANSWER:

1. Brown Stain

What was the brown stain on the paper?

Pen

Dye

2. Cola Test

Was there sleeping potion in the cola?

Yes

No

3. Fingerprints

Who drank from the cups?

Sam

Tina

Bill

Jan

Al

4. Smells

Whose perfume was on Mr. Bear?

Bill

Jan

5. White Threads

What kind of thread was near Mr. Bear?

Cotton

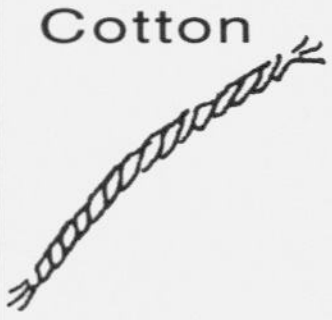

Wool

NAMES________________________________

____

CIRCLE YOUR ANSWER:

6. Mystery Crystals

What kind of crystals were on Mr. Bear?

Salt

Sugar

7. Ice Cube Test

Was there sleeping potion in the ice cubes?

Yes

No

8. Secret Note

Whose name was on the secret note?

Sam

Tina

Bill

Jan

Al

9. Powders

What kind of powder was on Mr. Bear?

Pie

Cookie

10. Tape Lift

What did you find on Mr. Bear?

Dog Hair

Grass
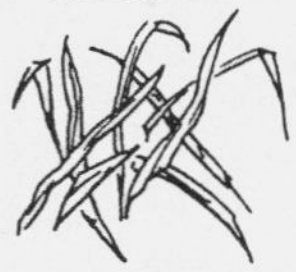

Mr. Bear MYSTERY 2 DATA SHEET

BROWN STAIN STATION SIGN

1 Get a piece of paper with a mystery dot on it.

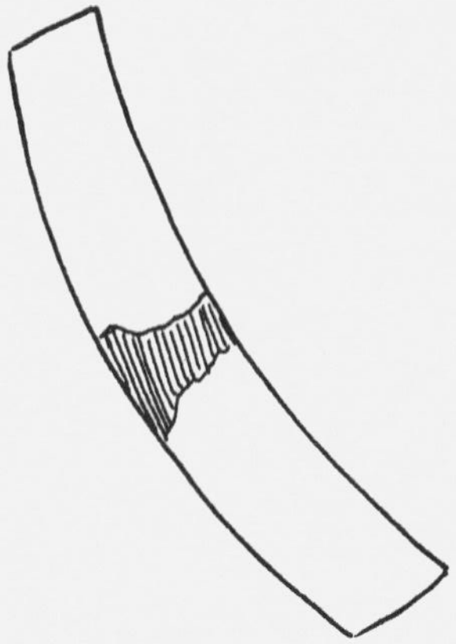

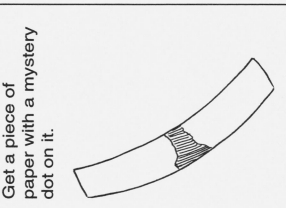

2 Tape the paper to a pencil.

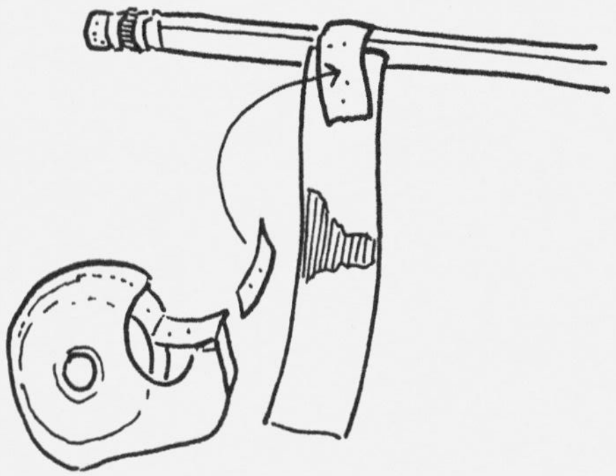

3 Set the pencil on a cup of water, so that the paper touches the water and the water starts climbing up the paper.

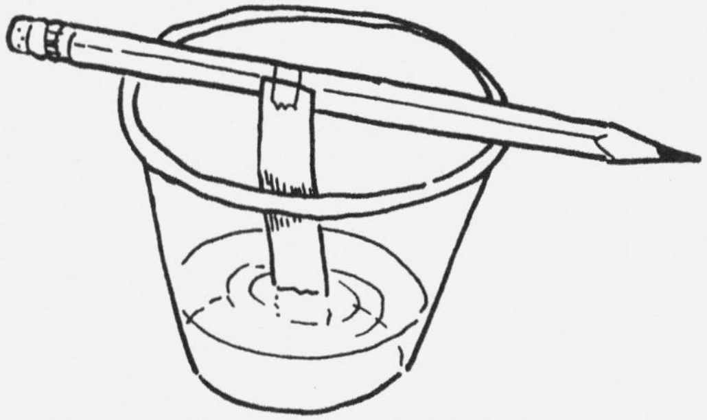

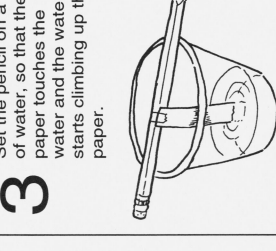

4 Look at the pen and dye samples. Which one matches the one you made?

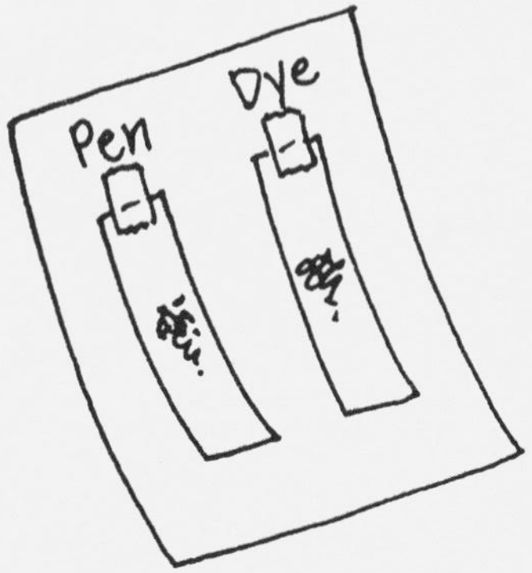

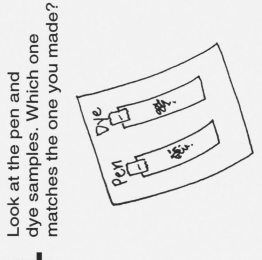

5 **What was the brown stain on the paper near Mr. Bear?**

or

COLA TEST
STATION SIGN

1 Take one piece of test paper.

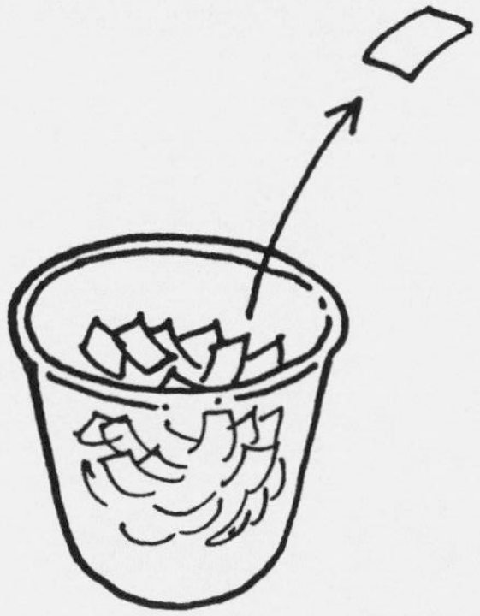

2 Dip the paper in the cola.

3

Green = sleeping potion = Yes

Yellow = No sleeping potion = No

4 **Was there sleeping potion in the cola?**

Yes or No

5 Throw away your used paper in the garbage can.

FINGERPRINTS STATION

1 Whose fingerprints are on the cup?

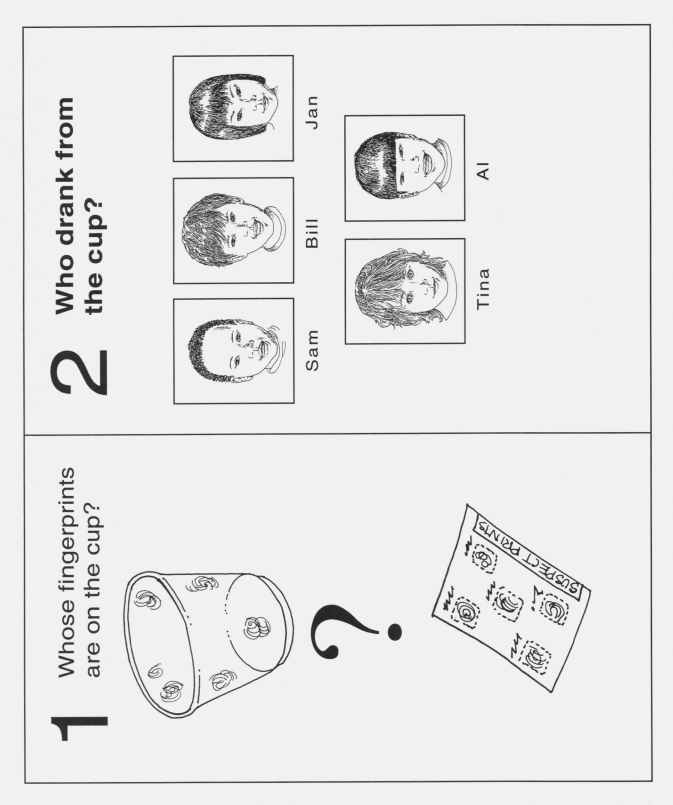

2 Who drank from the cup?

Sam Bill Jan

Tina Al

1 Which smell matches the one on Mr. Bear?

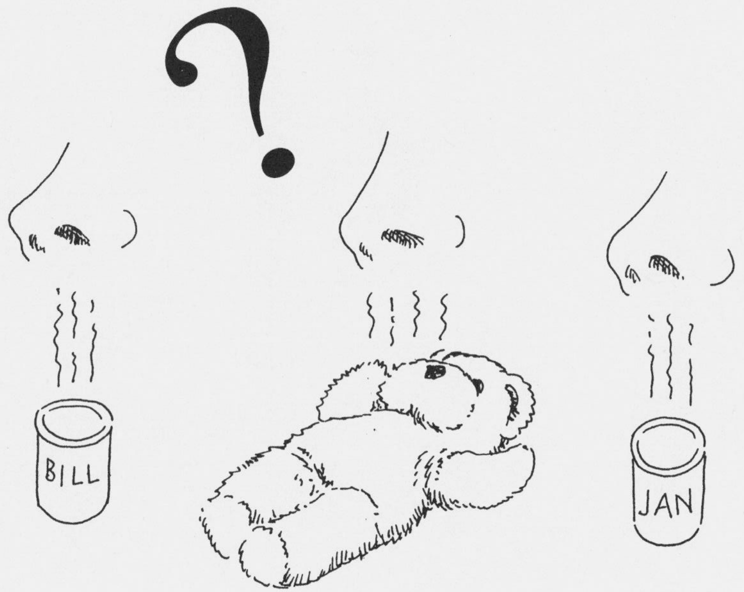

2 Whose perfume was on Mr. Bear?

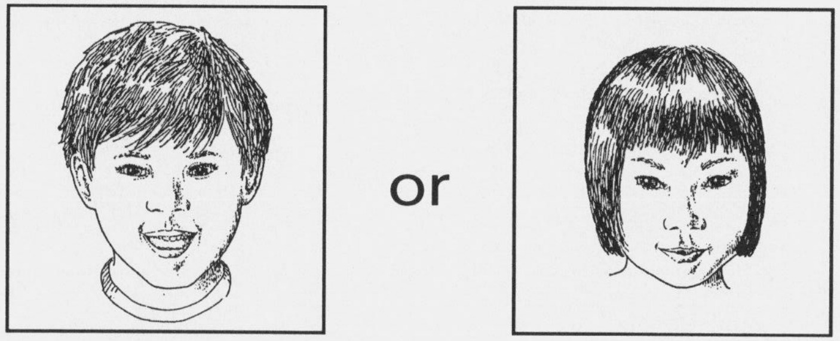

Bill

Jan

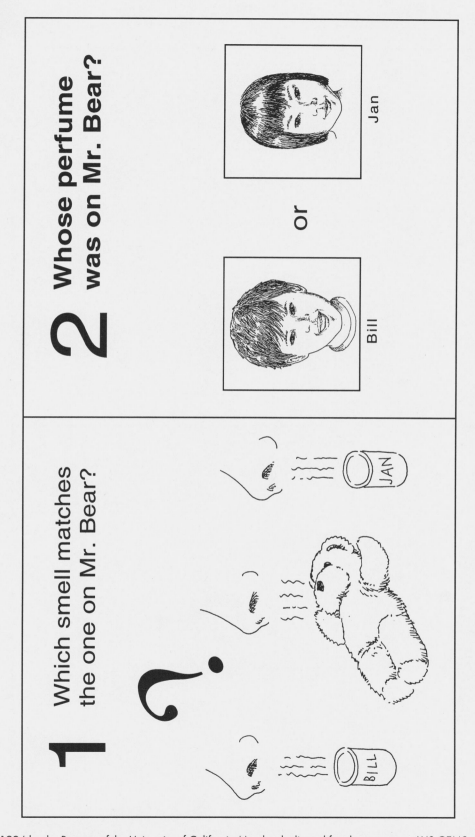

SMELLS STATION SIGN

1 Does the mystery thread look more like the wool or cotton thread?

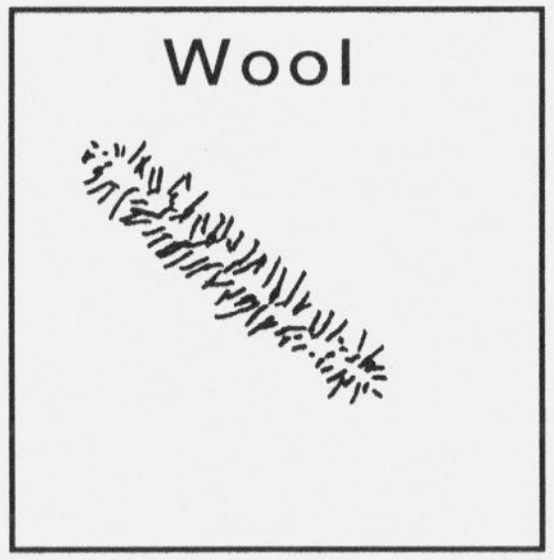

?

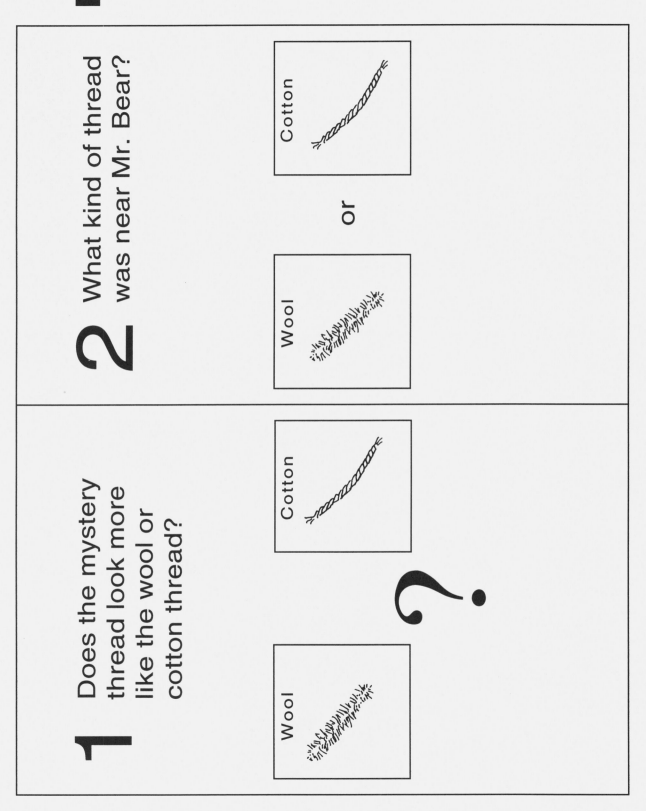

2 What kind of thread was near Mr. Bear?

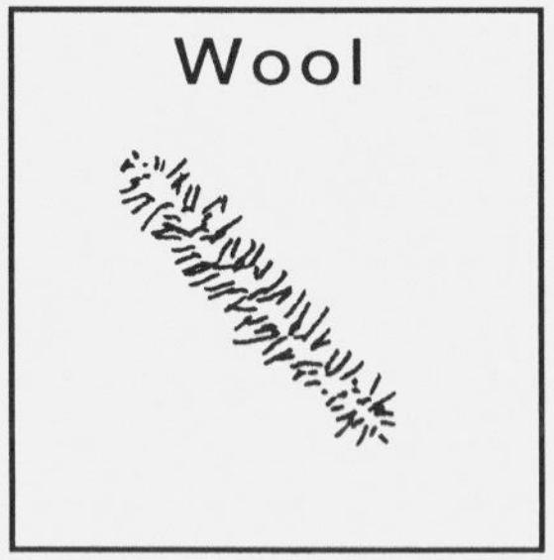

or

tinker toys

Mr. Bear Mystery Data Sheet

Session 4: Crime Lab Stations (Part 2)

Overview

This session follows the same format as Session 3, except the station activities are different, and are used to test different pieces of evidence. During this session the students conduct tests at the following five stations:

Mystery Crystals

Melted Ice Cube Test

Secret Note

Powders

Tape Lift

As before, students conduct tests on the evidence found at the scene of the crime during Session 1, and record their results on their data sheets. Illustrated signs tell students what to do at each station. At the end of the session, the class pools their results, and adds the new information to the Evidence Chart started in the previous session.

INFORMATION ON IODINE

Two iodine solutions are generally available from pharmacies: ***strong*** *tincture of iodine (85% alcohol, 7% iodine, 5% potassium iodide) or* ***mild*** *tincture of iodine (2% iodine).* ***We recommend that you obtain the mild tincture of iodine, then dilute it further to 1% iodine*** *by mixing one part water with one part of the 2% iodine solution. If you can only find the strong tincture, then dilute it to make 1% iodine, by mixing six parts water with one part of the 7% iodine solution. DO NOT USE TINCTURES OF IODIDES—clear solutions that do not contain iodine—because THEY WILL NOT WORK in the class tests!*

Iodine solutions have long been safely used topically, on human skin cuts and abrasions to disinfect wounds. Health authorities do recommend caution when handling the pure, solid form of iodine, but the dilute solutions used in these GEMS activities are not considered dangerous. Iodine is toxic when taken in large amounts internally. In general—as is a wise safety precaution when engaging in all chemistry-related experiments—make sure your students are aware that they should not taste or swallow ANY chemicals!

What You Need

For the Crystals Station:

- ❐ 3 clear plastic cups with sugar and salt crystals prepared in Session 1 "Getting Ready."

For the Melted Ice Cube Test Station:

- ❐ 2 cups
- ❐ ice cube tray from Session 1 crime scene
- ❐ the "baking soda water" from the tray in Session 1
- ❐ one roll of pH paper (use the same one as in Session 3 Cola Test station).

For the Secret Note Station:

- ❐ four small mirrors, preferably with stands (clay works as a make-shift stand)
- ❐ four copies of the backwards "Bill" note from Session 1 crime scene

For the Powders Station:

- ❐ 1 cup (to put powder in)
- ❐ 2 white test trays (Styrofoam egg cartons work well. If these are not available, you could use white plastic paint trays from an art store or white ice cube trays.)
- ❐ 1 large plastic trash bag
- ❐ about 4 tablespoons of cornstarch
- ❐ 1 sponge
- ❐ paper towels
- ❐ 1/8 teaspoon
- ❐ 1-4 small dropper bottles (empty medicine dropper bottles, saline fluid bottles, or similar small bottles are fine)
- ❐ about 1/2 ounce of iodine

For the Tape Lift Station:

- ❐ Mr. Bear stuffed animal
- ❐ 2 white sheets of paper (8 1/2" x 11")
- ❐ about 30 strands of pet hair (dog or cat hair is fine)
- ❐ about 1 handful of grass
- ❐ 1 roll clear tape from Session 3

Getting Ready

To help you keep track of the preparation tasks below, there is a Preparation Checklist on page 98.

Before the Day of the Activity:

1. Make four copies of each station sign (or fewer if you don't need four).

2. Have the student data sheets from Session 3 handy, along with a pencil for every pair of students.

3. To save time on the day of the activity, you can prepare the materials for the "Melted Ice Cube" and "Powders" stations before the day of the activity, as detailed below:

Melted Ice Cube:

1. Cut the pH paper up into strips about one inch long, one for each pair of students.
2. Put these into a cup.

Powders:

1. If you are using white styrofoam egg cartons as test trays, cut them into four trays with six compartments each.
2. Slit the large plastic garbage bag so that you have one large sheet of plastic to protect the table from iodine spills.
3. Label the cup: "Mr. Bear Powder."
4. Put about one inch of cornstarch and the spoon (or stirrer) in the cup.
5. Fill one to four small dropper bottles with iodine and label them.

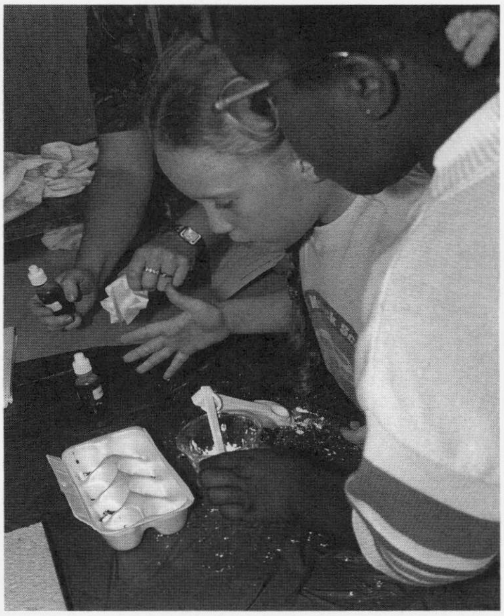

4. Decide if you will have two stations of the "Powders" activity. In Session 4, this is the station where students may tend to "pile up," because it takes longer. If you want two "Powders" stations, you'll need to double the materials listed under *Powders* in "What You Need" to make two stations, as described above.

5. Most teachers of young students feel that, because iodine stains clothes, and because this is a potentially messy station, it is important to have an adult volunteer at the "Powders" station. The volunteer can also help rinse out the test trays before the next group does the test. If you decide that you

need a volunteer, arrange to have one for this session. If you have two "Powders" stations, set them up close to each other, and one volunteer can probably supervise both.

On the Day of the Activity:

If you have adult volunteer(s), orient them to the station activity(ies) they will be helping with, and make sure they understand **the central importance of allowing the students to make their own discoveries and conduct the experiments themselves.**

1. Mystery Crystals

Prepare the materials:
1. Label one of the salt crystal cups you prepared in Session 1, "Mr. Bear Mystery Crystals."
2. Label the other salt and sugar crystal cups, "Salt Crystals" and "Sugar Crystals."

Set out these materials at the station:
1. The three labeled cups
2. The Crystals station sign

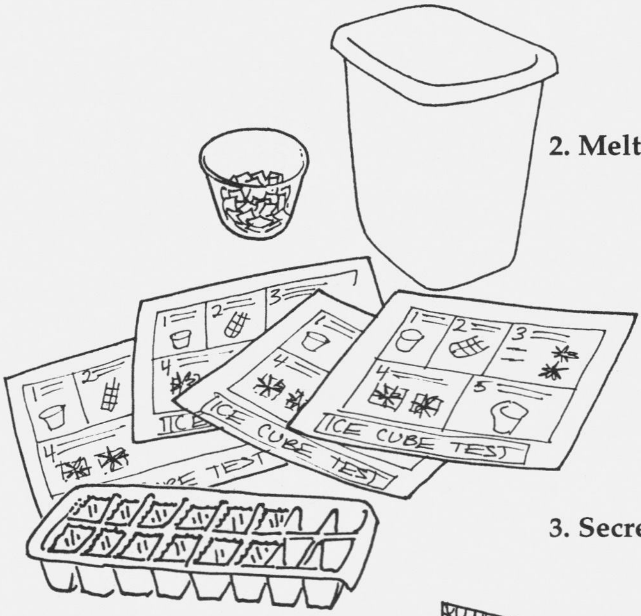

2. Melted Ice Cube Test

Prepare the materials as described under "Melted Ice Cube Test" in "Before the Day of the Activity," above (pH paper strips in a cup, and the ice cube tray with baking soda from Session 1).

Set out these materials at the station:
1. Ice cube tray from Session 1 crime scene with baking soda water filling all but four compartments
2. The pH paper strips
3. The Melted Ice Cube Test sign

3. Secret Note

Set out these materials at the station:
1. 4 small mirrors, preferably with stands (clay works as a make-shift stand).
2. Four backwards "Bill" notes.
3. The Secret Note sign.

4. Powders (Note: Locate this station near a sink if possible. If you want two Powders stations, double the materials.)

Prepare the materials as described under Powders in "Before the Day of the Activity" above.

1. Gather the materials previously prepared.
2. Use the large plastic garbage bag to protect the table from iodine spills. **Before laying down the plastic sheet, dribble a small amount of water onto the table surface. The plastic will adhere to the wet table.**

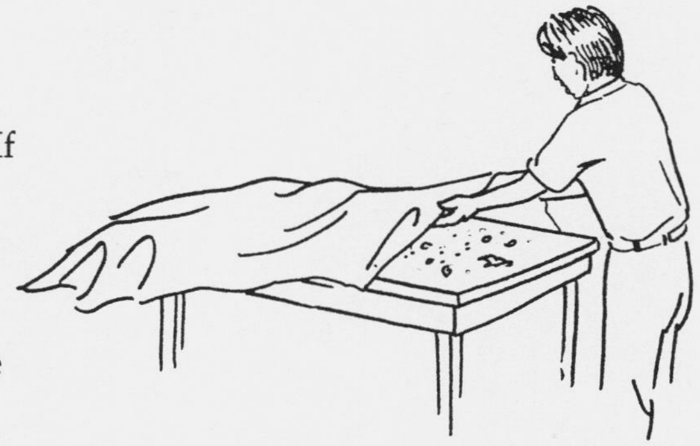

Set out these materials at the station:

1. 1 sponge
2. paper towels
3. 1/8 teaspoon (a popsicle stick or wooden stirrer could also be used)
4. The Powder Test sign
5. egg carton trays
6. iodine bottles
7. cup of powder

5. Tape Lift

Prepare the materials:

1. Put the pet hair and grass on Mr. Bear
2. Label the white sheets of paper next to Mr. Bear, "What we found on Mr. Bear."

Set out these materials at the station:

1. 1 roll clear tape
2. The Tape Lift sign.
3. stuffed bear with dog hair and grass stuck to it
4. paper next to the bear

Introduce the Stations

1. Explain to the students that today they will perform five more scientific tests on the evidence found at the scene of the crime.

2. Review the general station procedure, if necessary.

3. Point out each station, read the sign, and give a brief tie-in with the mystery. Again, demonstrate the procedure at each station, without actually doing the test or giving away any results, as in the following:

If your students wonder why they didn't see any crystals on Mr. Bear, you could say that these were gathered from down in his fur, or that they've appeared since the first day, or that it may have something to do with his fur being damp, or that you don't know!

Mystery Crystals : "We found tiny crystals on Mr. Bear. What kind of crystals are they? There are samples of sugar crystals and salt crystals for you to try to match them."

Melted Ice Cube Test station: "Some of the suspects drank straight from the *can* **without** ice cubes, and some drank from a *cup* **with** ice cubes. Was there sleeping potion in the ice cubes?" Say that each team should use only **one** piece of pH paper for their test, or if you have enough pH paper, say that each student should use only one piece.

Secret Note station: "We found a secret backwards message. Try to read what it says. It may be a clue that helps solve the mystery."

Powders station: "We found some white powder on Mr. Bear. All the suspects brought either cookies or pie with white powders in them. Find out what kind of powder was on Mr. Bear, cookie powder or pie powder." Be sure to mention that the iodine **stains** so they should handle it very carefully and leave their trays clean for the next group.

Emphasize also that their job is to see if the **powder** turns yellow or purple or black when mixed with iodine, and that they may need to watch carefully for a few moments, not just glance at the first drop. (Sometimes students only watch the drop of iodine itself and conclude that it stays yellow, even though the powder has turned purple or black.)

Note: If you set up two "Powders" stations, explain that they are both the same, and students only need to test at one of them.)

Tape Lift: "Use tape to look for other clues on Mr. Bear, which might tell us where he was taken." Emphasize that they should **touch the tape to only one part of the bear**, so there will be evidence left for other scientists to do the tape lift. In this activity, they will each get to lift off and look at just a little bit of the evidence. Explain that real crime lab scientists might have only **one** hair or a single blade of grass as a clue.

Crime Lab Testing and Recording Results

1. When they understand what they are to do, ask the students to get together with their partners from Session 3.

2. Tell students to walk. Ask them to be patient if there's not room at a station when they get there. Suggest that they can look at the charts and think about the evidence as they wait for a station.

3. Remind the students to record all their results. Hand out their data sheets and pencils, and assign them to their first stations.

Pooling Class Data

1. When all, or at least most, of your students have completed the stations, gather them in partners with their data sheets in front of them, near the Evidence Chart. Give them a couple of minutes to discuss among themselves, to make sure that they agree on the results they recorded on their data sheet.

2. Together as a class, go through stations #6 through #10, asking first for volunteers to give their results from each test. After hearing one group's results, ask those who agree to raise their hands. Then ask those who disagree to raise their hands. Find out the results of those who disagree, and discuss how/why they might have gotten different results, and how the class should decide which results to use.

3. Once they've agreed on a set of results, record them on the Evidence Chart in the results column.

4. Compare these results with the information on the Clue Board, and ask your students which of the suspects they think each piece of evidence points to or might implicate. Record their responses under the "Who looks guilty?" column. A list of probable results is also included below for the teacher, and is written in italics.

Session 4

Station	Results	Who Looks Guilty?
6) Crystals	*Salt*	*Bill (he wanted to go swimming in the salty ocean)*
7) Melted Ice Cube Test	*Yes — sleeping potion*	
8) Secret Note	*Bill*	*Bill*
9) Powder Study	*Pie powder*	*Bill and Jan (Both brought pie)*
10) Tape Lift	*Dog hair & Grass*	*Jan (She owns a dog, and wanted to play in the grass)*

Look for significant evidence:

1. Ask: which pieces of evidence make any of the suspects look guilty?

2. Encourage discussion about ways to tie these results together in a story so that they make logical sense.

3. Tell the students that in the next session they'll use their data to attempt to solve the crime.

4. Collect data sheets so students will have them for the next session.

MYSTERY CRYSTALS STATION SIGN

1 Look at the small crystals in the cup marked "Mr. Bear Mystery Crystals."

2 Look at the crystals in the sugar crystal cup and the salt crystal cup.

3 Which one looks like the mystery crystals?

Sugar? Salt?

Melted ICE CUBE TEST STATION SIGN

1 Take one piece of test paper.

2 Dip the paper in the ice cube liquid.

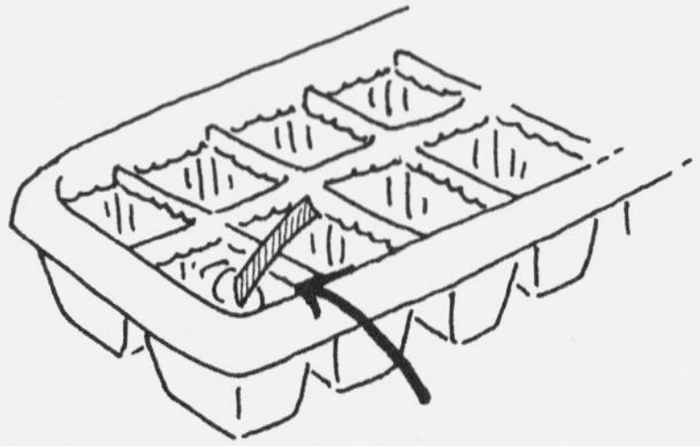

3

Green = sleeping potion = Yes

Yellow = No sleeping potion = No

4 **Was there sleeping potion in the ice cubes?**

Yes or No

5 Throw away your used paper in the garbage can.

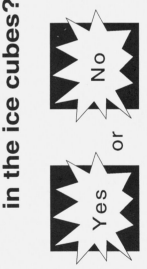

1 Use the mirror to read the name in the backwards note.

2 Whose name was in the secret backwards note?

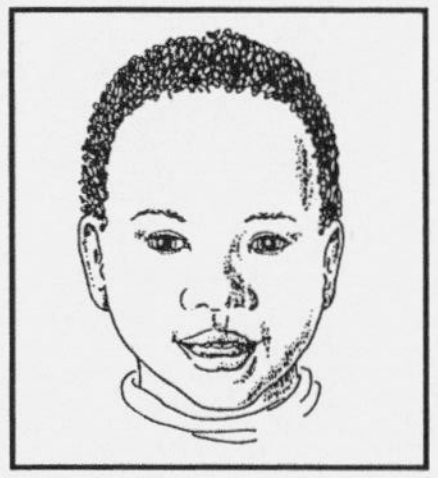

Sam

Tina

Bill

Jan

Al

SECRET NOTE STATION SIGN

POWDERS STATION SIGN

1 Put 1 tiny spoonful of Mr. Bear powder into a compartment.

2 Add 2 drops of iodine, and look at the color of the powder.

Color?

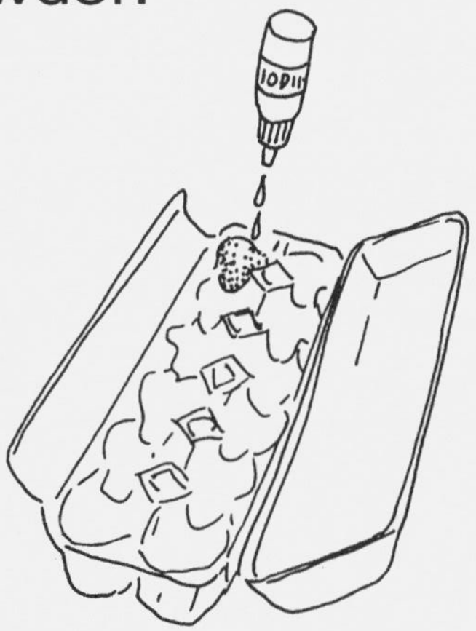

3 If it turned **purple** or **black**, then it is pie powder. If it is **yellow**, then it is cookie powder.

purple or black = Pie

yellow = Cookie

4 **What kind of powder was on Mr. Bear?**

Pie

or

Cookie

1 Take one piece of tape and touch the sticky side to one spot on Mr. Bear.

2 Stick it on the paper next to Mr. Bear.

3 What did you find on Mr. Bear?

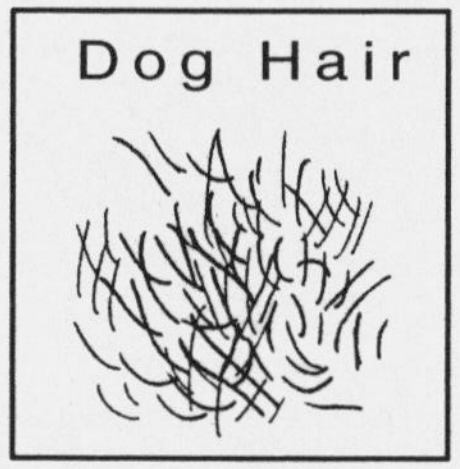

or

TAPE LIFT STATION SIGN

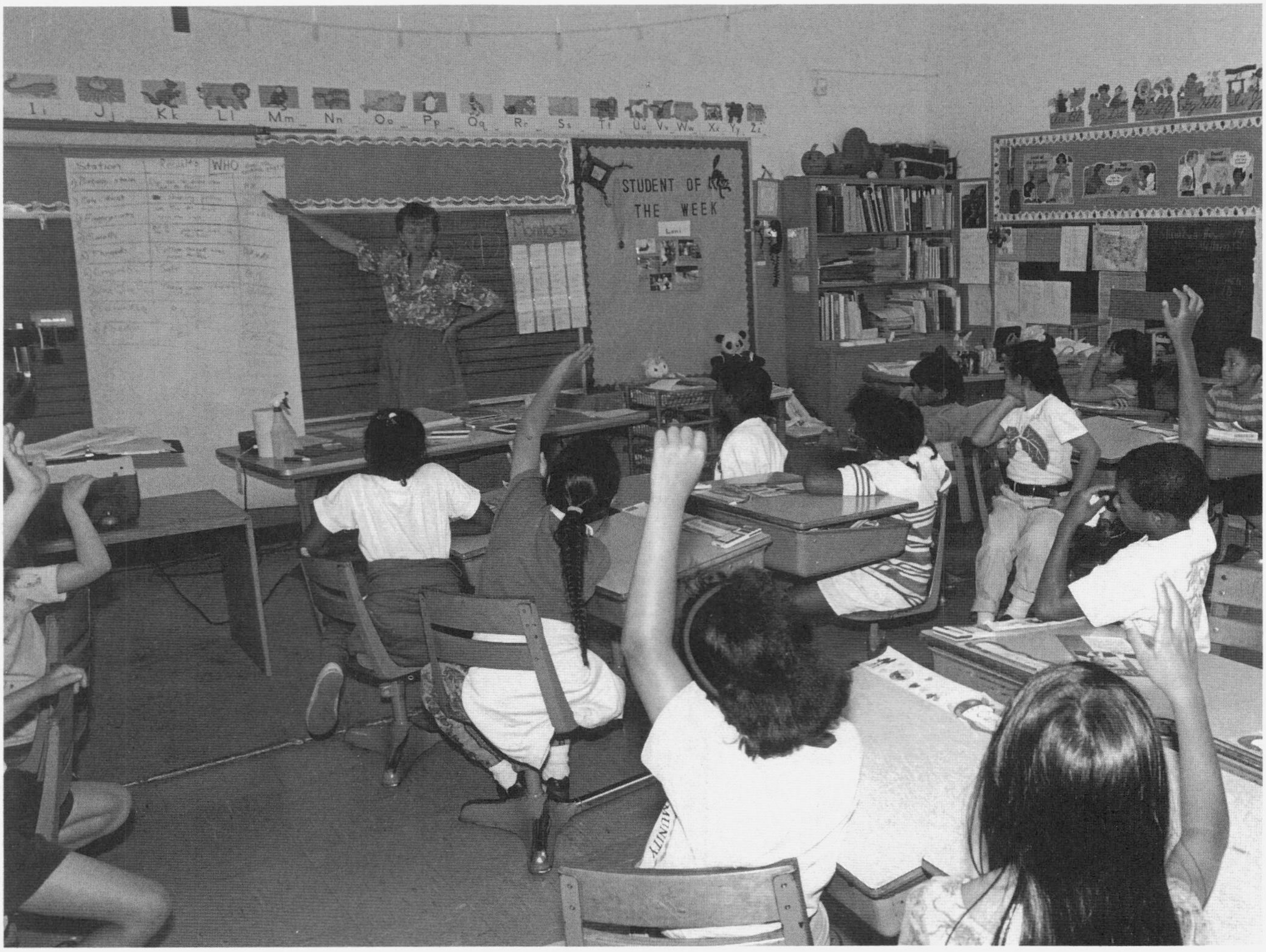
STUDENT OF THE WEEK
Monitors
Station
WHO

Session 5: Solving the Mystery

Overview

In this session your students bring together all their findings and attempt to solve the mystery. Depending upon the ability level of your students, and on your own preferences, we have provided several options for solving the mystery.

It is well worth emphasizing that whatever "verdict" your students come up with, the process involves your students in attempting to bring together their findings into a conclusion, drawing upon their findings from their crime lab testing stations and related clues. This is powerful and compelling practice in logical thinking and problem solving.

You may want to do one or all of the options, or come up with a variation of your own. Several "Going Further" ideas are included at the end of the session.

One teacher told us: "My students were so happy to finally get to tell what they think happened!"

What You Need

(from the previous sessions)
❐ The Crime Scene Map
❐ Clue Board
❐ Evidence Chart

Depending on the option you choose you may also need:
❐ pencils and paper
❐ crayons or colored markers
❐ a chalkboard and chalk.

Getting Ready

Choose one or more of the following mystery-solving activities—whichever you feel is appropriate to your class' interest and skill levels, as well as your time frame.

Solving the Mystery: Who Borrowed Mr. Bear?

1. Explain to the class that now they will have the chance to solve the "crime" of "Who Borrowed Mr. Bear?" Encourage them to take into account all the evidence they observed at the crime scene, along with the results of the many crime lab tests they've conducted as crime lab scientists, as well as their charts and discussions.

2. Depending on which option or options for "solving the mystery" you've decided on for your class, introduce and explain that option to your students and have them begin.

Option #1 - "Who Done It?" — Write/Draw Your Own Story

1. After reviewing the Evidence Chart, have each student write, draw, or dictate their own version of the crime story. Using paper, crayons and pencils, have your students either draw a picture of what happened, write what happened, or do a combination of the two. You may want to allow your students to use "invented spelling" for this writing assignment, so they concentrate on their narrative and thinking process, rather than worrying about exactly correct spelling.

2. Have volunteers read their versions to the class and share their drawings.

Option #2 : Class Vote

1. Ask the students to decide which character(s) they believe committed the crime. Allow some time for discussion before the vote.

2. Have your students vote on who they think is guilty. To enliven the proceedings, you may want to have five students stand up front to represent the five characters: Sam, Bill, Jan, Tina, Al. These students could even hold up the pictures of these characters. Sam's name is included in case any students decide that Sam borrowed his own Mr. Bear. Before voting, emphasize "thinking for yourself," and elicit student ideas about what might happen at the end of a real courtroom case:

> *For example:*
>
> 1) **Guilty** : the jury agrees, and convicts one or more of the suspects.

2) **Not Guilty (Innocent)** : the jury decides there is not enough evidence to convict anyone.

3) **Hung Jury** : the jury cannot agree and a mistrial is declared.

Note: It's important to stress beforehand that any of these outcomes is a success, because any one of these outcomes can and does happen in the real world of crime-solving and the courtroom.

One teacher used a bar graph to show the results of the vote.

Option #3- Put Your Name on the Line (15–30 minutes)

1. Write the five character names on the board: Sam, Bill, Jan, Tina, Al, with space left blank under each. Sam's name is included in case any students decide that he borrowed his own Mr. Bear.

2. Allow each student an opportunity to write his or her name on the board under the name of the character who they think did it. Don't require, but encourage students to share with the group why they chose that character, and how they see the story as having taken place. You may also choose to include a category for undecided.

Note: You may simplify this activity by first allowing the students to decide on one or two characters they wish to vote on, instead of voting on all four. Draw a line across the board with the words "guilty," and "not guilty" at either end. In the middle write, "undecided."

Mr. Bear Mystery - The "Real" Story

Although the Felix Mystery for 4th through 8th grade students is complex, with no right or wrong answer, the Mr. Bear version is designed so the evidence does point to two obvious culprits: Bill and Jan.

Your students may have come to several different conclusions about what "really" happened. That's fine! Ask them to explain the reasons for their conclusions, and accept everyone's ideas. Perhaps the "Case of the Borrowed Bear" will remain "open," as cases often do in real life! Some teachers prefer not to read the story, when they feel doing so will make students feel their answers were "wrong." Other teachers, after allowing students to come up with their own stories of what happened, and validating all the students' conclusions, then read the story on the next three pages, or tell it in their own storytelling way. •

Mr. Bear Mystery - The "Real" Story

"Mom, can I take some cookies with me?" Sam yelled up the stairs as he pulled on his red T-shirt. "Where are you going," Sam heard his mother ask through the upstairs bathroom door. "To the Stuffed Animal Adventure Club, mom, remember? We're building a clubhouse today." • "Oh, that's right Sam. I'm sorry, I forgot. Sure, go ahead and take some cookies. There's some in a bag on the counter. Why don't you take some drinks too. It looks like it's going to be a hot day. You and Mr. Bear should take your bathing suits!" • "No, that's O.K. mom. I don't feel like going swimming today." • "Up to you... be sure to be back in time for dinner." • "Sure mom." • Sam grabbed the cookies, some colas, and Mr. Bear, and started to run out the door. Just then he thought about bringing some cups and ice cubes. When he looked in the kitchen, he saw that there was only one plastic cup left, so he grabbed it. He looked in the freezer, but he couldn't find any ice cubes. • Sam's mother was a scientist/inventor, and he knew she had another freezer in her lab in the garage. He wasn't supposed to go in there alone, but he wanted ice cubes badly, so he went in anyway. Sure enough, he found some ice cubes, and took the whole tray. Sam didn't know that his mother had been experimenting with a new sleeping potion, and that she had put some in the ice cubes for one of her science experiments. • When Sam met his friends, he set his treats in a cool spot, and they all started to work on their clubhouse. Because it was a hot day, they got tired quickly. They sat down in the shade, and started to argue over what to do next. Sam wanted to play hopscotch, but they just couldn't agree. • "Let's stop arguing and cool off with some cola," said Al. • "I only have one cup, so if you want ice cubes, you'll have to share the cup," said Sam. • "No thanks, I'll just drink from the can," said Bill. • "Me too," said Jan • Sam put the melting ice cubes into the cup, and poured cola in it. Sam, Tina and Al took turns passing the cup around and drinking from it. While they were drinking, their fingerprints got all over the cup. Bill and Jan each drank from their own cans of cola. Since

continued . . .

they never touched the cup, they didn't get their fingerprints on it. • "Man, I'm getting sleepy," said Sam as he yawned a huge yawn. • "Me too," said Al. • "Yeah," said Tina, "I think I'm going to take a little nap. I think that.... ZZZZZZZ..." before she could finish her sentence, Tina was snoring up a storm. Sam and Al both fell asleep too. • "That's weird," said Bill, "I don't feel sleepy at all." • "Me neither," said Jan. "Hey, I've got a great idea. Let's go play while they're asleep. Let's grab our stuffed animals." • "Good idea," said Bill. "I'm going to take Mr. Bear too, because Sam never lets me play with him. Let's go swimming!" • "But I don't want to go swimming," said Jan. "I want to play in the grass." • "What if we go swimming first, then we play in the grass afterward?" • "O.K., but I'm going over to my house to get Puppy too. You wait here." • "Great," said Bill. • As Bill reached for Mr. Bear, his bottle of brown dye fell out of his pocket. Since the cap wasn't on very tight, some brown dye leaked out onto a paper towel. • He picked the bottle back up, put the lid on tight, and put it back in his pocket. Just then, Jan came back with Puppy. Puppy was so glad to see the other kids that he pulled away from Jan. Dragging his leash behind him, he ran up to each of the kids, licking their faces and slobbering all over them. Even Puppy's licking didn't wake up Tina, Sam and Al. • "Grab his leash, Bill," said Jan. • Bill yelled back, "I'm trying!" • Just then, Puppy knocked over the paint and stepped right in it. As they tried to catch Puppy, Bill stepped in the paint with his right foot. Jan stepped in it with both feet. The three of them left footprints of paint all over the ground. Puppy thought they were playing a game, so he picked up Bill's white cotton sweater to play with it. • "Let go of my sweater, Puppy," said Bill, "You're ripping it." Puppy finally let go, but some of the threads were already ripped off and lying on the ground. • "I've got him," said Jan, "let's go." • "O.K., I've got our stuffed animals and Mr. Bear," said Bill. • First they went to the beach. They left their stuffed animals lying on the sand while they played in the waves with Puppy and Mr. Bear. Afterward, they played in a grassy meadow nearby. As Mr. Bear started to dry, little salt crystals formed in his fur. • "We'd better get back before they all wake up," said Jan. On the way back they stopped by Jan's house, and put Puppy inside. When they got back the other kids were still asleep, so they ate some pie. There was some white "pie powder" on the side of the pie pan, and they accidentally spilled some on Mr. Bear while they were eating. Because Jan's perfume had washed off at the beach, she put on some more. Some perfume got on Mr. Bear. • "Quick, I think they're starting to wake up," Bill whispered. "Let's pretend we're asleep!" • Jan put Mr. Bear back in his place. She was afraid Sam was going to find out that they had borrowed Mr. Bear. She decided to try to make it look like Bill had done it by himself. She took her felt pen and wrote Bill's name backwards on a piece of paper. She set the paper out where the other kids would see it, and then pretended she was asleep. • When the other kids woke up, Sam was very upset—not just because Mr. Bear was wet—but also because he didn't like it that someone had borrowed Mr. Bear without asking permission first. The kids did their own experiments, and decided that Bill borrowed Mr. Bear, even though they couldn't figure out why there were dog prints all over the ground. Jan felt bad, because she knew it was her fault too. • "You guys," she said, "I did it too—I'm really sorry Sam, but Bill and I borrowed Mr. Bear together. To make up for it, how about if I let you borrow my stuffed animal for a whole week." • "Yeah, you can borrow mine too," said Bill, "I shouldn't have taken Mr. Bear without permission." • Sam was kind of quiet. The other kids weren't sure if he might cry or yell at Bill and Jan. Then he said, "It hurt my feelings that you took Mr. Bear when I told you not to, but maybe I should share him more when you ask. I'm glad you told me and said you were sorry though. I don't feel so mad anymore, so let's be friends and work on this clubhouse some more." The whole group quickly joined in. Mr. Bear sat with the other stuffed animals and let the sun dry his fur. ■

Going Further

1. Popsicle Stick Puppets

a . Make copies of the Popsicle Puppet characters (five suspects, Mr. Bear, and Puppy) on the next page and hand out one page to each group of four students.

b. Demonstrate how to cut out the pictures and tape each to a popsicle stick.

c. In their groups of four, let the students work as a group to act out with their puppets what they think happened.

d. Reassemble the whole class, and have any group of four that feels comfortable doing so, perform their version of the story for the class.

2. Plays and Skits

Have students put on skits or plays to dramatize the events that happened while the members of the Stuffed Animal Club slept.

3. Stories about Motive

Have the students write a story speculating about why the "crime" was committed.

4. Read Mysteries

Be sure to see the "Literature Connections" section on page 241. You may also be interested in obtaining the GEMS literature connections handbook entitled *Once Upon A GEMS Guide: Connecting Young People's Literature to Great Explorations in Math and Science*, which lists and annotates literature connections for the entire GEMS series.

5. Further Adventures

Have students write another mystery story that describes a further adventure of the "Stuffed Animal Adventure Club."

Popsicle Puppet CHARACTERS

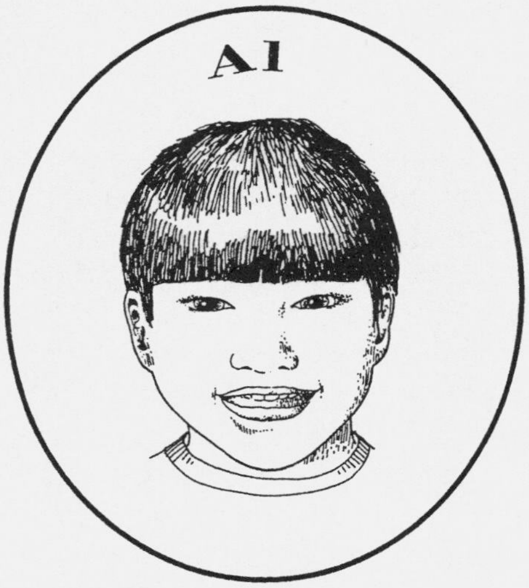

Mystery Festival Modifications for First Grade

Although first grade classes will greatly enjoy the *Mystery Festival*, classroom testing has shown that many of the key skills and concepts can elude many students. While all first grade students have fun doing the experiments and gain science experience, many first graders may have difficulty keeping in mind all of the clues and their possible relation to the mystery. Reading and following the directions on the signs is not possible for many first graders. Understanding the experimental techniques and interpreting the results in some of the crime lab activities, such as the "Brown Stain" and "Fingerprinting" stations, can be difficult even with extensive pre-teaching.

For these reasons, we don't recommend that you set up a Mystery Festival for *just* first grade. However, if you are co-presenting a Mystery Festival, and wish to include first graders along with older students, the suggested modifications below will help the younger students succeed.

1. Use all of the pre-teaching activities on page 12 of the introduction, and add more of your own!

2. If possible, take Polaroid photos of the "crime scene," rather than mapping it. If you map the crime scene, do so while students are still gathered around it and able to see.

3. Have an adult volunteer at every learning station.

4. Replace the "Fingerprinting" station in Session 3 with a footprint-identification activity. Use the Suspect Footprint Sheet (page 31) to create your own matching activity.

Dear Parents,

Your child's class will soon begin a unit called Mystery Festival, in which students act as crime lab scientists to help solve a make-believe mystery. In an effort to discover who borrowed a stuffed animal called "Mr. Bear," the students examine clues and do tests on evidence, while learning important science skills and concepts. This program was developed by the Great Explorations in Math and Science (GEMS) program at the Lawrence Hall of Science and tested in classrooms nationwide.

There are many materials that we need for this highly motivating unit, so we are asking for your help. Please see if you have any of the following items to donate, or if you know of others who do. Any items crossed out have already been gathered. We will need the materials by ____________________.

Thank you very much!

- 5 stuffed animals (one of which must be a bear)
- 1 paintbrush (any kind)
- 1 paint container (a plate or cup is fine)
- 24 clear plastic cups (flexible, wide-mouthed, 9-ounce cups)
- 1 box of baking soda
- 2 empty cola cans
- 1 can of cola, any kind
- 1 ice cube tray
- red and green food coloring (small squeeze bottles are fine)
- about 6 feet of white cotton yarn
- about 6 feet of colored cotton yarn
- about 6 feet of colored wool yarn
- about 40 feet of string or rope to barricade "crime scene" (or yellow plastic barrier tape)
- 4 rolls of transparent adhesive tape
- one roll plain white paper towels
- 1 brown felt water-base marker
- 2 rolls of Universal pH paper, with color chart
- 3 empty film canisters, with lids, preferably plastic
- 2 colognes or perfumes, as different from each other as possible (samples from department stores, bathroom cabinet, magazines etc.)
- 1 set measuring spoons, including 1 teaspoon, 1/2 tsp., 1/4 tsp., 1/8 tsp.
- eight 1/8 teaspoons (or 1/2 or 1/4 teaspoons)
- 1 container salt
- 1 box granulated sugar
- 1 box cornstarch
- plastic stir stick
- 4 small mirrors, preferably with stands
- 4 or more white styrofoam egg cartons
- 3 large plastic trash bags
- 2 sponges
- 4 small plastic dropper bottles
- 1/2 ounce of iodine (strong or mild tincture of iodine; diluted by teacher before student use)
- pet hair (about 30 strands—dog or cat hair is fine)
- about 1 handful of grass

Preparation Checklists
&
Summary Outlines

(for Mr. Bear Mystery)

▶ Mr. Bear Session 1: Scene of the Crime

Getting Ready Before the Day of the Activity:

___ 1. Decide where the crime scene will be.

___ 2. Make one copy of each of the 21 footprint pages and make 16 copies of the "Suspect Footprint Sheet."

___ 3. Prepare the "brown stain" paper towels.

___ 4. Cut the cotton yarn.

___ 5. Put perfume on Mr. Bear.

___ 6. Make the secret note.

___ 7. Prepare sugar and salt crystals (for Session 4).

Getting Ready On the Day of the Activity:

For Scene of the Crime

___ 1. Cover crime scene area with butcher paper and rope it off.

___ 2. Tape 21 footprint pages to butcher paper according to diagram.

___ 3. Put cornstarch and threads on Mr. Bear.

___ 4. Fill all but four compartments of ice cube tray with baking soda solution.

___ 5. Add cola to clear plastic cup and stir in baking soda.

___ 6. Set out the following clues according to the diagram of the crime scene:

- one paper towel with brown stain
- Mr. Bear and other stuffed animals
- ice-cube tray
- clear cup with cola
- two empty cola cans
- secret note
- paintbrush
- spilled paint and container
- cotton threads

For Class Crime Scene Map

___ 1. Tape up butcher paper.

___ 2. Have marking pens and Suspect Footprint Sheets handy.

Introducing the Challenge

1. Gather away from the crime scene. Discuss mysteries and how they can be solved.

2. Explain that they are going to observe a make-believe crime scene, and ask them to go to the scene and observe carefully for a few minutes, staying outside the "rope."

Recording Their Observations

1. Regroup away from the crime scene. Explain that they will each study five things.

2. As a group, practice describing an object in detail.

3. Have the students go observe five objects at the crime scene.

4. Regroup near the "Crime Scene Map" and have students describe objects while you draw them on the map. Also record the location of the footprints.

Using the Suspect Footprint Sheet

1. Discuss patterns on bottom of shoes. Have partners compare shoe types, then groups of four students compare.

2. Have partners use Suspect Footprint sheet to focus on different patterns.

3. Send the students back to identify the footprints at the crime scene.

4. Regroup and ask whose footprints were at the scene. If there's disagreement, send a few students back to double check.

▶ Mr. Bear Session 2: The Story

Getting Ready

___ 1. Jot down which stuffed animal belongs to each character in the story.

___ 2. Copy suspect pictures and other illustrations for the Clue Board.

___ 3. Put up the butcher paper for the Clue Board and tape the five suspect pictures along the top edge.

___ 4. Draw the grid on the Clue Board as in the diagram.

___ 5. Lay out the illustrations in the order you will be giving them as clues in the story.

Presenting the Story

1. Ask what the class remembers from the crime scene in Session 1. Tell them that today they will learn more about what happened there.

2. Explain that the Clue Board will be a place to record what they learn.

3. Read the story. Stick clues onto Clue Board at appropriate points in the story. Reread the story once or twice.

Introducing the Next Sessions

1. Remind them not to jump to conclusions about who borrowed Mr. Bear.

2. Explain that in the next two sessions they will use science to learn more about the clues.

▶ Mr. Bear Session 3: Crime Lab Stations

Getting Ready Before the Day of the Activity:

___ 1. Make four copies of each of the station signs.

___ 2. Make four copies of the "Whose Fingerprints are on the Cup?" sheet and the "Suspect Fingerprints" sheet.

___ 3. Make one copy of the data sheet for every two students in your class and have pencils ready.

___ 4. Decide how many "Brown Stain" stations you want to set up.

___ 5. Prepare Brown Stain Station:

- _____ Cut up the "brown stain" paper towels from Session 1.
- _____ Make samples for PEN and DYE sample sheet.

___ 6. Prepare Cola Station:

- _____ Label cup and fill with cola mixed with baking soda.
- _____ Cut the pH paper into 1 inch strips and put into labeled cup.
- _____ (optional) Color code signs.

___ 7. Arrange for any volunteers and prep them on discovery approach to learning.

___ 8. Set up Mr. Bear Evidence Chart.

Getting Ready On the Day of the Activity:

1. Brown Stain Station

Prepare the Materials

- _____ Gather strips and sample sheet prepared previously for "Brown Stain" station
- _____ Pour water into cups.

Set out:

- _____ Brown stain paper strips
- _____ PEN and DYE sample sheet
- _____ Roll of clear adhesive tape
- _____ Five pencils
- _____ Brown Stain Station signs
- _____ Four cups with water

2. **Cola Test Station**

Prepare the Materials:

_____ Gather cola cup and pH strips

Set Out:

_____ Cup with cola

_____ Cup with pH paper strips

_____ Wastebasket

_____ Cola Test Station signs

3. **Fingerprints Station**

Set Out:

_____ Four copies of "Cup with Fingerprints" page

_____ Four copies of "Suspect Fingerprints" page

_____ Fingerprints Station signs

4. **Smells Station**

Prepare the Materials:

_____ Label two containers "Jan" and "Bill."

_____ Add drops of perfume to each.

Set Out:

_____ "Jan" and "Bill" perfume containers

_____ Scented Mr. Bear

_____ Smells Station signs

5. **Threads Station**

Prepare the Materials:

_____ Cut the yarn samples into three inch pieces.

_____ Label cups for the three types of yarn.

Set Out:

_____ Three cups containing yarn samples

_____ Thread Test Station signs

Introducing the Stations

1. Say that they will work in partners to do scientific tests on the clues found at the Crime Scene.

2. For each station, hold up the station sign and read each step, demonstrating the procedures without actually doing the tests.

3. Explain briefly how each test ties in with the mystery.

Crime Lab Testing and Recording Results

1. Show data sheets and explain how to record results.

2. Explain that after their first station, they may go with their partner to any other available station until they have done five station activities.

3 Mention that if they have extra time, they may return to the Crime Scene Map or Clue Board.

4. Assign each team to a station, and have them begin.

Pooling Class Data

1. Give teams a few minutes to discuss results.

2. Refocus the whole group and gather results for the five tests. Emphasize that disagreement is okay and accept all answers.

3. Ask first for a volunteer to report, then ask who agrees and disagrees by counting hands raised. Find out results of those who disagree.

4. Record results on the Evidence Chart and compare them with the information on the Clue Board. Ask which suspect each clue points to, and record this in the last column.

5. Say that in the next session, they will do five more tests. Collect their data sheets to be used again next time.

▶ Mr. Bear Session 4: Crime Lab Stations

Getting Ready Before the Day of the Activity:

___ 1. Make four copies of each station sign.

___ 2. Have student data sheets from previous session and pencils handy.

___ 3. Decide if you want two "Powders" stations.

___ 4. Arrange for volunteer(s).

___ 5. Prepare Ice Cube Station:

_____ Cut pH paper into 1 inch strips.

_____ Put strips into a cup.

___ 6. Prepare Powder Test Station:

_____ Cut egg cartons into test trays

_____ Label and fill cup with "Mr. Bear powder" (cornstarch)

_____ Fill and label four dropper bottles with iodine

Getting Ready On the Day of the Activity:

1. **Mystery Crystals Station**

Prepare the Materials:

_____ Label the three cups with crystals prepared in Session 1.

Set Out:

_____ Three cups with crystal samples

_____ Crystals Station signs

2. **Melted Ice Cube Test Station**

Prepare the Materials:

_____ Gather pH strips you prepared

Set Out:

_____ Ice cube tray with baking soda water from Session 1

_____ Cup of pH paper strips

_____ Melted Ice Cube Test signs

_____ Wastebasket

3. **Secret Note Station**

Set Out:

_____ Four mirrors

_____ Four backwards "Bill" notes

_____ Secret Note Station signs

4. **Powder Test Station**

Prepare the Materials:

_____ Gather the test trays, "Mr. Bear powder" and iodine.

Set Out:

_____ Plastic sheet to cover table
_____ Sponge and paper towels
_____ Four test trays
_____ Cup of "Mr. Bear powder" with spoon or stir stick
_____ Four iodine bottles
_____ Powder Test Station signs

5. **Tape Lift Station**
Prepare the Materials:

_____ Put pet hair and grass on Mr. Bear
_____ Label blank sheets of paper "What We Found on Mr. Bear"

Set Out:

_____ Roll of clear adhesive tape
_____ Mr. Bear
_____ Paper next to Mr. Bear
_____ Tape Lift Station signs

Introducing the Stations

1. Say that they will do five different tests today. Review general procedures.

2. Use the signs to demonstrate the procedure at each station.

3. Provide a brief tie-in with the mystery for each station.

Crime Lab Testing and Recording Results

1. Have students rejoin their partners and hand out their data sheets.

2. Remind students to look at the charts and reflect on clues if they have extra time. Assign them to their first stations and have them begin.

Pooling Class Data

1. Gather the class with their data sheets near the Evidence Chart.

2. Gather results in the same way as you did in the last session, and record on Evidence Chart.

3. Ask which clues implicate which suspects and record in the last column.

▶ Mr. Bear Session 5: Solving the Mystery

Getting Ready

1. Choose one or more of the mystery-solving activities:

- Option #1 Write/Draw Your Own Story
- Option #2 Class Vote
- Option #3 Put Your Name on the Line

Solving the Mystery: Who Borrowed Mr. Bear?

1. Have students share their conclusions. Ask them to explain the reasons for their conclusions and accept everyone's ideas.

2. After validating students' conclusions, you may want to read "The 'Real' Story," starting on page 91.

The Mystery of Felix

" The Case of the Missing Millionaire "

(a mystery for "older" detectives: Grades 4–8)

PLAIN
m&m's

Session 1: Scene of the Crime

Overview

As your students enter the classroom they are intrigued to discover a roped-off "crime scene" full of curious items. After a brief introduction, the students observe and list the clues they find as a class. The crime scene is then divided into eight sections, with a team of students assigned to each.

Students use drawings to record what their section looks like before anything is touched or moved. They also record detailed observations of any clues found in their section on the class "Crime Scene Map." This map is used as a reference throughout the rest of the *Mystery Festival* activities.

Depending on the experience and background of your students, you may want to present some preliminary observation activities, such as those described on page 12.

What You Need

See page 200 for a sample letter asking parents to contribute materials.

For the Crime Scene:

- ❒ 3 or 4 seven-foot lengths of white butcher paper to cover the floor under the crime scene
- ❒ 1 paintbrush (any kind)
- ❒ 1 paint container (a plate or cup is fine)
- ❒ 2 clear plastic cups
- ❒ 2 one-gallon ziplock plastic bags
- ❒ about 1 1/2 tablespoons of baking soda
- ❒ about 1 tablespoon cornstarch
- ❒ 2 empty cola cans
- ❒ about 1/4 cup cola
- ❒ 1 ice cube tray
- ❒ 1 wastebasket
- ❒ 1 chocolate candy wrapper
- ❒ 1 white cotton towel
- ❒ 1 comb with several strands of human hair
- ❒ 2 white paper towels
- ❒ 2 tablespoons of red food coloring and 1 tablespoon of green food coloring (to make the brown stain)
- ❒ 1 additional tablespoon red food coloring (to make the fake blood)

- ❒ a container with lid to store food coloring (a film can is fine)
- ❒ about 10 inches of white cotton yarn
- ❒ 1 "broken" alarm clock
- ❒ 1 piece of tagboard ~8 1/2 x 11 inches (the cardboard back of a notepad works fine)
- ❒ 1 long piece of string or rope to barricade the 7 x 10 foot crime scene
- ❒ 1 roll 3/4" clear tape
- ❒ five colognes or perfumes, as different from each other as possible (get samples from department stores, your bathroom cabinet, friends, magazines etc.).
- ❒ masking tape (for making labels)
- ❒ a roll of string (at least sixty feet) for dividing the crime scene into eight sections
- ❒ 3 x 5 cards or "post-its" to label the sections with numbers

The following items are optional, but are great for "spicing up" the crime scene:

- ❒ 1 guitar pick
- ❒ 1 pair of sunglasses with Gene's name on them
- ❒ 1 empty, or partially empty container of Gene's favorite cologne (one of those mentioned above)
- ❒ 1 package of carpet tacks
- ❒ 1 clip-on earring
- ❒ about 1 pint of black tempera paint
- ❒ plastic, yellow "caution" tape for "roping off" the crime scene
- ❒ Video camera (or Polaroid) for recording pictures of the crime scene

For the Crime Scene Map:

For each of your 8 Groups: (These items would need to be provided for each class.)

- ❒ at least 1 pencil
- ❒ 1 piece of drawing paper
- ❒ 1 "Suspect Footprints" sheet (page 129)
- ❒ about five lined 3 x 5 index cards

For the Class:

- ❒ 2 marking pens (1 permanent for labeling cups, the other for drawing lines and labels on Crime Scene Map)
- ❒ a roll of transparent adhesive tape to put 3 x 5 cards on Crime Scene Map
- ❒ one piece of butcher paper about 3 x 5 feet

Getting Ready

To help you keep track of the preparation tasks below, there is a Preparation Checklist on page 201.

Before the Day of the Activity:

1. Decide where the scene of the crime will be:

You'll need a rectangular floor area, at least 7 x 10 feet, preferably not against a wall, around which your class can gather to observe.

2. Prepare the footprints:

• Make one copy of each of the 21 pages of footprints (pages 211-231).

• Make 8 copies of the Suspect Footprints sheet (page 129)

3. Prepare the Suspect Fingerprint Sheet:

Note: While this suspect sheet is not used until Session 3, it is easiest to make it now.

• You will need to make 3 different fingerprints to add to the two already on the Suspect Fingerprint Sheet (page 130). If you have three prints that are easily distinguished from each other on your own hands, you could use all your own prints for the three suspects. If not, you can use your prints and the prints of anyone else who happens to be around. Make a note of which finger is printed by each person and whose prints are to be Alfredo's, Felix's and Kendra's.

• Don't let your accomplices leave yet! For the "Prepare the Cups" step below, you will need to put these *same* prints on the plastic cups.

• To make graphite prints for the Suspect Fingerprints Sheet:

a. Scribble with a #2 pencil to make a 1 inch graphite patch on a piece of scratch paper.

b. Rub the pad of your finger on the graphite patch until your finger is dirty from the tip to the first bend-line.

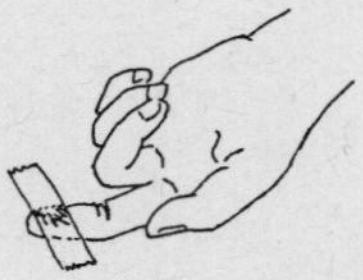

c. Take a piece of transparent tape and put it across the pad of your dirty finger.

d. Remove the tape (which now has the graphite fingerprint on it) and stick it to the Suspect Fingerprint Sheet under one of the suspects' names.

• Repeat this procedure two more times, until you have a different print under the names of Alfredo, Felix and Kendra.

4. Prepare the Cups:

• Use a permanent marker to label the two clear plastic cups. In small lettering, label one cup, "Alfredo's cup," and the other, "Felix's cup."

• Use a cloth to wipe the inside and outside of the cups to eliminate any fingerprints that might already be on them.

• Use the skin oil fingerprinting technique (the next step, below) to leave prints on the two cups.

On Alfredo's cup: put several of Alfredo's prints on the outside of the cup.

On Felix's cup: Put several of Felix's and one of Kendra's prints on the inside.

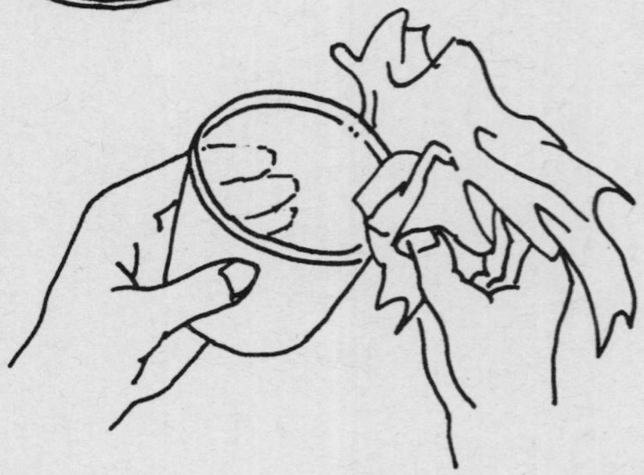

• To make prints using the skin oil fingerprinting technique:

a. Rub the face of the finger on the bridge of your nose or on your temples, to pick up extra natural skin oil.

b. Press the finger onto the cup where you want the print to be. Be careful not to smudge the print.

c. The print should be *faintly* visible to you at this point. If it is not, use a cloth to wipe the cup clean and try again.

5. Prepare the "brown stain" paper towel:

Note: Although you will put only one brown stain paper towel at the crime scene, you need to make two. The reason to make two is so that your students will have enough pieces of towel to test in Session 3. Just set aside the second paper towel until Session 3.

• Make brown food coloring by mixing 2 tablespoons of red food coloring with 1 tablespoon green. Save what you don't use now in a sealed container (a film canister is fine) labeled, "brown food coloring" for use in Session 3.

• Cut two strips of white paper towel 3 inches by about 10 inches.

• Use the brown food coloring to make a stain across the middle of the strips of paper towel, using a stir stick, straw, or cotton swab dipped in brown food coloring (see diagram).

• Allow the stain to dry.

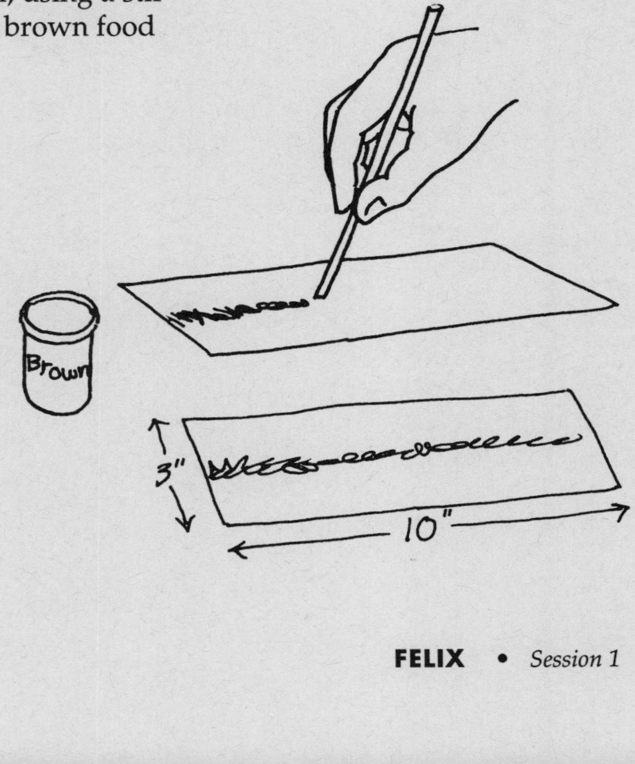

6. Make the Secret Note:

• Lay a sheet of paper on top of a piece of tagboard. Write the following message in your own **printed** handwriting (not cursive). It should be written in the four lines shown below on the paper with a ballpoint pen. Press hard so indentations of the writing appear on the tagboard below.

Dear Martha,

The deed is done.

Felix is dead and I'll

be rich soon. love, Vera

• Discard the paper and save the tagboard for when you set up the scene of the crime.

7. Prepare the cotton threads:

Cut five 2" pieces of white cotton yarn.

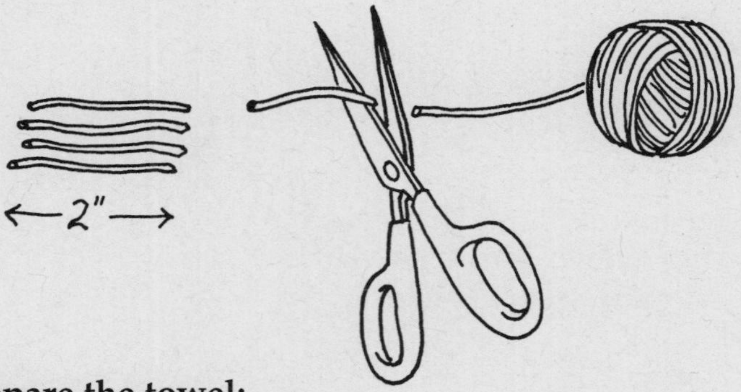

8. Prepare the towel:

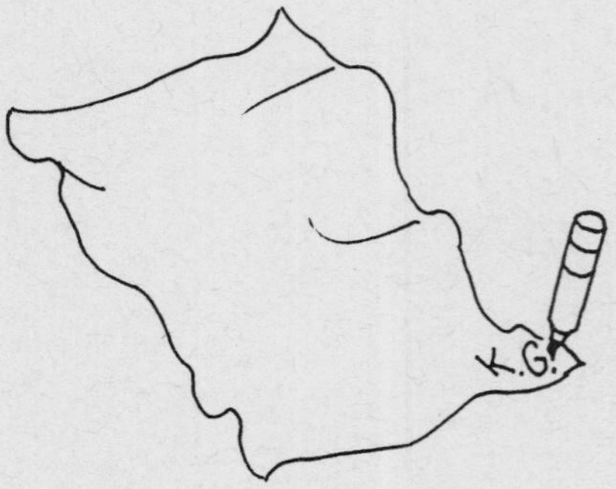

1. Use a permanent marker to write the initials "K.G." on one corner of the white cotton towel.

2. Tear the towel so that it looks chewed by a dog (unless you have a canine pal to help you!)

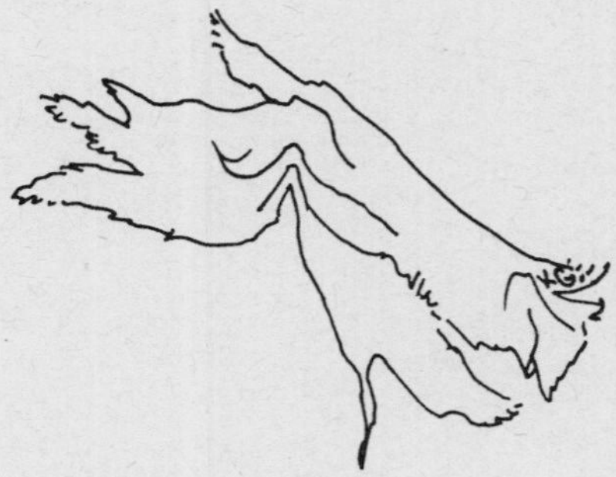

3. Scent the white towel with a few drops of one of the colognes, which will represent Gene's cologne. Choose a cologne that smells as different as possible from the other colognes. Make a note of which cologne you used, and set that cologne aside with the other four colognes/perfumes for later use in Session 3.

9. Make the fake blood:

Mix 1 tablespoon of cornstarch with 1 tablespoon of red food coloring to make fake blood.

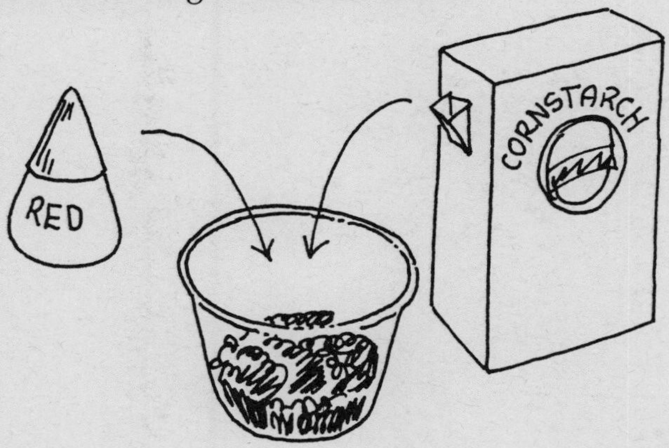

10. Prepare the Crime Scene Map:

You may want to consider using a Polaroid or other camera to record what's at the scene of the crime, instead of (or in addition to) having the students draw it. If you choose the camera method, but do not have a Polaroid, you will need to set up the crime scene the afternoon before the day of the activity, take the photos, and have them developed overnight. Stand on top of the chair to take your photos. You may need to take more than one photo per section, depending on the size of your sections.

1. Dedicate a bulletin board to be used for the duration of this unit or post a sheet of butcher paper on the wall. This is where your students will record what they see at the crime scene. The map area should be about 3 x 5 feet.

2. On the day of the class, when you start up the crime scene, you will use string to make eight sections, with a group of students assigned to each. The paper map should be sectioned in the same way. (See the crime scene set–up diagram on page 116.) Use a marker to divide the Crime Scene Map into eight sections.

FELIX CRIME SCENE SET-UP

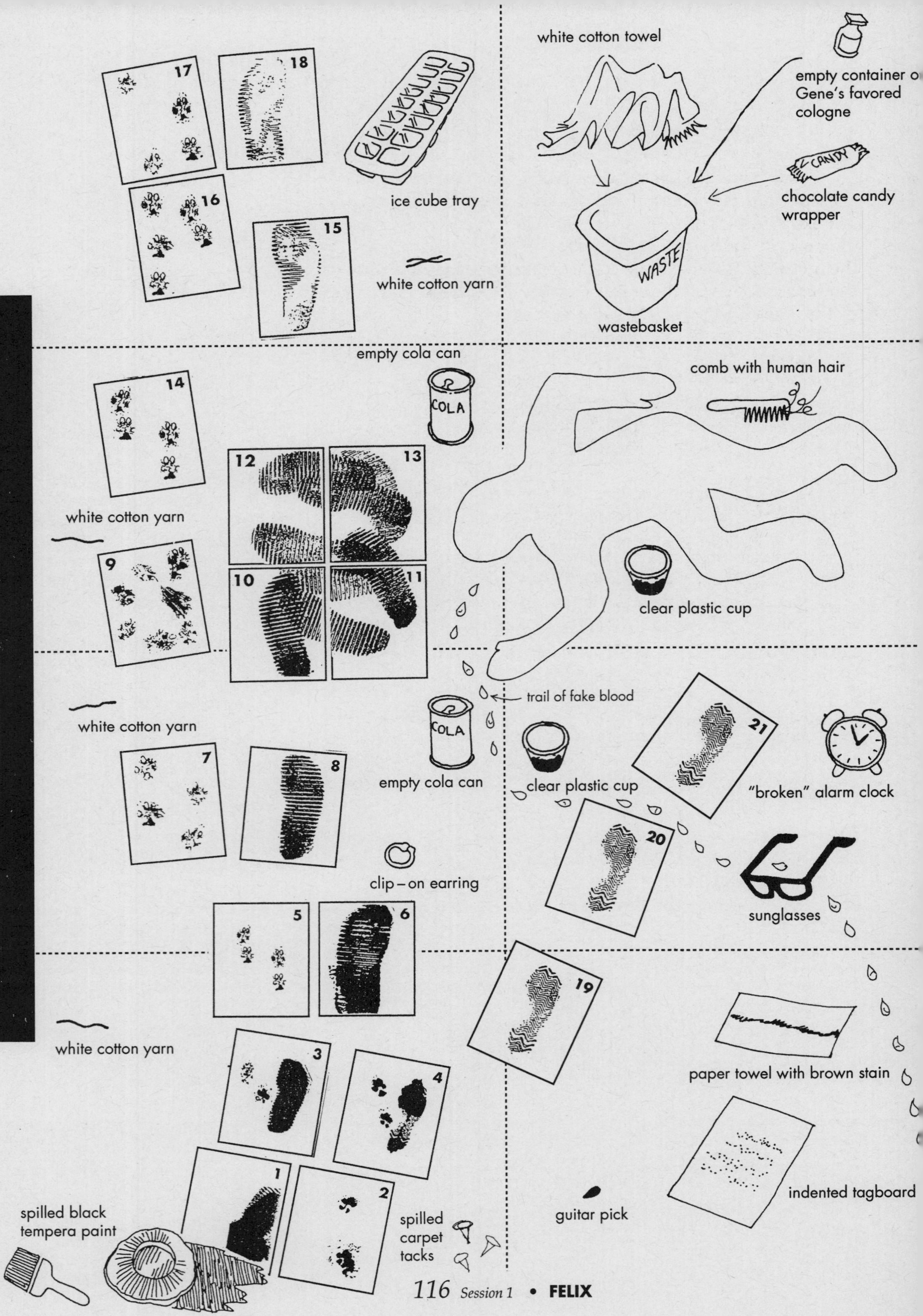

17
18
16
15
ice cube tray
white cotton yarn
white cotton towel
empty container of Gene's favored cologne
CANDY
chocolate candy wrapper
WASTE
wastebasket
empty cola can
COLA
14
comb with human hair
12
13
white cotton yarn
9
10
11
clear plastic cup
trail of fake blood
white cotton yarn
COLA
7
8
empty cola can
clear plastic cup
21
"broken" alarm clock
20
clip – on earring
sunglasses
5
6
19
white cotton yarn
paper towel with brown stain
3
4
1
2
indented tagboard
spilled black tempera paint
spilled carpet tacks
guitar pick

The Day of the Activity:

Setting up on the day of the activity will take you about two hours (less if you have help). The first time you present a Mystery Festival, it is probably wise to allow yourself extra time, just in case. If possible, set up the crime scene after school the day before and start the activity first thing in the morning. Use the crime scene diagram on page 116 as a guide for placing all the clues. **Don't worry if your placement of the clues isn't *precisely* like the diagram.**

(**Note**: If you are sharing an already set up crime scene with more than one class, there is not very much extra preparation. However, since students have examined the evidence, you will need to do the following quick straightening up after each class, before a new class begins its observations:

• Use the diagram of the crime scene on page 116 to do a visual check to make sure that the last class has returned the items to approximately the same places.

• Take the cups with fingerprints (that students have examined) out of their ziplock bags and pour the cola back into them (Felix's cola is the one with the baking soda in it). Place the empty cups back on the scene in the original positions, being careful not to disturb the prints on the cups.

• Set aside the Crime Scene Map made by the last class and have the new class make their own.)

1. Spread butcher paper on the floor:

Clear a rectangular space on the floor, at least 7 x 10 feet, and cover the whole area with three or four lengths of white butcher paper. Use string, yarn or rope to "rope-off" the crime scene. Chairs make good corner supports around which to wind the string.

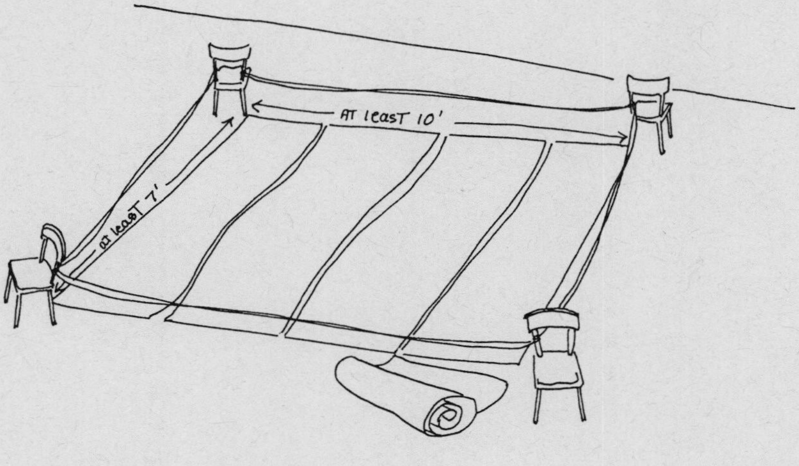

2. Draw the body outline:

Use a marker to trace someone lying down on the butcher paper in the location shown on the diagram.

When you introduce the Crime Scene to the students, you may want to emphasize that the "blood" is not real. Some teachers have discussed with their classes that, in situations where real blood is involved, such as at an accident, there are very important health and safety procedures that medical/health personnel, detectives, scientists and everyone else need to know and practice.

3. Add the fake blood:

Dribble some of the mixture of red food coloring and cornstarch in roughly the same pattern shown on the crime scene diagram.

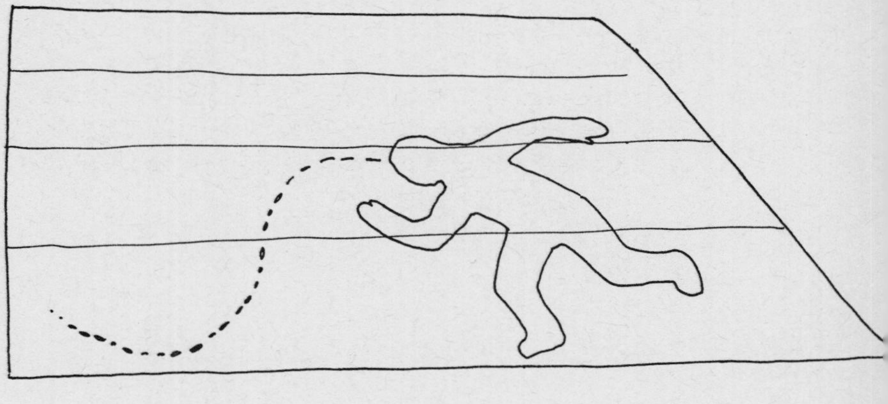

4. Add the footprints:

The 21 pages of footprints that you duplicated earlier need to be set out in the pattern shown by the numbered rectangles on the diagram. Tape the footprints to the butcher paper. (After the festival, roll up the butcher paper with the footprints, and save it for future festivals.) If you have black tempera paint—which is optional, since a print of a small spill already appears near the printed footprints—some of it could also be spilled onto the crime scene.

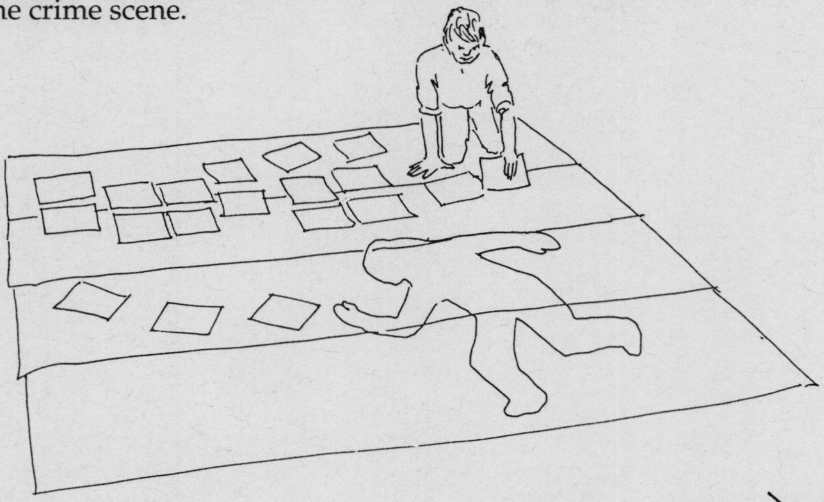

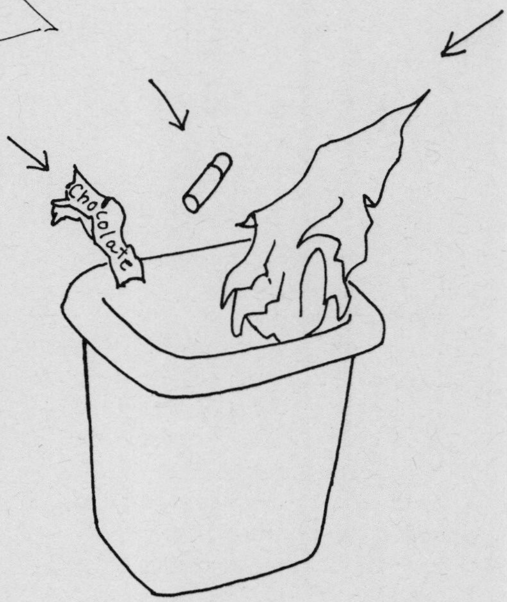

5. Do some last-minute preparation on four items:

1. The Wastebasket

- Put the towel that you have previously prepared with Gene's cologne scent in the wastebasket.
- Put the chocolate candy wrapper in the wastebasket.
- Optional: Also put the empty container of "Gene's" cologne in the wastebasket.

2. The Ice Cube Tray

- Place it right side up. Leave four compartments empty. Fill the other compartments with a baking soda solution. To make the baking soda solution, stir approximately 1 tablespoon of baking soda into 1 cup of water until dissolved. When you dismantle the crime scene, save the ice cube tray and baking soda water for use in Session 4.

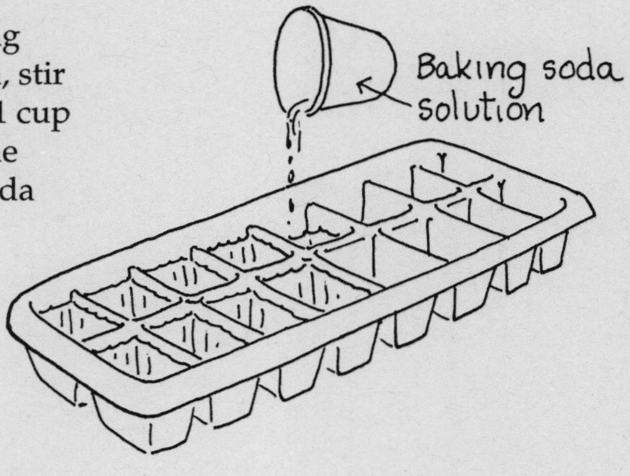

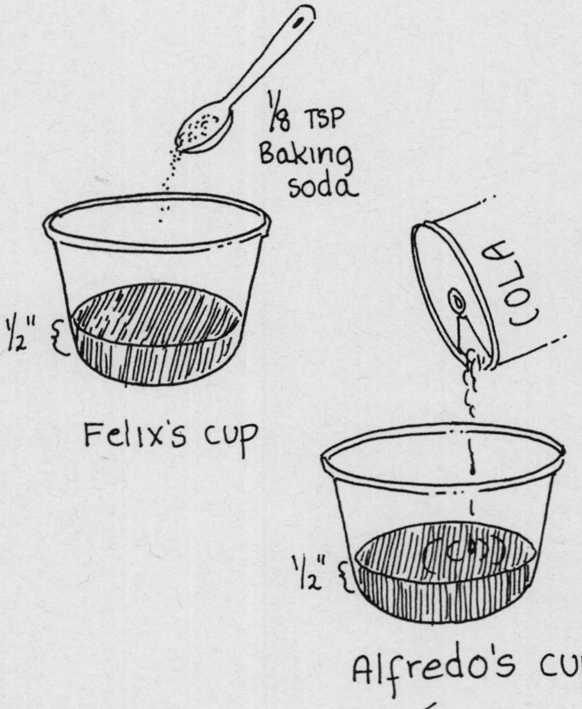

3. Two Cups of Cola

- Being careful not to disturb the fingerprints on the cups, add approximately 1/2" of cola to each cup. Into Felix's cup stir approximately 1/8 teaspoon of baking soda until it's dissolved.

- Have two one-gallon size plastic ziplock bags handy in which to put Felix's and Alfredo's cups after the students have observed the scene. You will need to pour the colas from the cups with fingerprints into two other cups and save it for the lab test in Session 3. To be ready, label the two extra cups now: label one "Alfredo's Cola," and the other "Felix's Cola."

4. The Alarm Clock

- Make sure the hands are not moving, so that it appears broken (either remove the battery or let the clock wind down). Set the time at 2:57 p.m.

6. Place all the clues on the crime scene:

Assemble these four clues (wastebasket, ice cube tray, two cups of cola, alarm clock) and all the other items and place them in the appropriate places. Use the diagram to place each item on the scene:

- 2 empty cola cans
- comb with strands of human hair
- 1 paper towel with brown stain
- five 3" pieces of white cotton yarn near footprints #9 and #14 on the diagram
- Indented tagboard secret note
- Paintbrush
- Paint container

The following items are optional, but highly recommended:

- guitar pick
- sunglasses
- spilled package of carpet tacks
- clip-on earring

7. Divide the Crime Scene into Sections:

Use string taped to the floor at each end to divide the crime scene into eight sections as shown in the diagram. Number the sections by placing a numbered 3 x 5 card or "post-it" note in each.

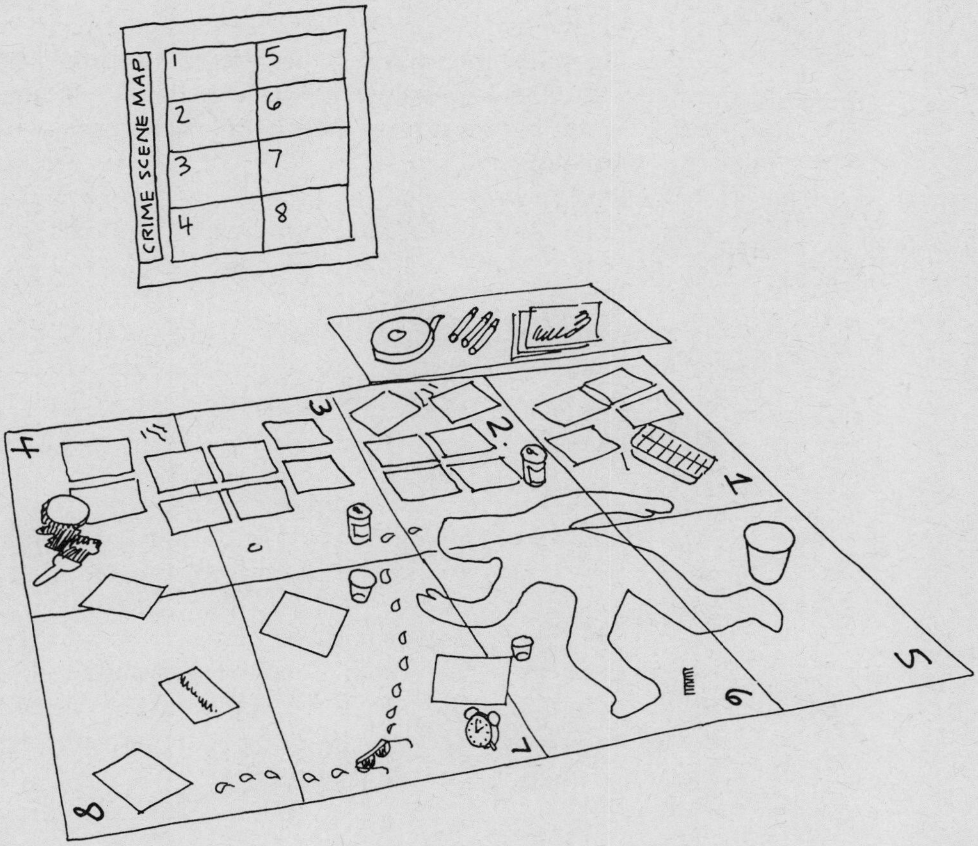

8. Set up the Crime Scene Map:

a. Draw lines on the butcher paper to create eight sections like the ones you made on the crime scene.

b. Number the sections to correspond with the crime scene sections.

c. Place several pens and masking tape (to tape on the index cards) nearby.

d. Have handy the eight copies of the Suspect Footprint sheet, as well as pencils, drawing paper and index cards.

If you decided to take photos, post them on the board. They could either take the place of or supplement student drawings. One group of students suggested using a video camera to record the crime scene.

9. Decide on student teams.

During the activity you will need eight teams of students. If you wish to assign students to the groups yourself, you may want to do so ahead of time.

Introducing the Challenge

1. Gather the class *away from the crime scene* and tell them that today they will take the first step in trying to solve a "made-up" mystery. Tell them that for the several days they will be crime lab, or forensic, scientists, using science to solve a crime.

2. Tell your students that they will observe the scene of the crime today. At this point all they know is that the scene is the patio of a two-bedroom, one-bathroom beach house, and that it is a warm day.

3. Explain that more information will come later, but that's all they know for now.

4. To prepare your students for the challenge, and to discourage the tendency to jump to conclusions, tell them that although this is a simulated crime, it is just as complicated as a real mystery.

5. Remind the students to try to keep an open mind, so that they won't be fooled. Point out that although some of them may decide right away that the victim was murdered, they don't have any proof of that yet. Say that if they think that they've solved the mystery early on, they've probably been tricked, because it's too complicated to solve without considering *all* the evidence. Remind them that in mystery books and movies the suspect who appears to be obviously guilty in the beginning is rarely the culprit in the end!

A First Look at the Scene of the Crime

1. Tell the students they'll begin by spending five minutes taking a first, careful look at the scene of the crime. Remind them to look for anything that looks unusual, but also to take note of *every* detail. Anything they see could be an important clue. Mention that the string and numbered labels they will see in the eight sections were not part of the crime scene, but were added to help them examine it in an organized way.

2. For now, tell them they must remain behind the barrier. Let them know that later on during the session they will have an opportunity to examine items closely, but for now they must not touch anything or enter the crime scene.

3. Let the students observe the scene. In some cases, the class may have difficulty gathering around the scene in a way that allows everyone to see. If this is your situation, there are several possible ways to adjust:

- Have the students walk slowly around the scene in one direction.
- Have small groups view the scene while other students prepare their 3 x 5 cards (see #5 under "Examining the Crime Scene" below).
- Have some students kneel near the barrier, with others standing behind them. (Some teachers prefer to have this first visit to the crime scene be a silent activity, so students are focused on looking at the scene themselves, rather than talking and listening to each other.)

4. After they have observed the crime scene for approximately five minutes, bring the class together away from the scene, and ask for their observations, listing them on the chalkboard. Encourage discussions of what they've observed.

Examining the Crime Scene

1. Tell them that they will have to record information about the crime scene accurately and in detail, since the crime scene will be dismantled at the end of the day. They will have to depend on their records to help solve the mystery.

2. Take one item from the scene of the crime to use as an example. Ask for suggestions on how to describe the item.

3. Help students begin to understand the distinction between something we can directly observe and know for certain ***(evidence)*** and the conclusions we draw or "infer" from the evidence ***(inferences).*** Encourage students to record *only what they can directly observe* about the clues at the crime scene, using their senses of sight, smell, and touch. For instance, if you chose the comb, its color, where it was found, whether or not it had hair in it—this is all evidence. Some examples of inferences are, "It was Felix's comb," or, "He was combing his hair right before he died."

4. Point out that there are eight numbered sections of the crime scene. Explain that there will be eight teams, each examining *one* assigned section of the crime scene. Each team will share the tasks of drawing their section, examining the evidence and recording details on index cards.

Throughout Mystery Festival you are asked to help students make "inferences," that is, to derive possible explanations or conclusions based on evidence and reasoning, and also to distinguish evidence from inference. As they become more and more involved in solving the mystery, students also gauge the strength and validity of various pieces of evidence, while refining and adjusting their earlier inferences. Although the process of making at least simple inferences is appropriate for students of all ages, it is not necessary to use the word "inference" itself, especially not with younger students. You may want to use a more common word, such as "explanation" or "good guess." The very process your students are so involved in—looking for and analyzing "clues" to find out more about what happened—provides them with great practical and direct experience differentiating evidence from inference! Older students who work on the Felix mystery, such as those in middle school/junior high, can be encouraged to examine this distinction more directly. Assessment activities could focus on, for example, a fictional newspaper article reporting on a crime, which students are asked to edit to clearly distinguish facts from inferences, to eliminate unfair inferences, and to qualify as appropriate those inferences that can reasonably be reported. The new edition of the GEMS guide Fingerprinting includes such an assessment activity.

5. Emphasize that they have to proceed carefully so that they can examine each item without disturbing any other evidence. Explain the procedure and establish rules for who may enter the crime scene:

- Teams sit in an area separate from the crime scene.

- One student from each team will go to the crime scene, stay outside the barrier, and make a labeled drawing of the team's *undisturbed* section. You may prefer to have the entire team do this. *(If you took photos, students may skip this step.)*

If only one class is using the Crime Scene, you may want each team to keep their evidence in a bag or shoebox.

- After the first student (or the team) has finished drawing the section, **one** student from the team may enter the crime scene to get a piece of evidence from their section. That student must walk carefully and not disturb any of the sections.

- The student may pick out only one item from the team's section, and bring it back to the team. The team writes down every detail they observe about the item on an index card. When the team has finished recording details about that item, a different student from their team puts it back where it was and gets one more item, and so on.

• If there are any footprints in their section, tell them to fill out an index card for each type of footprint found. Show them the "Suspect Footprints Sheet," and say that it has information that will help them identify the footprints. Tell them to also try to tell if whoever made the prints was walking, running, struggling, etc.

• Do the following steps as the students watch, explaining what you are doing as you go along. Say that these steps will help protect the evidence as the students examine it in this session and later.

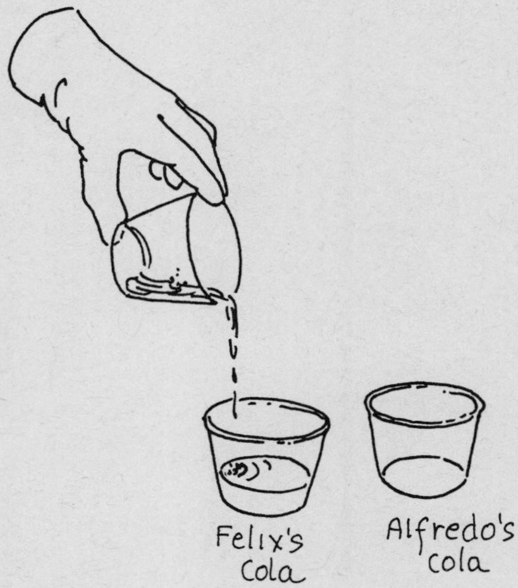

a. After asking a student to note carefully exactly where the two cups of cola are on the crime scene, pick them up carefully by the rims and bottoms, explaining how important it is to avoid smudging any possible fingerprints. If you have gloves, wear them.

b. Pour out the cola into the extra cups you labeled earlier, "Felix's Cola" and "Alfredo's Cola." Set these cups of cola aside, telling the students that they will get to do lab tests on the colas in Session 3.

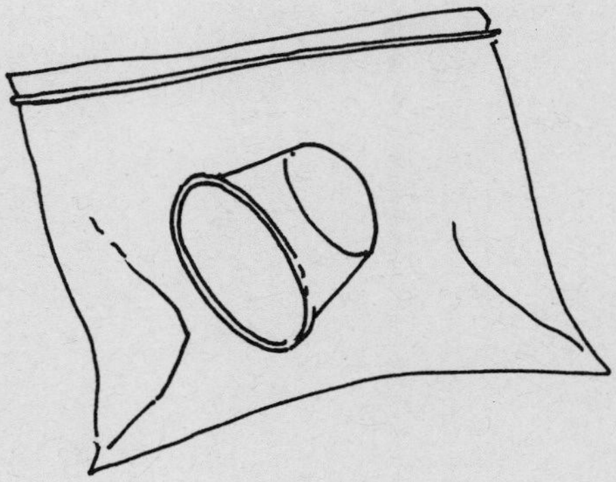

c. Put each of the now-empty cups with fingerprints into a ziplock bag, and set them back where they were on the crime scene. Explain that now students will be able to examine them closely without smudging any fingerprints that might be on them.

5. Show your students how to set up their index cards. Have them divide each card up into three sections. In the top section, they write the name of the object with bold letters, so it can be read from a distance. In the second section (which should be the largest) they write their observations of the object. They leave the remaining section blank for now; later that's where they'll record the results of the chemical and physical crime lab tests they conduct on the evidence. Here's an example:

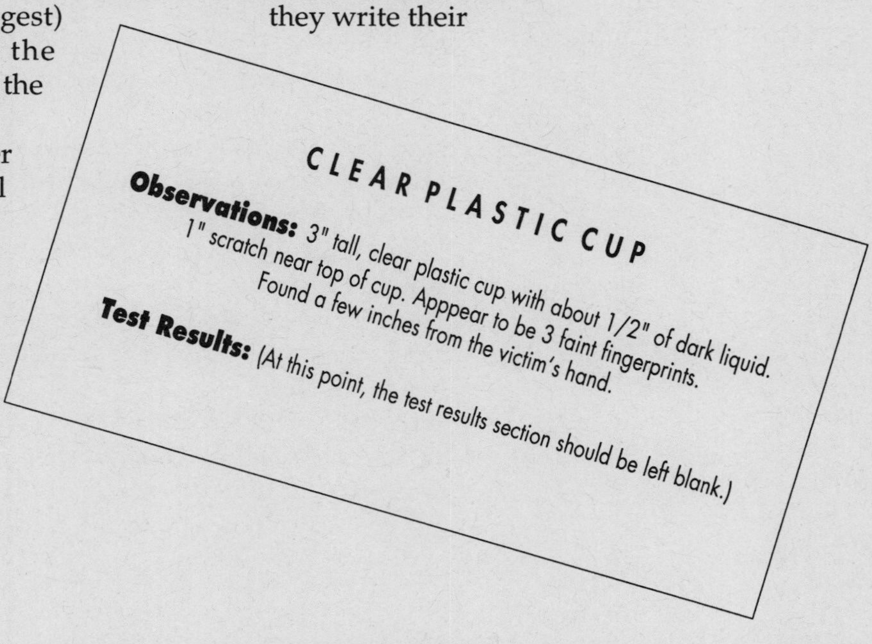

CLEAR PLASTIC CUP

Observations: 3" tall, clear plastic cup with about 1/2" of dark liquid. 1" scratch near top of cup. Apppear to be 3 faint fingerprints. Found a few inches from the victim's hand.

Test Results: (At this point, the test results section should be left blank.)

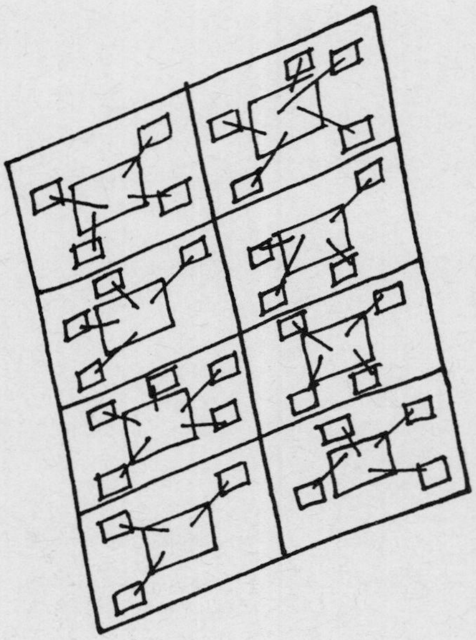

6. Ask the students to tape their drawings (or photos) of their section in the corresponding section of the Crime Scene Map. Tell them also, that as they fill out their index cards, to tape them on the Crime Scene Map around the drawing (or photo) in their section. Show them how to draw a line from each index card to the location of the object in the drawing. (See illustration on page 128.)

7. When you are sure that the students understand the procedure, assign them to teams and tell the teams which numbered section is theirs.

8. Distribute drawing paper, pencils, index cards, and the "Suspect Footprints" sheets, and have them begin. Circulate as needed to make sure teams are cooperating well, observing carefully, putting clues back, and recording their observations on the index cards.

9. When the class has finished, explain that during the next session they're going to learn more about the events that happened at this crime scene, and the suspects involved.

Breaking Down the Crime Scene

The evidence has been recorded by the class on the Crime Scene Map, so the crime scene can be dismantled after Session 1. Most of the materials can be put away and stored for a future Mystery Festival. **However, keep the following items handy for use in later sessions of this Festival:**

Keep on hand these items you prepared, but didn't place on the crime scene:

- the second, extra brown stain paper towel
- the Suspect Fingerprint Sheet
- the container of brown stain dye
- the five colognes or perfumes you gathered
- the baking powder and cornstarch

Keep on hand these items from the Crime Scene:

- the brown stain paper towel from the scene
- Felix and Alfredo's cups with fingerprints
- the cola that was poured from Felix and Alfredo's cups
- the ice cube tray with the "melted ice cube water" that you made by mixing baking soda and water in the ice cube tray.
- the towel with perfume on it
- the indented tagboard secret note
- yarn pieces found at scene

Going Further

Have a member of the local police department as a guest. The guest could explain to the students how they will be working just as real detectives and forensic scientists do to solve a crime.

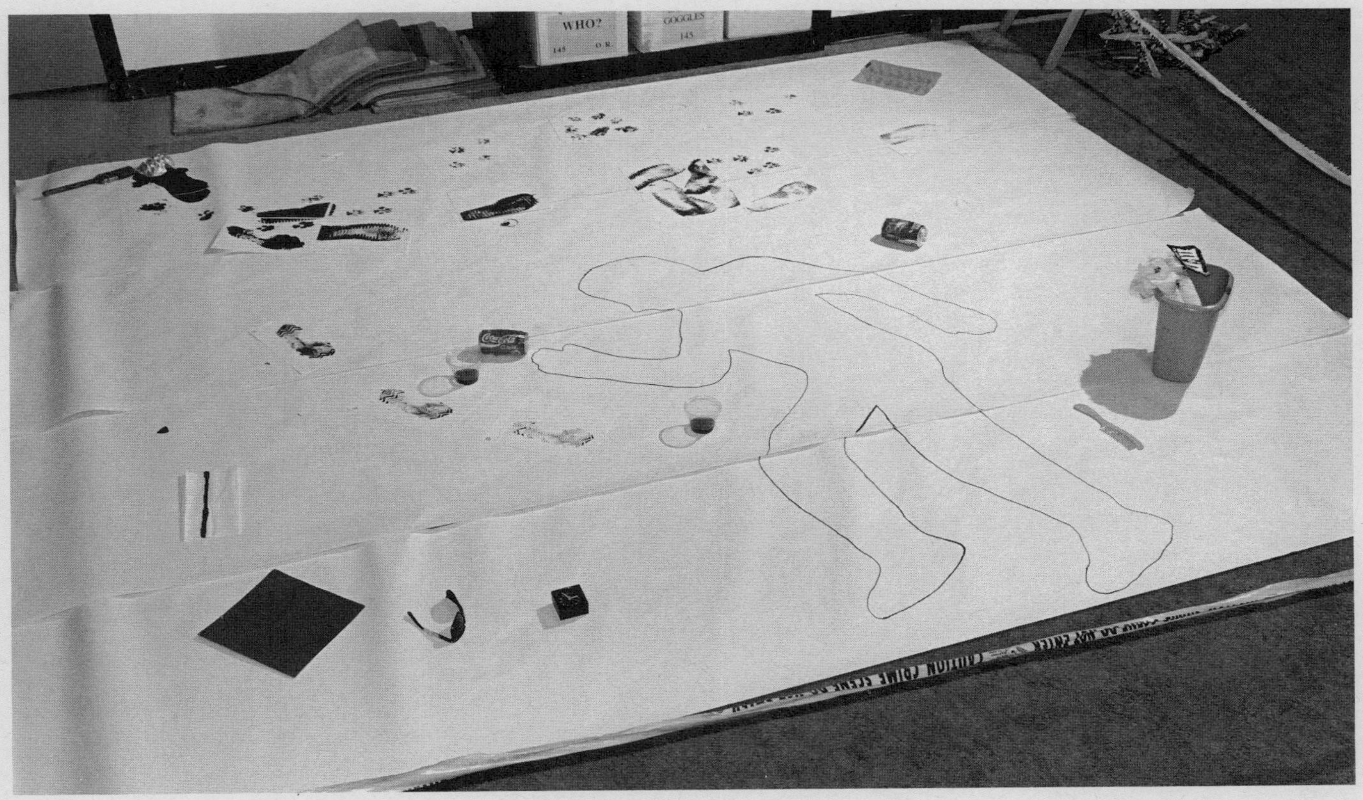

CRIME SCENE MAP

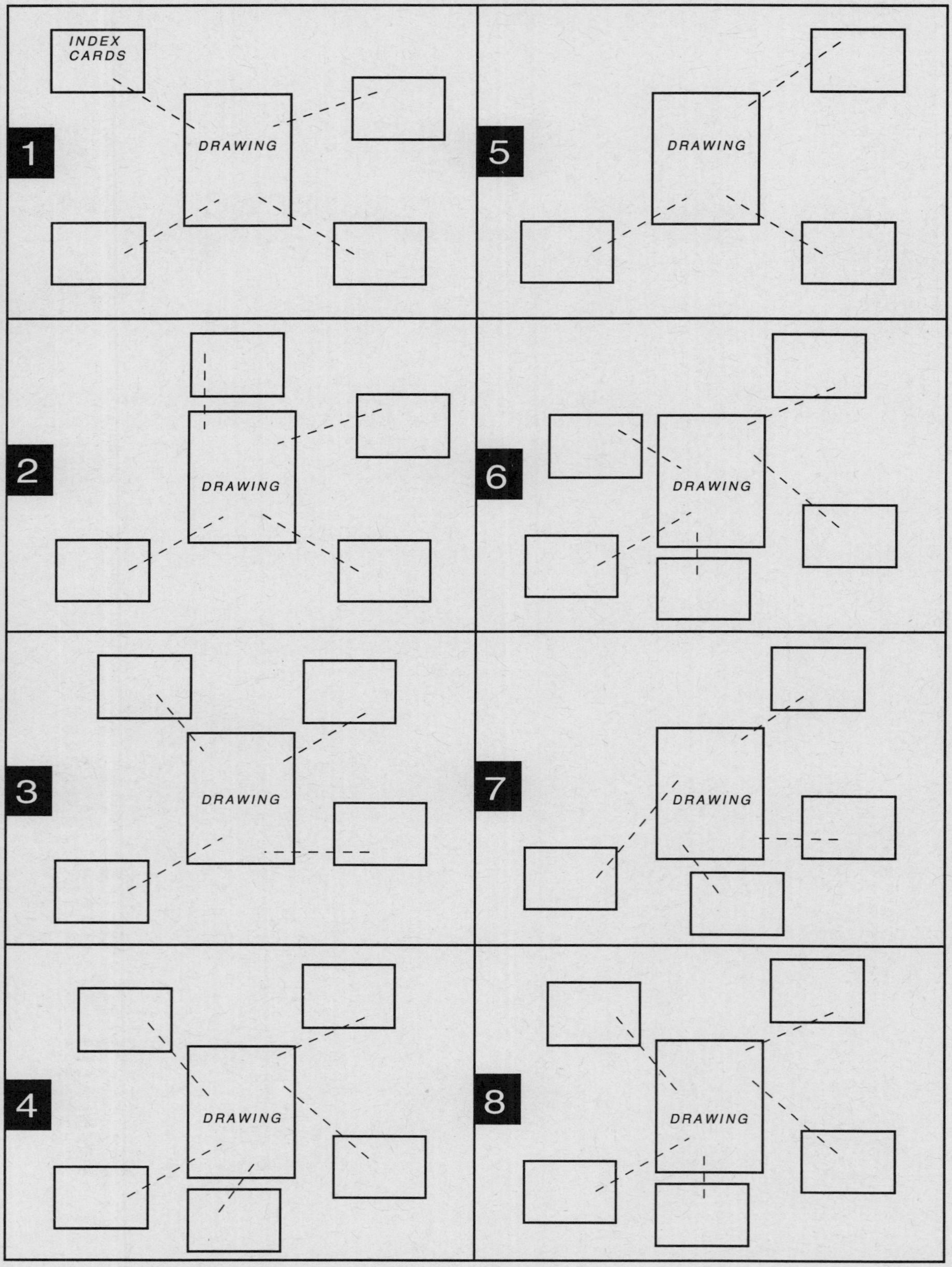

Suspect FOOTPRINTS

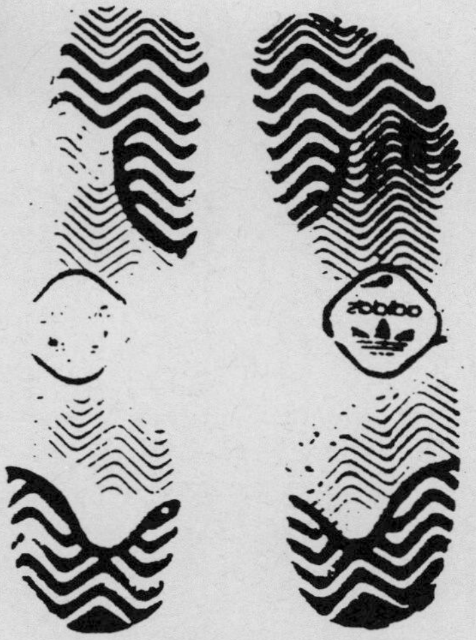

Name: VERA CRUISE
Brand: ADIDAS
Size: 8 WOMENS
Notes:

Name: FELIX NAVIDAD
Brand: ADIDAS
Size: 7 1/2 MENS
Notes: GUM ON SHOE

Name: ALFREDO FETTUCINE
Brand: REEBOK
Size: 9 MENS
Notes:

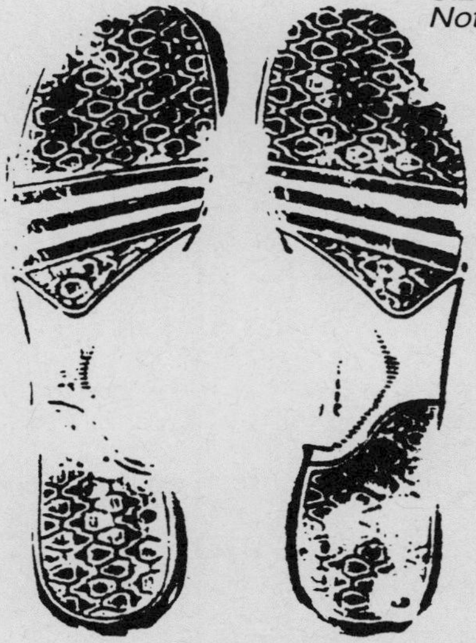

Name: KENDRA GOODE
Brand: ASICS TIGERS
Size: 8 WOMENS
Notes: CARPET TACK IN HEEL

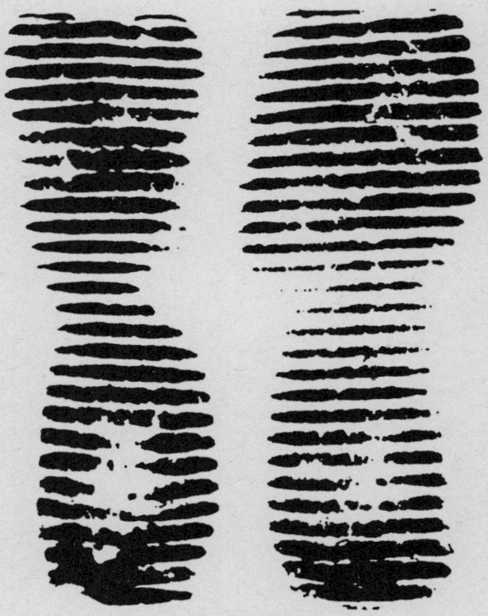

Name: GENE POULE
Brand: BEACH SANDAL
Size: 10 MENS
Notes:

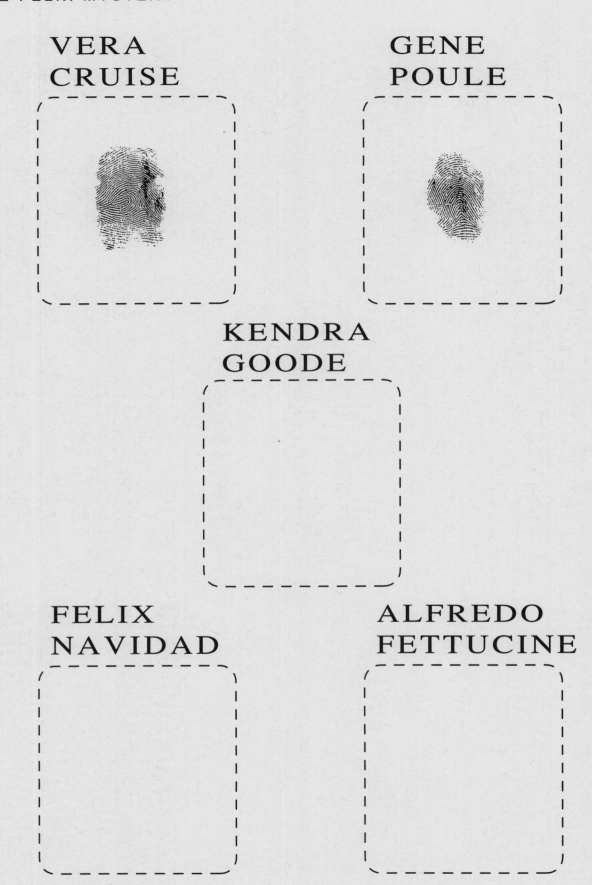

SUSPECT FINGERPRINTS

VERA CRUISE

GENE POULE

KENDRA GOODE

FELIX NAVIDAD

ALFREDO FETTUCINE

Felix
coke can
paper towel
Paint
Paint spill
Towel
Comb
SAVE THE PLANET
Best

Session 2: The Story

Overview

During this session, students learn more about the suspects and what is known about the crime. Student volunteers read the statements by four suspects, and the teacher adds other potentially pertinent information.

The students use a "Clue Board" to list clues that seem to point to specific suspects beneath those suspects' names. Clues which at this point do not seem to incriminate anyone in particular are also listed as such. The class will refer to the Clue Board in later sessions, and change the positions of some of the clues as they conduct tests on the evidence.

At the end of this session, the teacher uses a simple fingerprinting technique that involves Krazy Glue to check for fingerprints on the cups found at the scene of the crime.

What You Need

- ❐ pictures of suspects (masters on pages 141–144)
- ❐ a sheet of butcher paper or a chalkboard space about 5' x 4' feet for making the Clue Board
- ❐ a meter or yardstick for drawing lines on Clue Board
- ❐ 1 pad of 100 3 x 5 inch Post-it® notes (not needed if you make a chalkboard Clue Board—see #2 in Getting Ready, below.)
- ❐ 1 small container of Krazy Glue®
- ❐ 1 pair plastic gloves
- ❐ 2 plastic cups from the crime scene, with fingerprints on them, in ziplock bags

Getting Ready

1. Duplicate one copy of each suspect's picture and statement (pages 141-144).

2. Decide if you want to make your Clue Board on butcher paper or on the chalkboard. "Post-it" notes will allow students to move the clues around on the butcher paper Clue Board. If you decide to use the chalkboard, you won't need "post-its." You will need to reserve that part of the chalkboard for the Clue Board until the end of the Mystery Festival.

3. Have the Clue Board in a place where all the students can see it during the class discussion.

4. Tape or staple each suspect's picture and statement along what will be the top (one of the five-foot edges) of the Clue Board, as shown below. In addition, leave room on the right for a "Can't Decide" column, for clues that don't clearly point to any suspect. Use the marking pen and yardstick to draw vertical lines to form six columns under the suspects and the "Can't Decide" heading. (See page 140.)

5. For the closing demonstration, have on hand the Krazy Glue and the two cups with fingerprints, from the crime scene, in ziplock bags.

Introduce the Session

1. Have the students gather in their eight groups. Hand out about eight to ten "post-it" notes to each group and have them write on them the names of the evidence in their section of the crime scene (for instance, one might say, "paper towel with brown stain"). Each group will need about five post-its, plus a few extra in case certain clues need to go in more than one column of the Clue Board.

2. Encourage the groups to review their evidence for a few minutes and be ready to share their observations and ideas with the class.

3. Refocus the group as a whole. Tell them that before the class discusses the evidence, they need to learn a little more about who the suspects are and what they were doing at the time of Felix's demise.

Present the Scenario

Set the scene by reading the following information, which our detective squad has "dug up" since the last session:

The victim in this case is Felix Navidad. Felix grew up with a lot of expensive things, but not very much love. He dropped out of college in his freshman year, and never kept a job for more than a month at a time. Felix was not very well-liked because he continually criticized everyone and everything around him. He was not a very happy person. To make matters even worse, less than a year ago, Felix's parents were killed in a freak bungee-jumping accident. As a result of this tragedy, however, Felix inherited a considerable amount of money.

continued . . . continued . . . continued . . .

Felix had just recently bought a new place to live. It was a two-bedroom one-bath beach house located in a very expensive neighborhood. He was still in the process of remodeling his cottage when he decided to throw a weekend housewarming party for four of his closest friends. Although Felix considered these people to be his best friends, none of them liked him very much, and they probably only accepted the invitation because he had recently announced that they were all named equally in his will.

All four of Felix's guests are suspects in the case. Alfredo, one of the suspects, says he found Felix's body at 3:00 in the afternoon, and then called for the others to come. When the police arrived, they found no external injuries, and no blood on the victim's body. The body was sent to the morgue, but unfortunately was stolen before an autopsy could be performed to figure out how he died. We not only don't know who killed Felix, if it was a murder, but we don't even know how he died! There is even some speculation that Felix is not dead, but staged the crime for his own reasons. Reports that he has been seen at the local bus station have not been confirmed.

The task of solving this crime now rests in the hands of the detectives and forensic scientists assigned to collect and examine the physical evidence left at the beach house. It is up to them to try to piece together the story of how Felix came to this bitter end, if indeed he did.

Present the Suspects and their Statements

1. Read out loud to the class the "What We Know" information for each suspect from under their pictures on the Clue Board.

2. Choose four students who are comfortable reading in front of a group to stand, and read the suspects' statements. As each student finishes and sits down, ask another volunteer to make a brief summary of each suspect's statement.

3. Point out to the class that everything they have observed or heard about the crime or suspects may or may not be an important clue. If someone did kill Felix, they would probably do everything they could to make it look like someone else did it.

4. Explain that it's up to them to decide if each piece of evidence they've found or heard is something important, or something designed to throw them off the track.

5. Point out that this is an *imaginary, made-up* mystery, and has no "real" answer, no real solution, except what *they* come up with as detectives and scientists. It is up to them to come up with the best "answer" they can, and as in a real crime situation, no one is going to tell them, "that's the right answer," or, "sorry, you were wrong!" Tell the class that:

- Different students or classes may come up with different "answers" or solutions to this mystery.

- They might decide that they can't decide, like courts in real life sometimes do. The decision that there is not enough conclusive evidence to convict anyone should be considered a more successful outcome than convicting someone simply so the "detectives" can walk away with a "solution." Remind the class that some crimes remain unsolved for years and years.

- As long as they're thinking, learning, exploring and having fun, all of these solutions are fine!

Discussing and Classifying the Clues

1. Have each crime scene section group report their findings from the previous session. As each group reports, lead a discussion about the evidence from that section:

- Start by having a student from that group suggest where on the Clue Board each piece of evidence should be placed and why.

- Check to see if the class agrees by a quick show of hands. Ask those who disagree to explain why.

- If a clue incriminates more than one suspect, have students use extra "post-its" to put it in the appropriate columns.

Some teachers have re-ordered the clues in each column, putting what the class decides are "unimportant clues" at the bottom of the column.

- Put the clue in the column(s) where the majority think it should go. Remind the class that they can move clues again later if they need to.

- Have them put clues they are unsure about into the "Can't Decide" column.

2. As the students classify each piece of evidence, encourage them to evaluate its strength and/or relevance to the solution of the mystery:

- Is it **"hard evidence"** (looks *very* incriminating to a particular suspect or is very directly connected to the crime)?

- Is it **"shaky evidence"** (not very informative or reliable, or possibly even planted to frame someone)?

- Or, is it **"unimportant"** (probably has nothing to do with the crime or suspects)?

3. After deciding together as a class, make an identifying mark, such as an asterisk, next to all the clues the class thinks are "hard evidence." Point out that their ideas may change considerably after the tests have been performed on the evidence in the following sessions.

Please Note: If the discussion becomes too long, consider splitting it into two class sessions. You could have the first four teams of students present the evidence from their sections of the crime scene on one day, and the other four teams the next.

Develop the Fingerprints

1. Tell the class that you are going to demonstrate a forensic technique to check for fingerprints on the plastic cups from the scene of the crime.

2. Hold up each of the two ziplock bags with the empty plastic cups with fingerprints from the crime scene. Add three or four drops of Krazy Glue to each of the ziplock bags. Place the glue so that it won't directly touch the cup. Seal the bag and let it sit.

3. Explain that over several hours, the Krazy Glue gas will adhere to the oils on the fingerprints and make them appear white, and easier to see. Tell your students that they will attempt to identify these prints during the next session.

4. Tell the class that in the next two sessions they will conduct crime lab tests on the evidence to find out more about the mystery.

Felix Mystery CLUE BOARD

Kendra	**Gene**	**Vera**	**Alfredo**	**Felix**	**Can't Decide**

What We Know

- **Gene has a faithful blind dog, Sasha, that always follows him, and no one else.**
- **Gene was wearing beach sandals and a white wool sweater.**
- **He had a brown felt pen in his pocket.**
- **He has a pierced ear.**

Suspect's Statement:

"My name is Gene and I am an office manager. I took my dog Sasha down to the beach for a walk at noon. After taking off my sandals, I fell asleep with Sasha lying next to me. When Alfredo called out at about 3:00 p.m., I woke up, and brought Sasha up right away. I never let Sasha come inside or on to the patio."

What We Know

- **Kendra has white powder on her tennis shoe.**
- **She has pierced ears.**

Suspect's Statement:

"My name is Kendra and I am an artist. I went upstairs to take a shower in the bathroom at about 2:30 p.m. I think that I heard a woman's voice downstairs. I came downstairs as soon as Alfredo called out at about 3:00."

What We Know

- **A white powder was found on Vera's tennis shoe.**
- **Vera was wearing a white wool sweater.**
- **She loves candies with brown coating.**
- **She has pierced ears.**

Suspect's Statement:

"My name is Vera and I am a chemist. I went for a walk at about 2:00 p.m. in the hills behind the house. I came back to the house when I heard Alfredo call for help at about 3:00."

What We Know

- **Alfredo has a cut on his left hand.**
- **He had a brown felt pen in his pocket.**
- **He plays guitar.**
- **He was wearing tennis shoes and a blue sweater.**

Suspect's Statement:

"My name is Alfredo and I am a computer programmer. I saw Felix sitting on the patio, so I joined him at about 2:00 p.m. We each had a can of cola, but we poured them into cups to drink. I set down my cup of cola and went to the bathroom at about 2:45 p.m. When I came back 10 minutes later, I found Felix lying dead on the floor, so I called out to the others at about 3:00."

SUSPECT PRINTS
GENE POULE
ALFREDO FETTUCINE

Felix's
SUSPECT PRINTS
VERA CRUISE
ALFREDO FETTUCINE
FELIX NAVIDAD
GENE POULE
DATA SHEET

Session 3: Crime Lab Stations (Part 1)

Overview

During this and the following session, your classroom is transformed into a crime lab. In all, there are ten forensic test stations, five of which are used in this session, and the other five in the next. During this session the students will be performing tests at the following five stations:

Brown Stain
Cola Test
Fingerprints
Smells
Threads Test

At each of these stations, students perform tests on the evidence and clues found at the scene of the crime during Session 1. Detailed signs, with a series of pictures and written instructions, explain the procedure at each station.

At the end of each of the forensic station days, the class pools their results on the Crime Scene Map from Session 1. With this new information, the class revises the Clue Board from Session 2. If time is short, consider doing these concluding discussions at a separate time.

*A note on stations: Three of these stations are set up to accommodate eight students at a time. However, two stations: "Threads" and "Fingerprints," are set up for only **four** students each. This provides total station space for only 32 students; if you need more space for students at stations, consider duplicating the "Brown Stain" station and having it available at two stations. (See # 4 and #5 under "Getting Ready Before the Day of the Activity," below.)*

What You Need

For every two students:

- ❒ 1 copy of the "Felix Mystery Data Sheet" (master on pages 165–166). (This data sheet is used in both this session and Session 4.)

For the Brown Stain Test Station:

- ❒ four cups (about 3 inches high with a wide mouth)
- ❒ the 2 brown stain paper towels from Session 1
- ❒ brown food coloring (1 part green to 2 parts red)
- ❒ 1 brown felt water-base marker
- ❒ 1 roll of clear tape
- ❒ five pencils
- ❒ 1 dropper bottle (old medicine dropper bottle or saline fluid bottle or similar small bottles are fine)
- ❒ white paper towels
- ❒ 1 pair scissors (for the teacher)

For the Cola Test Station:

- ❒ 2 cups of cola from Session 1 labeled, "Alfredo's cola," and "Felix's cola."
- ❒ 1 cup (the same kind as Felix's and Alfredo's)
- ❒ 1 roll of Universal pH paper with color chart (this can also be used in the next session's Melted Ice Cube Test station).
- ❒ 1 metric ruler
- ❒ A wastebasket for used pH paper (or other small container)

Please note: *Usually, Universal pH paper comes with a color chart calibrating the colors to pH numbers. If a chart is not included, a written description of the colors is given. In this case, either use the written description to make your own color chart, or order a Universal pH paper color chart separately. Inexpensive Universal pH paper is available from scientific supply houses and catalogs. Flinn Scientific, Inc., for example, carries Hydrion 1–14 pH paper, sold by the roll (a roll is 15 feet).*

For the Fingerprint Station:

- ❒ Suspect Fingerprint Sheet made in Session 1 "Getting Ready"
- ❒ Alfredo and Felix's empty cups from the Session 1 crime scene

For the Smells Station:

- ❒ white cotton towel from Session 1 crime scene
- ❒ five empty film canisters
- ❒ five colognes or perfumes, as distinctive as possible (these are the samples you got in Session 1 from department stores, your bathroom cabinet, magazines etc.)
- ❒ masking tape (for making labels)

For the Thread Test Station:

- ❒ 3 cups
- ❒ 2 sheets of aluminum foil about 12" x 16"
- ❒ 2 votive candles
- ❒ 1 book of matches (for teacher to carry)

❒ At least 1 pair of safety goggles (4 pairs would be ideal).
❒ 2 pairs of metal tweezers, tongs or equivalent
❒ ~ 6 feet of white cotton yarn
❒ ~ 6 feet of colored cotton yarn
❒ ~ 6 feet of colored wool yarn

Getting Ready

To help you keep track of the preparation tasks below, there is a Preparation Checklist on page 201.

Note: Some teachers have used swimming, snorkeling, or ski goggles. Safety requirements vary from state to state, and you should be familiar with local requirements. If safety goggles are required in your region, and you do not already have them, you can probably borrow several pairs from upper level chemistry or physics classes.

Before the Day of the Activity

1. Make four copies of each station sign.

2. Make one copy of the data sheet (pages 165 and 166) for every two students in your class. Have pencils handy (one for every two students).

3. Most teachers recommend having an adult volunteer for the Threads station because of the candle flames. It is also helpful to have a volunteer to help at the Brown Stain station. Arrange now for volunteer(s).

Synthetic yarn is not recommended, because it gives off unhealthy fumes when burned. If it is difficult to find cotton or wool yarn in your area, ask for donations of old cotton or wool sweaters to take apart and use.

4. Please note that the "Threads" and "Fingerprint" stations are set up to accommodate only four students at a time. Smaller groups at the Threads station are necessary for safety in using the candles. At the Fingerprinting station, smaller groups allow students to share the two cups with prints.

Having four copies of the sign spread out on the surface of each station allows eight students to see the directions without crowding. At "Threads," "Fingerprints" or other stations where you decide to have fewer than eight students, just make as many copies of the sign as you need. Some teachers prefer to mount just one sign on the wall or on a manila folder to stand at the station so that more students can see.

5. Decide if you will make two stations of the "Brown Stain" activity. This is the station where students tend to "pile up," because the activity takes longer. If you want two Brown Stain stations, you'll need to double the materials under *Brown Stain,* in What You Need, above, and set up two identical stations like the one prepared below and listed in "On the Day of the Activity." The only items you will not have to duplicate for the second station are the two brown stain paper towels you prepared in Session 1; when you cut them into strips, just put half the strips on the second station.

6. To save time on the day of the activity, you can prepare some of the materials for the Brown Stain, Cola, Smells, and Threads stations before the day of the activity, as detailed below:

Brown Stain Station

Prepare the materials:

1. Cut the brown stain paper towels that you prepared in Session 1 into one-inch by three-inch strips, one for each pair of students, plus a few extra.

2. Cut enough 1" x 3" **blank** pieces of white paper towel for each team to have two pieces, plus a few extra.

3. Fill the dropper bottle with the brown food coloring used in Session 1 (one part green to two parts red). Label the bottle, "brown candy food coloring."

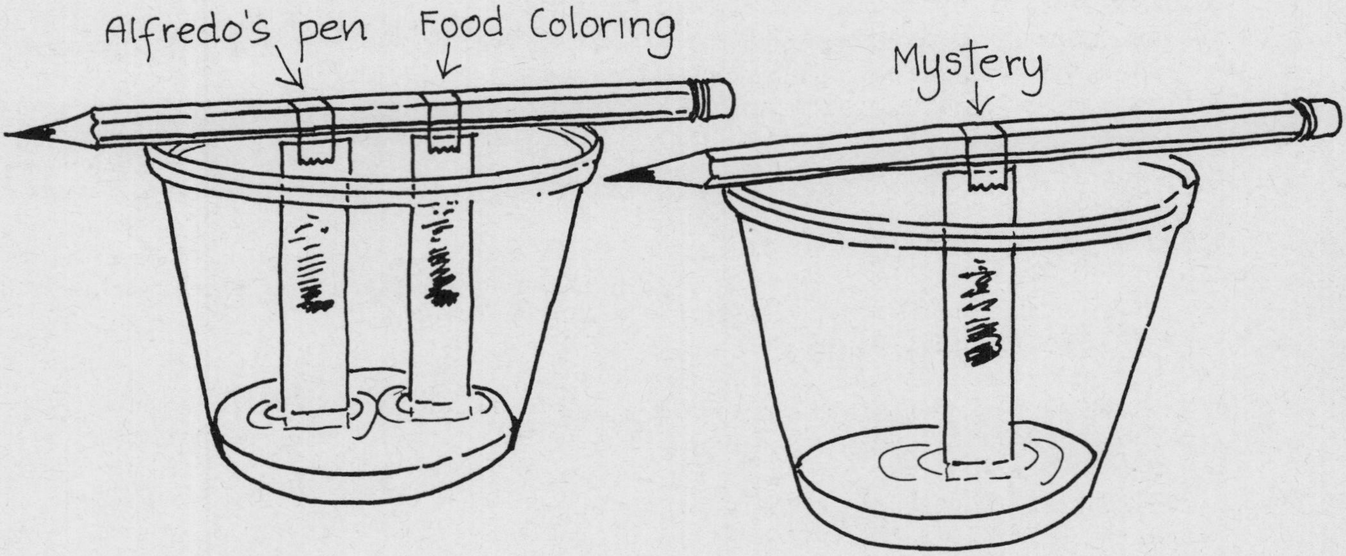

Cola Station
Prepare the materials:

If a color-coded pH chart did not come with the pH paper, then make one. Use a pen to mark on the pH chart which numbers are acids (#'s 0-6), bases (#'s 8-14) and neutrals (# 7).

Many teachers feel it is worth the extra effort to make a big pH chart, so that all students at the station can see it at once. If you do make a big chart, color it with crayons as closely as possible to the one that comes with the Universal pH paper.

Smells Station
Prepare the materials:

1. Label the five film canisters with the names of Felix and the four suspects: Kendra, Gene, Vera and Alfredo. You may also want to label the lids, if you have time.

2. In the container labeled, "Gene," put a few drops of **the same cologne that you already put on the white cotton towel.** Put a few drops of each of the other four perfumes/colognes in the other four containers.

Threads Station

1. Tear off two sheets of aluminum foil about 12"x 16" each, and lay them out to protect the table top from the candles and burning yarn.

2. Cut the three types of yarn (white cotton, colored cotton, and colored wool) into 2" long pieces. Cut 25 of each, and put them into containers labeled, "Mystery thread" (white cotton thread), "Cotton thread" and "Wool thread."

On the Day of the Activity

Set up each of the five stations. Some teachers prefer to set up the stations before the day of the activity, and store them in bins or boxes for quick distribution and clean up. This also makes it easier to share with other teachers.

If you have an adult volunteer(s), go over the station activity that they will be helping with, making sure the volunteer understands the importance of allowing the students to make their own discoveries and conduct their own tests.

Try each of the station activities yourself to become familiar with all the procedures.

1. Brown Stain

At this station, students conduct a test in which they hang strips of paper towel from a pencil into a cup of water, so that the bottom end of the strips get wet. Water moves up the paper, causing a stain on the middle of the strip to separate into different colors. This kind of test is called "paper chromatography."

Prepare the materials:

1. Gather the brown stain paper towel strips, blank pieces of paper towel, and dropper bottle previously prepared, with four cups.

2. Into each of four cups, pour about 1/2" of water, or enough so that when the paper strip is suspended from a pencil, just the end of it will be in the water.

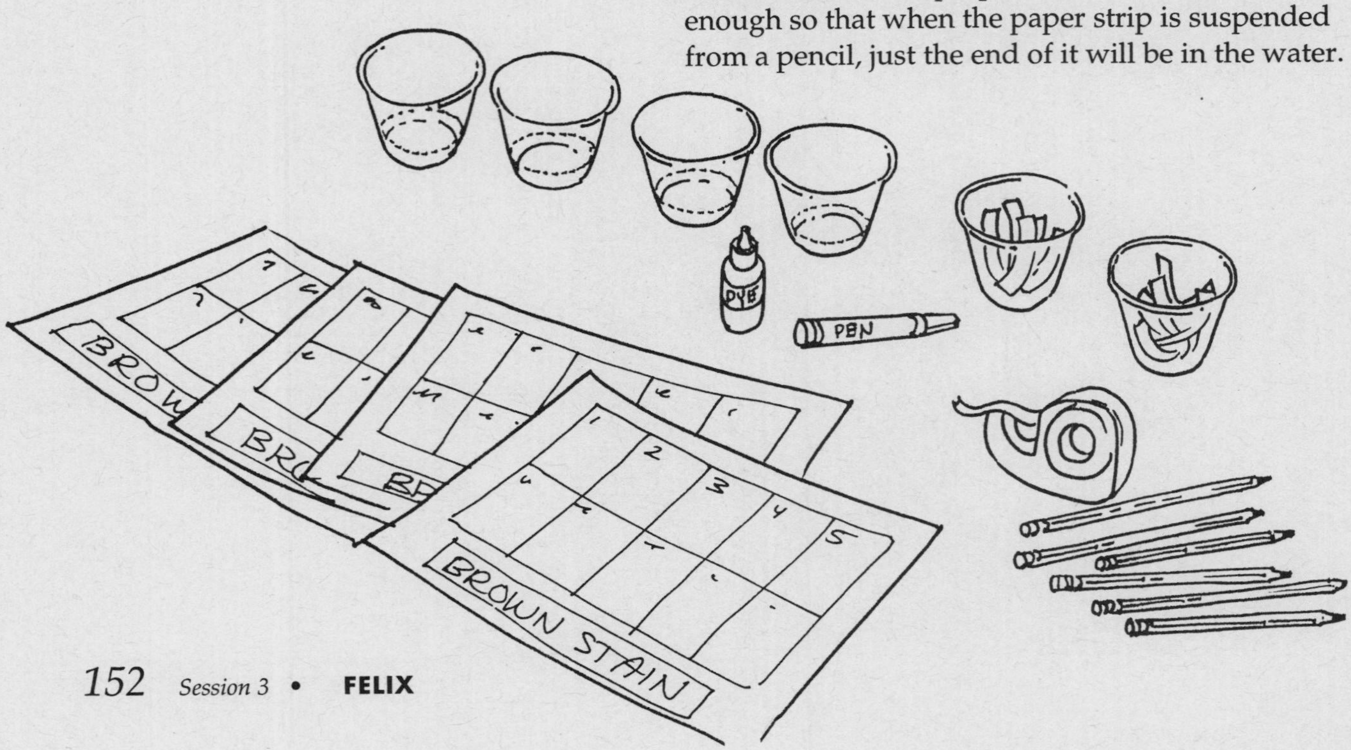

Set out these materials at the station:

1. The brown stain paper towel strips.
2. The blank white paper towel strips.
3. 1 roll of clear tape
4. At least five pencils
6. The Brown Pen
7. The eyedropper bottle with food coloring
8. The four cups, each about 1/2 inch full of water
9. The Brown Stain signs

(Note: If you decide to make two Brown Stain stations, you will need to duplicate everything except the brown stain strips and the blank pieces of paper towel. There should already be enough so that you can put half the strips on the second station.)

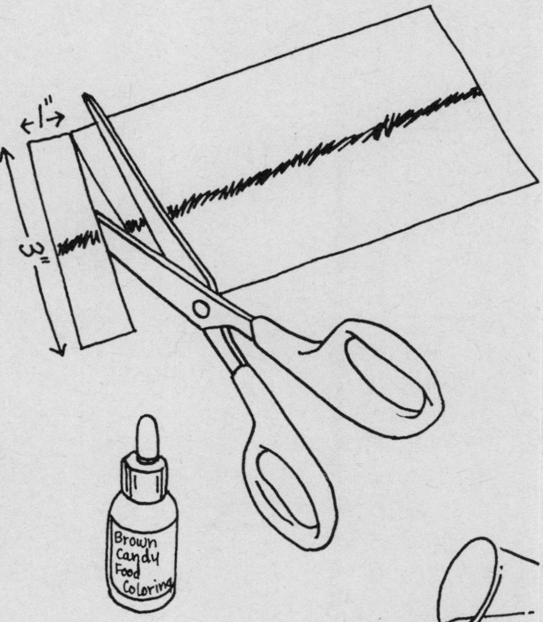

2. Cola Test

At this station, students test the pH of the cola in Felix's and Alfredo's cups and compare it to a cup of "regular cola."

Prepare the materials:

1. Get the cups with cola in them that you labeled during Session 1, "Alfredo's cola," and "Felix's cola." **(Felix's cola should still have about 1/8 teaspoon of baking soda stirred into it.)**

2. Make a third cup, and label it "regular cola." Each of the three cups should have about 1/2" cola in it.

3. Have available the color-coded pH chart.

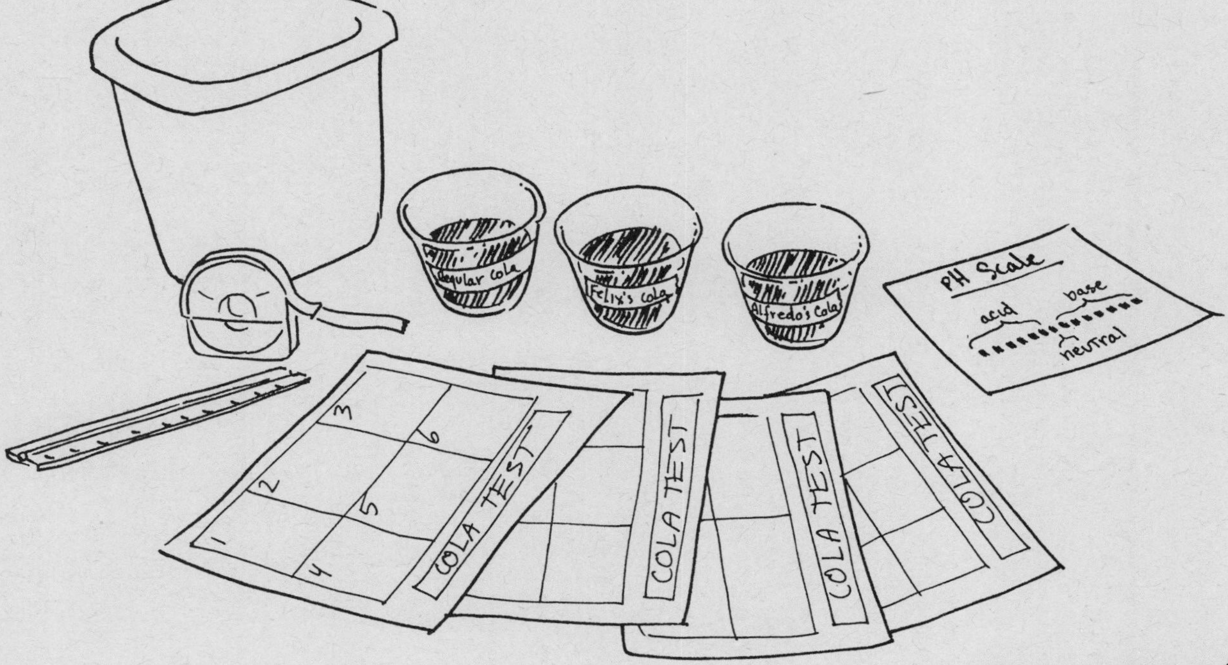

Note: You may want to use cabbage juice pH paper instead of the commercial type paper. Boil a red cabbage in water in a non-aluminum pan till the water is deep purple. Paint the cabbage juice on white paper with a paintbrush, set it out to dry, then do another coat and let it dry. Cut up into strips. Your simplified pH chart could then simply be pink = acidic, purple = neutral, green = basic. You could even avoid the need to boil the cabbage by using a blender and straining out the cabbage juice.

Set out these materials at the station:

1. The three cups of cola
2. One roll of Universal pH paper with chart
3. Metric ruler
4. The Cola Test signs
5. A wastebasket for used pH paper

3. Fingerprints

Prepare the materials:

1. Take the two cups out of their ziplock bags.(Krazy Glue technique should have made the prints show up white)

Set out these materials at the station:

1. Alfredo and Felix's cups from Session 1 crime scene
2. Suspect Fingerprint Sheet from Session 1 "Getting Ready."
3. The Fingerprints signs

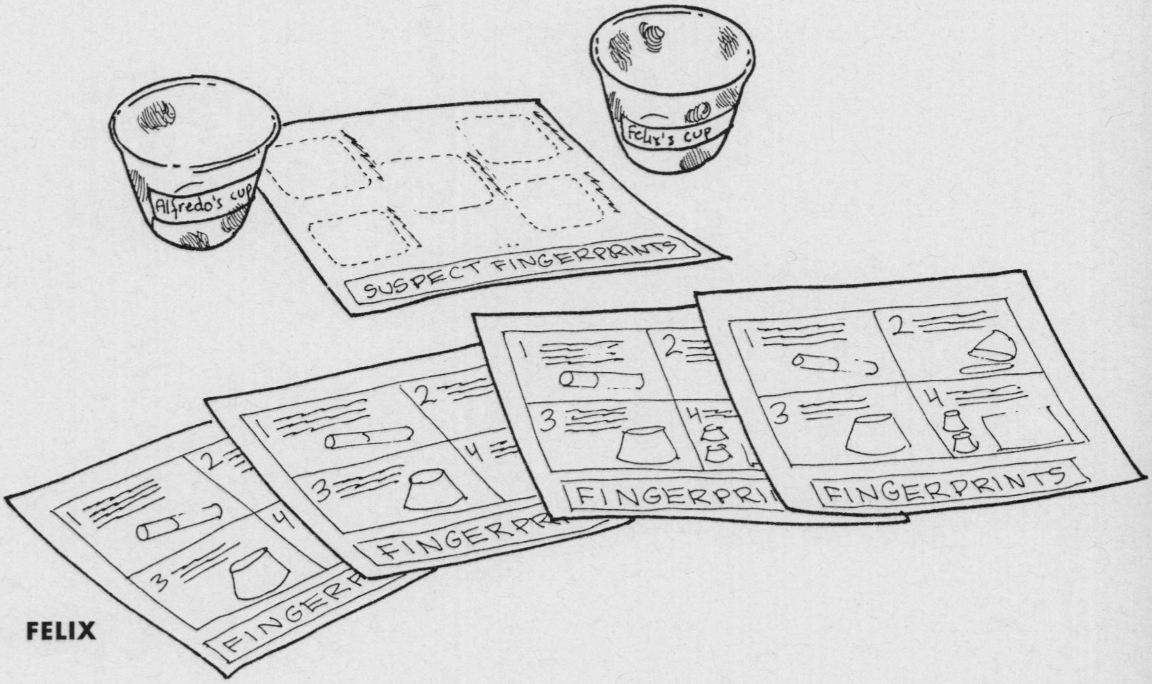

4. Smells

Prepare the materials:

Gather the five labeled film canisters previously prepared, with drops of cologne in them.

Set out these materials at the station:

1. White cotton towel from Session 1 crime scene
2. Labeled small containers
3. The Smells station signs

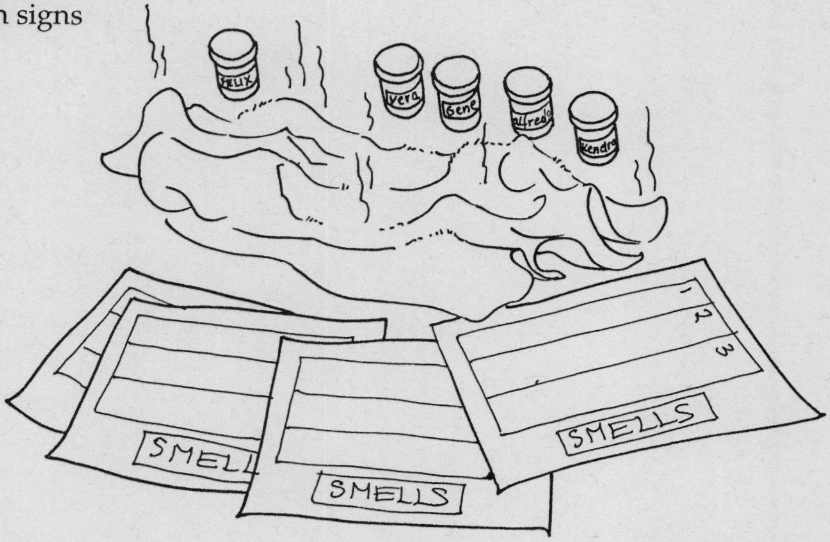

5. Threads

Prepare the materials:

Gather the two-inch pieces of yarn previously prepared, in three labeled containers/cups, along with candles, safety goggles, and tweezers. Teacher should have a book of matches.

Set out these materials at the station:

1. Two votive candles
2. One book of matches (for teacher to carry)
3. At least 1 pair of safety goggles (4 pairs would be ideal)
4. Two pairs of metal tweezers, tongs or equivalent
5. Yarn samples in labeled cups
6. The Thread Test signs

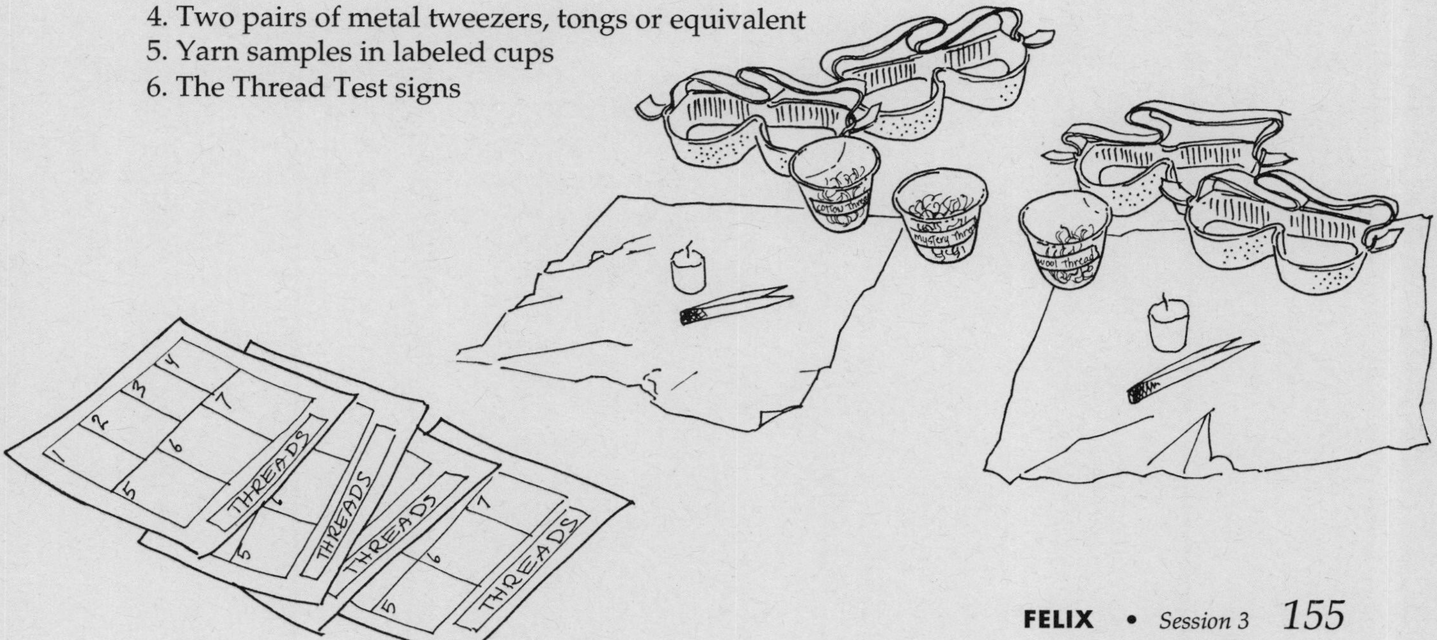

Introduce the Stations

1. Explain to the students that today they will conduct chemical and physical tests on the evidence found at the scene of the crime.

2. Tell the students they will each work with a partner to do the tests at each station. Say that the partners will share a data sheet on which to write the results of their tests.

3. Hold up a sign and tell them they'll need to read each step on the signs and look at the pictures to understand how to do each test.

4. Briefly demonstrate the procedure at each station without actually doing the tests or giving away the results. As you explain each test, read the sign and be sure that the students understand how the test ties in with the mystery, as in the following:

After you demonstrate how to set it up, you might want to set out your sample of how the cup, pencil and paper strips are set up, but without the water. This way, students will have a 3-dimensional model of the test, but not the result.

1. **Brown Stain Station:** Remind them that a brown stain was found on a piece of paper near the body. Ask why we might want to find out if the stain is food coloring or brown pen. [Alfredo and Gene had identical brown pens, and Vera loves candies with brown coating.] Demonstrate the steps, **emphasizing that the bottom of the paper strip must touch the water in the cup, but the brown stain on the paper must stay above the level of the water.**

*Please note: At this station (and at the Melted Ice Cube station in Session 4) it is not essential that your students understand **why** the pH paper changes color when dipped in the cola solution. The GEMS units Of Cabbages and Chemistry and Acid Rain explore the concepts of pH and acid-base chemistry further. Using these units or other pH activities before or after the Mystery Festival is recommended but certainly not necessary. Even if you don't teach your students about pH, their experiences during the Mystery Festival serve as a solid foundation of experience on which to build future concepts.*

2. **Cola Station:** Was anything added to Alfredo's or Felix's cola? Do a pH test to find out. Caution the students to be careful with these samples so that they aren't spilled or contaminated.

3. **Fingerprints Station:** "The Krazy Glue" has made the fingerprints left on the plastic cups turn white so they are easier to see. Whose fingerprints match the ones on Alfredo's and Felix's cups? Are there more than one person's prints on either of the cups?" **Note:** Since the fingerprints were "developed" with Krazy Glue, they won't rub off easily. Even so, remind the students to hold the cups by the rim and bottom so they don't alter the evidence.

4. **Smells Station:** A white towel was found in the wastebasket at the scene of the crime. The towel has a strong smell. Whose cologne or perfume matches the one on the towel?

5. **Threads Station:** Were the white "Mystery Threads" found at the scene of the crime cotton or wool? How would the results of this test connect to the mystery? [certain suspects were wearing wool...] **Emphasize safety at this station**, and tell students that only four students, instead of eight, can be there at one time. Mention that as soon as the thread starts burning, they should take it out of the flame. Keeping it in the flame makes it burn too fast, making the results harder to see. Also caution students not to let the thread get into the hot wax because that will change the way it burns and adversely affect the results.

Some students will probably have difficulty distinguishing between the scents at this station. That's to be expected! Let them know that smells are hard to tell apart and that scientists and detectives might have the same kind of difficulty. Suggest that they be careful to smell each sample one at a time, comparing it to the towel after each to see which smell is most similar. Have students do their best, and perhaps together the group will be able to reach a conclusion.

One teacher instructed her students to test the threads in the order given on their data sheet: Mystery, Wool, Cotton. This way the contrasting results are most obvious.

Crime Lab Testing and Recording Results

1. Explain to the students that each team carries with them a data sheet and pencil to record their results. Show them how to record results on the data sheet.

2. Tell the class that when they finish their first station, they may go to any other available station they like, until they have completed all five. Remind them not to run, and to go to uncrowded stations.

3. Tell them that in between stations, or if they finish early, they may return to the Crime Scene Map and the Clue Board to attempt to piece together the evidence.

4. Caution students not to jump to conclusions after doing only one or two stations. Solving a mystery is like putting together a big puzzle — it is very hard to see the whole picture if you have only one or two pieces.

5. When they understand what they are to do, choose partners, hand out data sheets and pencils, and assign the teams to their first stations.

6. Allow student teams to conduct their tests. Circulate as needed to assist.

Pooling Class Data on the Crime Scene Map

1. When all, or at least most, of your students have completed the stations, gather them with partners near the Crime Scene Map and the Clue Board, with their data sheets in front of them. Give them a couple of minutes to discuss among themselves, to make sure that they agree on the results they recorded on their data sheet. This helps to avoid arguments between partners in front of the class.

2. Refocus the group on the Crime Scene Map. You will be pooling the results from each of the five station activities and writing them on the index cards. In each case, ask first for a volunteer to report their results. Ask those who agree to raise their hands. Then ask those who disagree to raise their hands. Find out the results of those who disagree, and discuss how they might have arrived at different results, and how they could decide which to use.

3. Depending upon student ability, and how carefully they conducted their tests, observed, and recorded their results, there may be a lot of disagreement. Ask the students how they think that different people performing the same test could come up with completely different results. They may suggest impurities in the substances, procedure not performed identically, faulty equipment, students observing the same thing but describing it differently, errors in recording data, etc.

4. Make sure the students realize that scientists often disagree, and they shouldn't feel they have failed if their results are different from those of other teams. Below are three strategies to deal with a variety of results during the discussion.

- Write down all results on the chalkboard, but use only the results of the majority on the index card.

- If the students disagree completely, they may want to declare that particular piece of evidence inconclusive, and not use it. Or, you may want to have your students, or a small team of your students, return and redo this experiment with particular care.

- Simply record how many groups in your class came up with different results, and move on.

5. Once they've agreed on a set of results, record them in the section titled, "Test Results" on the index cards posted on the Crime Scene Map.

Putting Test Results on the Clue Board

1. Ask the students which suspects (if any) each piece of evidence points to, and record this with "post-its" on the Clue Board.

2. The students probably have some kind of evidence pointing to each suspect. Ask why some of the evidence might not be important or "significant." [it could have been "planted" by the murderer to make someone else look guilty. Or, some of the "evidence" may not even have anything to do with the crime and could be there just by coincidence.]

3. Ask which pieces of evidence seem the most difficult to explain away—the ones that make a suspect look *really* guilty? Encourage discussion about ways to tie these "significant" pieces of evidence together in a story so they make logical sense.

4. Tell the students that, based on future findings, their ideas may change! Explain that in the next session, their same teams of high-powered crime lab scientists will conduct five more scientific tests on the evidence.

5. Collect data sheets so that students will have them for the next session.

BROWN STAIN STATION SIGN

1 Make a dot in the middle of the blank piece of paper towel with Alfredo's brown felt pen.

2 On another piece of paper towel, make a dot with the brown food coloring.

3 Label the strips with a pencil.

4 Tape the strips to one pencil. Tape the mystery strip to another.

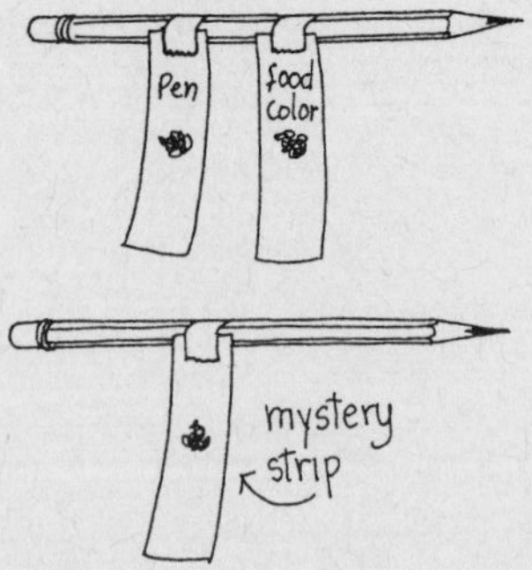

5 Set the pencils on two cups of water, so that the paper touches the water and starts climbing up the paper.

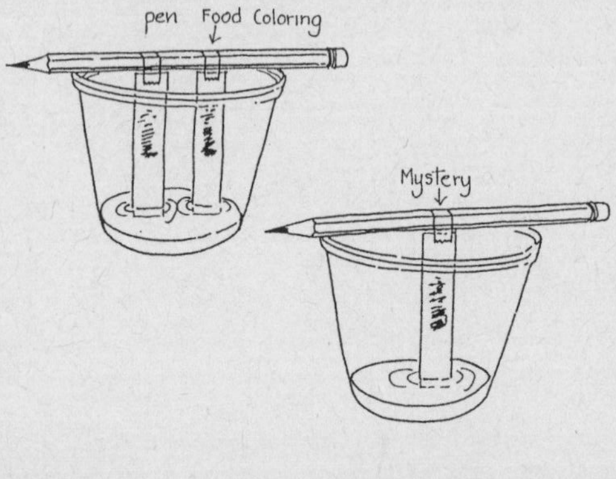

6 Watch what happens when the water moves through the dots.

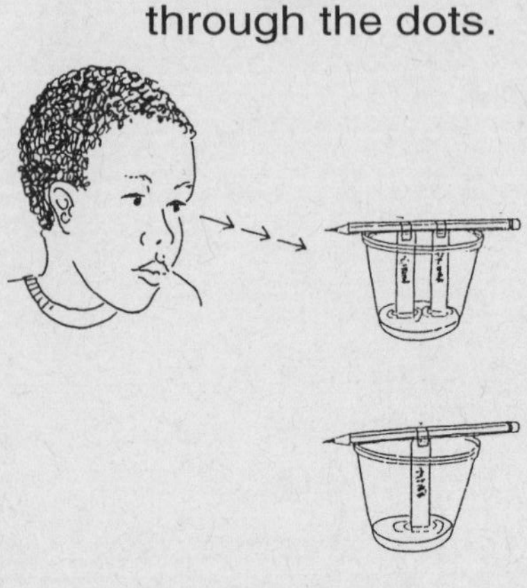

7 See if the pen or the food coloring matches the mystery dot. Circle it on your data sheet.

8 Tape the papers to your data sheet.

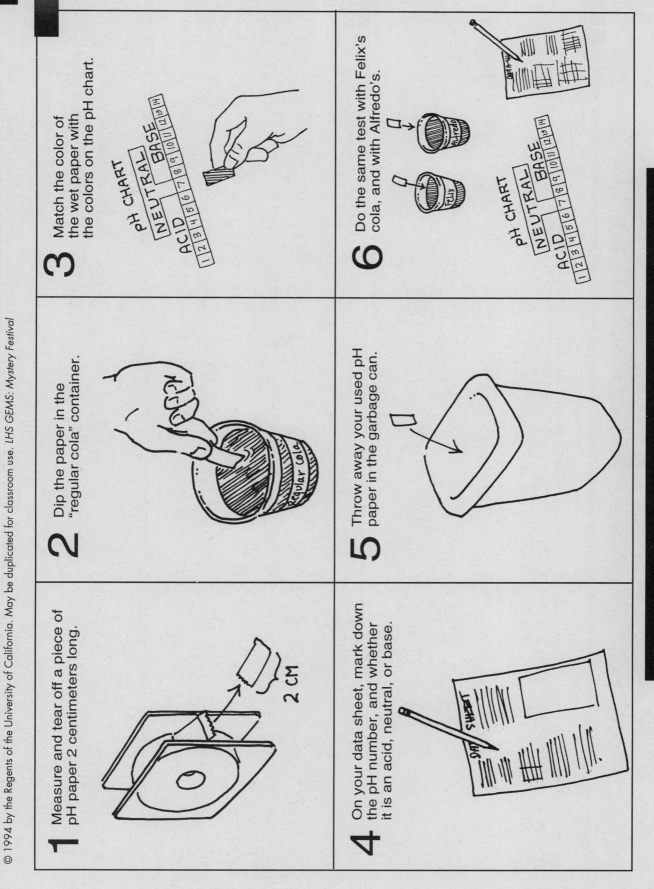

1 Measure and tear off a piece of pH paper 2 centimeters long.

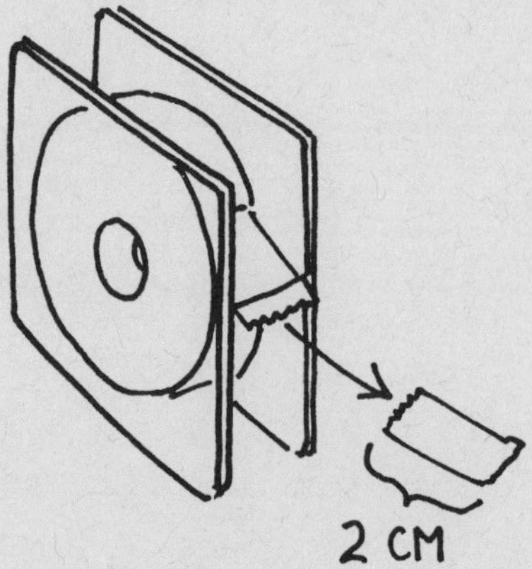

2 Dip the paper in the "regular cola" container.

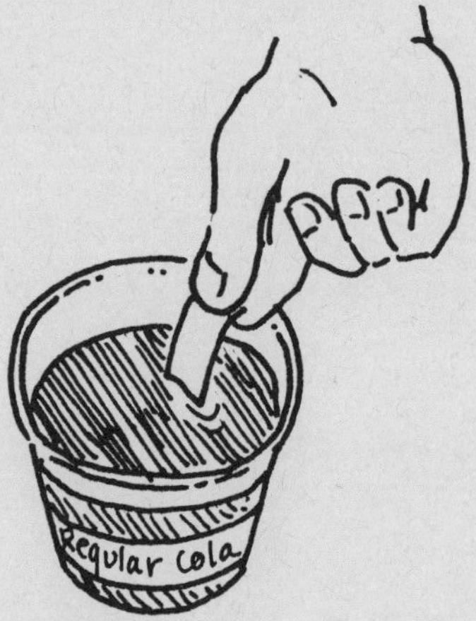

3 Match the color of the wet paper with the colors on the pH chart.

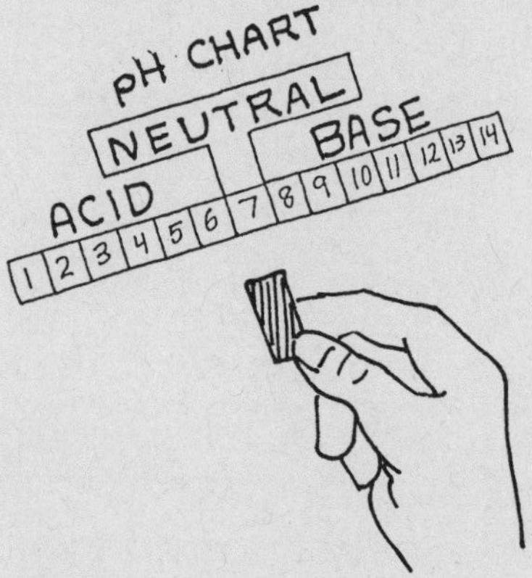

4 On your data sheet, mark down the pH number, and whether it is an acid, neutral, or base.

5 Throw away your used pH paper in the garbage can.

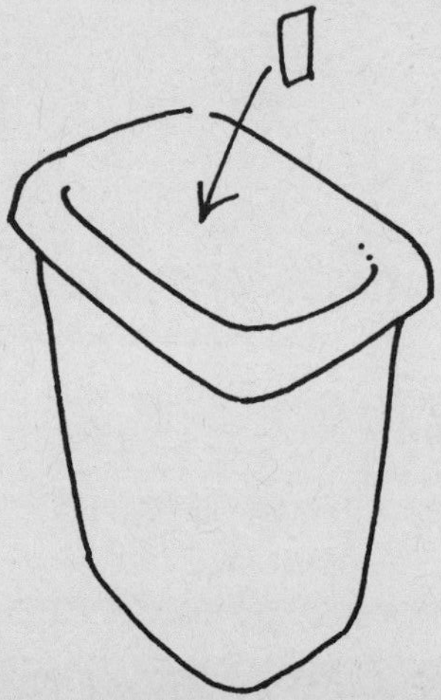

6 Do the same test with Felix's cola, and with Alfredo's.

COLA TEST STATION SIGN

FINGERPRINTS STATION SIGN

Whose fingerprints can you find on Alfredo's and Felix's cup?

Record the results on your data sheet.

1 When scientists smell an unknown substance they use "wafting" which helps protect the nose from smells that might be dangerous, or to which they might be allergic.

When smelling, use your hand to pull the air from over the chemical towards your nose. Don't stick your nose in the container.

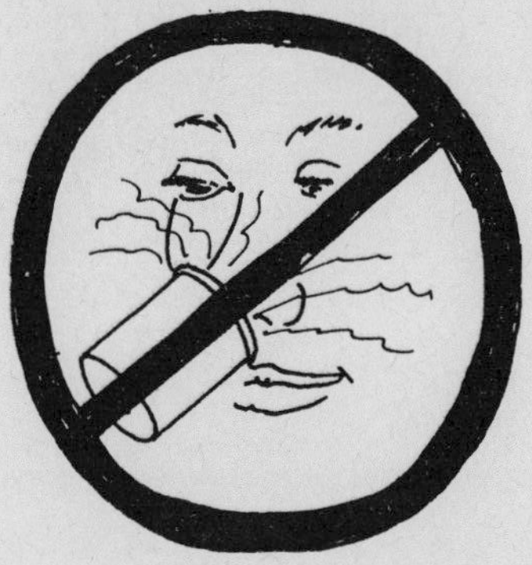

2 Smell the towel found at the scene of the crime.

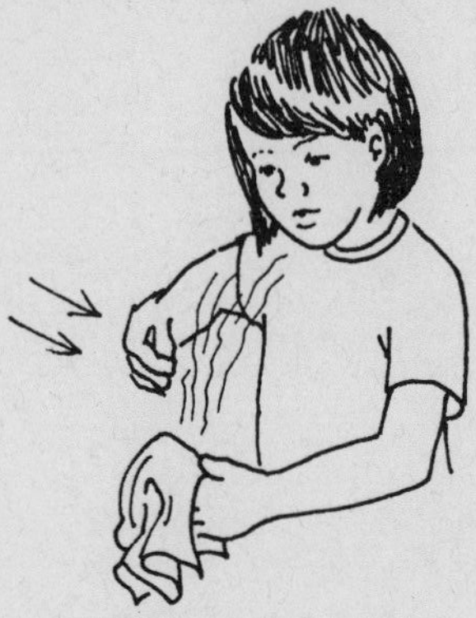

Compare the smell of the towel with the perfumes/colognes.

3 Write down on your data sheet which smell you think is on the towel.

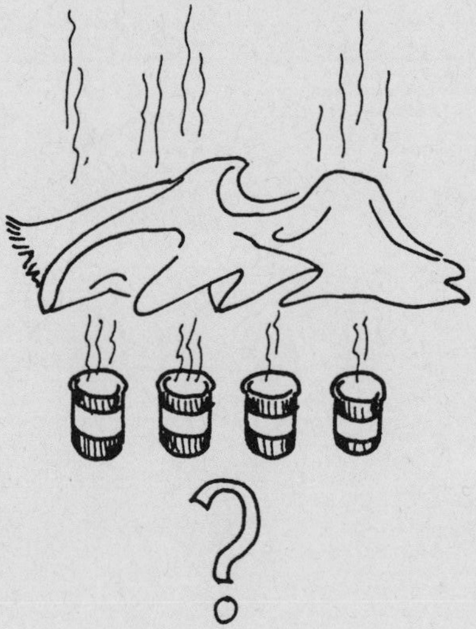

SMELLS STATION SIGN

THREADS STATION SIGN

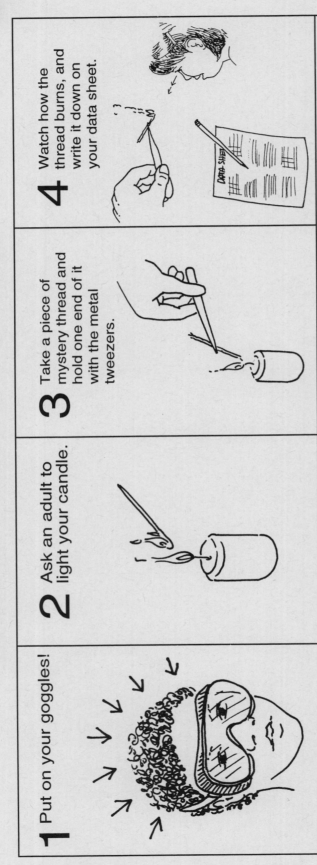

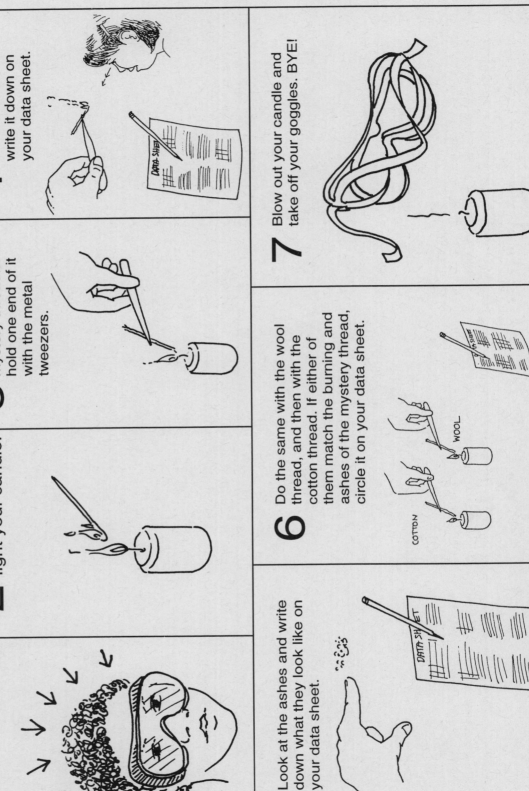

1 Put on your goggles!

2 Ask an adult to light your candle.

3 Take a piece of mystery thread and hold one end of it with the metal tweezers.

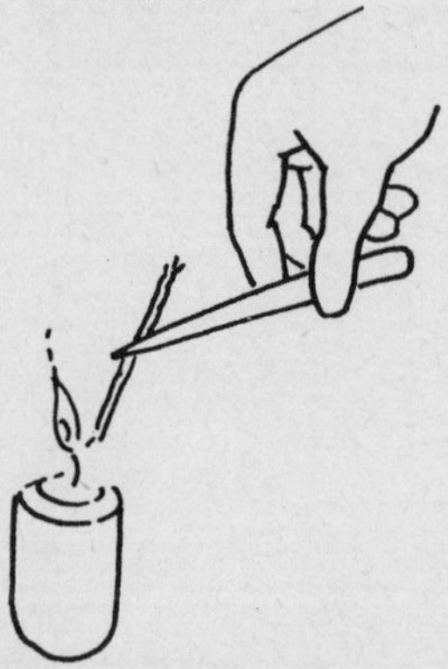

4 Watch how the thread burns, and write it down on your data sheet.

5 Look at the ashes and write down what they look like on your data sheet.

6 Do the same with the wool thread, and then with the cotton thread. If either of them match the burning and ashes of the mystery thread, circle it on your data sheet.

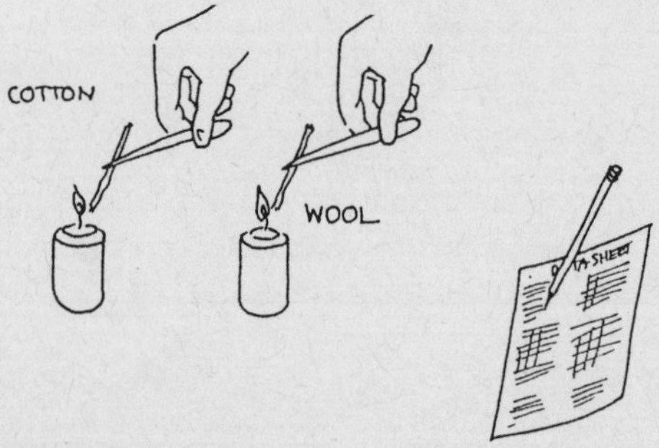

7 Blow out your candle and take off your goggles. BYE!

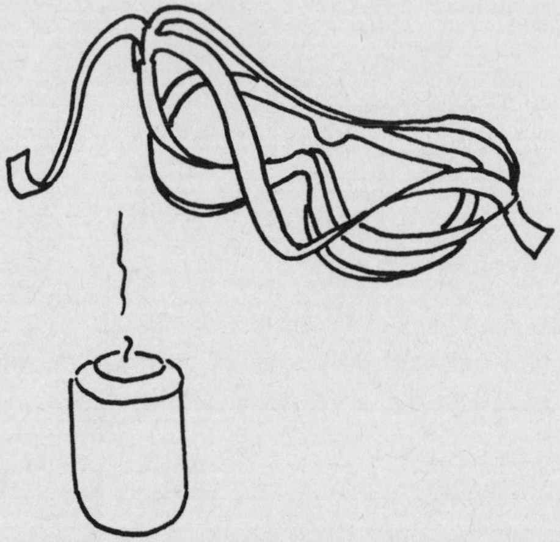

DATA SHEET

for Felix Mystery

Names: ____________________

____

1 Brown Stain

Tape your chromatography paper here. Circle the one which matches the mystery stain:

FELT PEN
FOOD COLORING

2 Cola Test

	pH#	acid, neutral, base
regular cola		
Felix's		
Alfredo's		

3 Fingerprints on Plastic

Whose fingerprints match those on:

Alfredo's cup ____________

Felix's cup ____________

4 Smells

Which smell/cologne matches the smell on the towel?

Gene's
Vera's
Kendra's
Alfredo's

5 White Threads

	BURNING		ASHES	
	Fast or Slow?	Smooth or not Smooth?	Black or Grey?	Powdery or Shiny?
MYSTERY				
WOOL				
COTTON				

Describe how each thread burns and what its ashes are like. Circle the one that matches the mystery thread.

DATA SHEET

for Felix Mystery

Names: ______________________

____

6 DNA Testing

Whose DNA matches the DNA of the cells of root hairs on the comb?

7 Ice Cube Test

	pH#	acid, neutral, base
tap water		
ice water		

8 Secret Note

If you found a message pressed into the cardboard, what did it say? Who do you think wrote it?

9 Powder Study

Write down what color the powder turns when you add 2 drops of iodine. Circle the powders that turn black or purple.

POWDER	COLOR IT TURNED
"blood powder"	
Kendra's shoe	
Vera's shoe	
cornstarch	
baking soda	

Circle the white powder that is in the fake blood:

BAKING SODA
CORNSTARCH

What kind of white powder was on the shoes of:

Vera –
Kendra –

10 Tape Lift

What did you find on the suspects' clothes?

Alfredo –
Vera –
Gene –
Kendra –

Felix's

pertaining to now murder?
body
paint spill
coke can
ice cube tray
garbage can
Felix cup
watch
coke can
paper towel
note

Session 4: Crime Lab Stations (Part 2)

Overview

This session follows the same general format as Session 3, except the five learning station activities are different, and are used to test five different pieces of evidence. During this session your students will be conducting tests at the following five stations:

DNA
Melted Ice Cube
Secret Note
Powders
Tape Lift

At each of these stations, students conduct tests on the evidence and clues found at the scene of the crime during Session 1. In this session, each station is set up to accommodate eight students at a time. At the end of the session, the students again pool their results on the Crime Scene Map. With this new information, the class revises the Clue Board from the previous session.

What You Need

For four teams of two at each station:
For the DNA Station:

- ❒ 4 copies of the "DNA Fingerprints" sheet, page 179

For the Melted Ice Cube Test Station:

- ❒ 1 cup
- ❒ Ice cube tray from Session 1 crime scene
- ❒ 1 roll of pH paper with color-coded pH chart from Session 3 Cola Station
- ❒ metric ruler from Session 3 Cola Station
- ❒ a wastebasket for used strips of pH paper

For the Secret Note Station:

- ❒ 4 small mirrors, preferably with stands (clay works as a make-shift stand)
- ❒ 2 "eggs" of Silly Putty™
- ❒ handwriting-indented Tagboard from Session 1 crime scene
- ❒ 1 copy of the "Suspect Handwriting Samples" sheet, p 185

INFORMATION ON IODINE

Two iodine solutions are generally available from pharmacies: strong tincture of iodine (85% alcohol, 7% iodine, 5% potassium iodide) or mild tincture of iodine (2% iodine). ***We recommend that you obtain the mild tincture of iodine, then dilute it further to 1% iodine*** *by mixing one part water with one part of the 2% iodine solution. If you can only find the strong tincture, then dilute it to make 1% iodine, by mixing six parts water with one part of the 7% iodine solution. DO NOT USE TINCTURES OF IODIDES—clear solutions that do not contain any iodine—because THEY WILL NOT WORK in the class tests!*

Iodine solutions have long been safely used topically, on human skin cuts and abrasions to disinfect wounds. Health authorities do recommend caution when handling the pure, solid form of iodine, but the dilute solutions used in these GEMS activities are not considered dangerous. Iodine is toxic when taken in large amounts internally. In general—as is a wise safety precaution when engaging in all chemistry-related experiments—make sure your students are aware that they should not taste or swallow ANY chemicals!

For the Powders Station:

- ❒ five clear plastic cups
- ❒ 2 white test trays (Styrofoam egg cartons work well. If these are not available, you could use white plastic paint trays from an art store or white ice cube trays.)
- ❒ 1 large plastic trash bag
- ❒ about 1 cup of cornstarch
- ❒ 1 sponge
- ❒ paper towels
- ❒ 1/8 teaspoon (have students estimate half of a 1/4 teaspoon)
- ❒ 1–4 small dropper bottles (empty medicine dropper bottles, saline bottles, or other small bottles are fine)
- ❒ about 1/2 ounce of iodine
- ❒ about 1 cup of baking soda

For the Tape Lift Station:

- ❒ 4 old sweaters or t-shirts
- ❒ 4 bags (Optional: these can be used for storing the sweaters for use in other classrooms or later presentations. Brown paper shopping bags or plastic bags are fine.)
- ❒ 4 white sheets of paper.
- ❒ about 30 strands of pet hair (dog or cat hair is fine)
- ❒ 1 roll transparent adhesive tape from Session 3
- ❒ tape lift examples sheet
- ❒ pinch of human hair, grass, threads, yarn, for tape lift examples sheet.

Getting Ready

To help you keep track of the preparation tasks below, the Summary Outlines include a Preparation Checklist, beginning on page 201 for "Felix."

Before the Day of the Activity:

1. Make four copies of each station sign. (If you plan to have fewer than eight students at a station, or if you prefer to mount signs on the wall or on manila folders to stand, just make as many copies of each sign as you need.)

2. Have available student data sheets from Session 3 and pencils (one for every two students).

3. Make four copies of the "DNA Fingerprints" sheet, page 178.

4. Make a copy of the "Suspect Handwriting Samples" sheet, page 185. PRINT: "**Hello, my name is Kendra**" in the space provided. This writing must match that on the indented tagboard. Make three copies of the completed sheet.

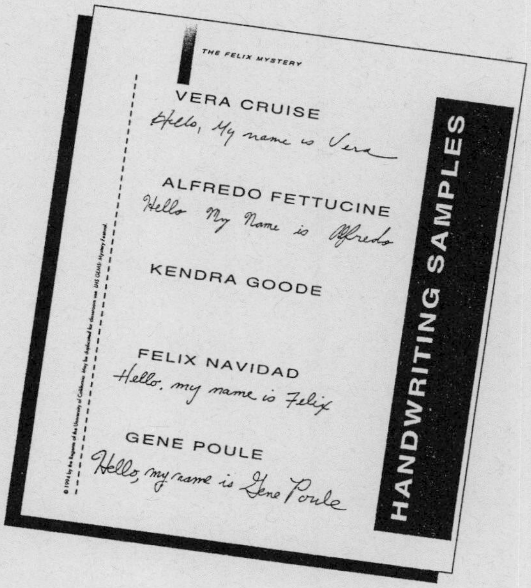

5. Many teachers recommend having an adult volunteer for the "Powders" station because the iodine can be messy. (See the note on iodine and safety considerations on page 170.) Although iodine is not toxic unless swallowed in large amounts, it does stain. Most teachers of young students feel that, because of the potential for stains and mess, it is important to have an adult volunteer at the "Powders" station. It is also helpful to have a volunteer to rinse out the test trays as new teams arrive at this station. If you decide you need a volunteer for this activity, arrange for one now. If you have two "Powders" stations, set them up close to each other, and one volunteer can probably supervise both.

6. Decide if you will have two stations of the "Powders" activity. In Session 4, this is the station where students may tend to "pile up," because it takes longer. If you want two Powders stations, you'll need to double the materials under *Powders* above, and set up two identical stations like the one described below. One adult volunteer can probably supervise two stations if they are next to each other.

7. To save time, you can prepare parts of the Powders and Tape Lift stations before the day of the activity:

Powders Station:

1. Cut the 2 white styrofoam egg cartons into 4 trays with 6 compartments each (or use other test trays)
2. Slit the large plastic garbage bag so that you end up with one large sheet of plastic.
3. Label the five cups: "Blood" powder, Kendra's shoe, Vera's shoe, corn starch, and baking soda
4. Put about 1" of cornstarch in all the cups, except the one marked baking soda.
5. Put about 1" of baking soda in the cup marked, "baking soda"
6. Fill one to four small dropper bottles with iodine

Tape Lift Station:

1. Label the four old sweaters or T-shirts with the suspect's names. Gene's and Kendra's need to have pet hair (supposedly Sasha, the dog's) on them.
2. Label the four white sheets of paper with the suspects' names.
3. Prepare the "Tape Lift Examples" sheet. Tape samples in the appropriate boxes on the tape lift examples sheet (including pet hair in the "dog hair" box) for students to compare with what they find.

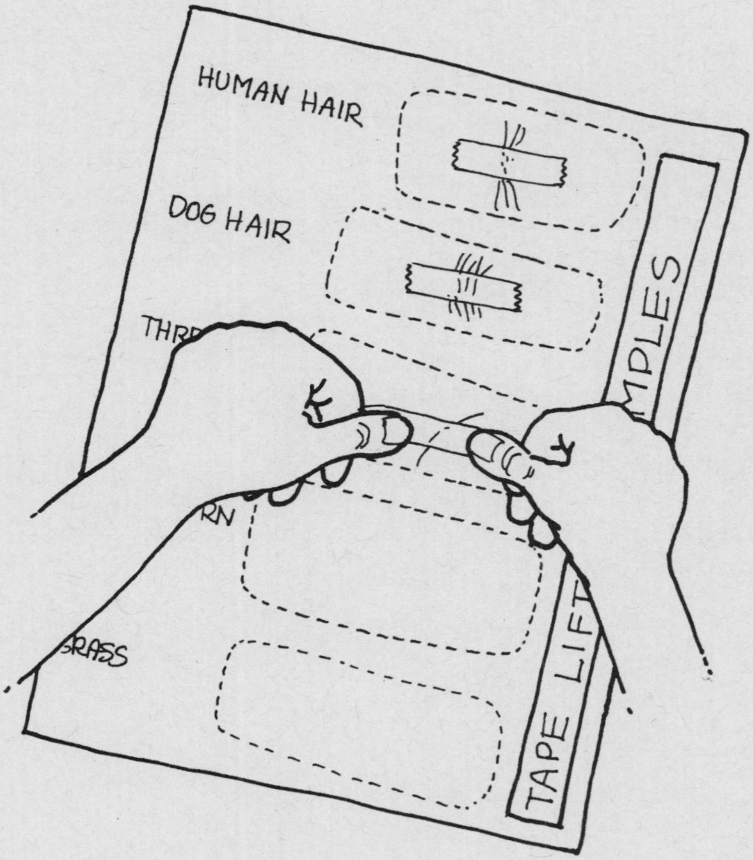

On the Day of the Activity:

(*Note*: Some teachers prefer to set up the stations *before* the day of the activity, and store them in bins or boxes for quick distribution and clean up.)

If you have adult volunteers, orient them to their assigned station activity(ies), making sure all volunteers understand the importance of allowing the students **to make their own discoveries and conduct their own tests.**

Try out each of the station activities to familiarize yourself with the procedure.

Set up each of the five stations:

1. DNA

Set out these materials at the station:

1. Four copies of the "DNA Fingerprints" sheet, page 178
2. The DNA signs

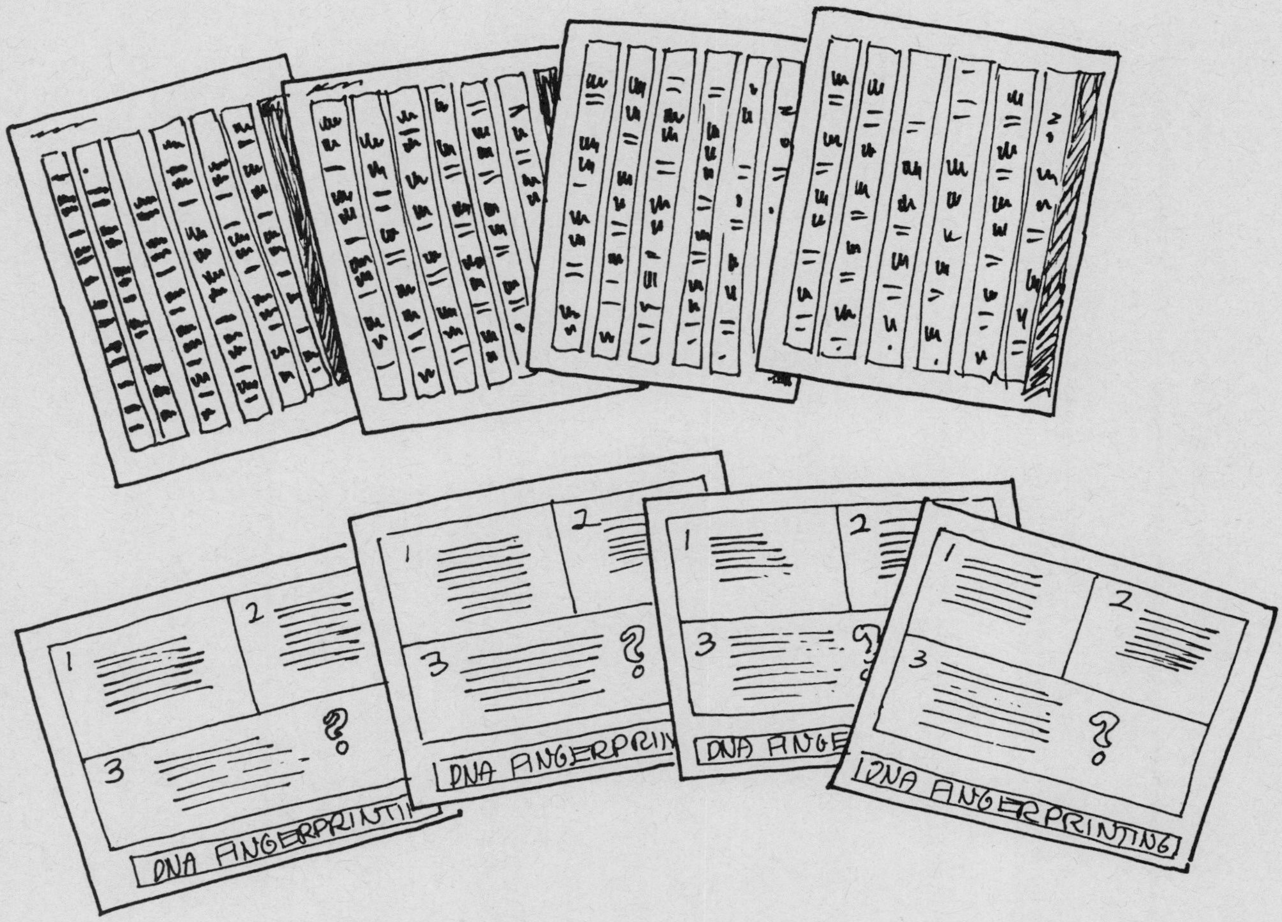

2. Melted Ice Cube Test

Prepare the materials:

1. Fill 1 cup with tap water, and label it "regular water."

Set out these materials at the station:

1. 1 roll of pH paper with pH color-coded chart
2. metric ruler
3. The ice cube tray from Session 1 with four empty compartments. (The other compartments should have water with baking soda stirred into it. The baking soda should not be visible.)
4. Melted Ice Cube test signs
5. Cup of regular water
6. A trash can.

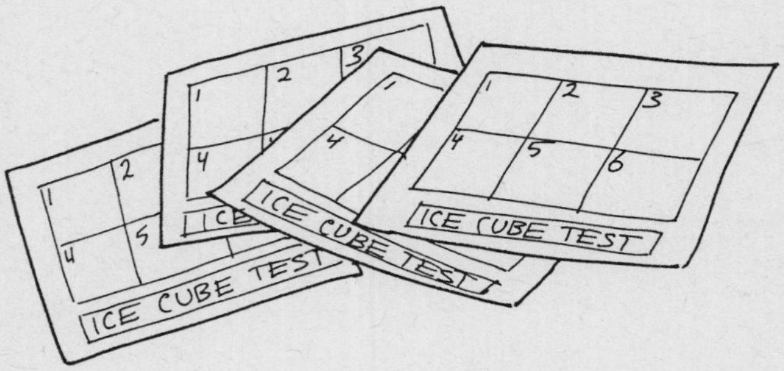

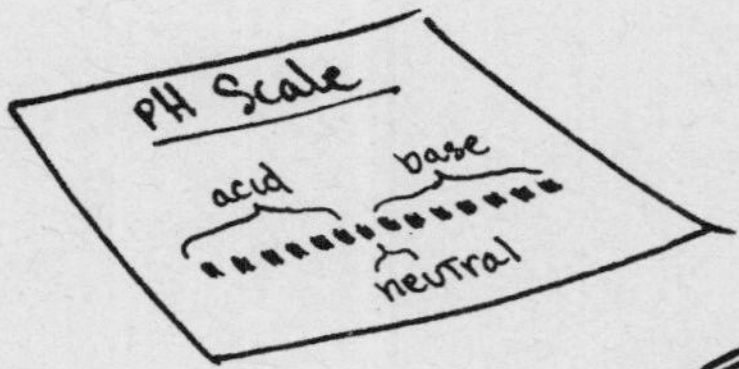

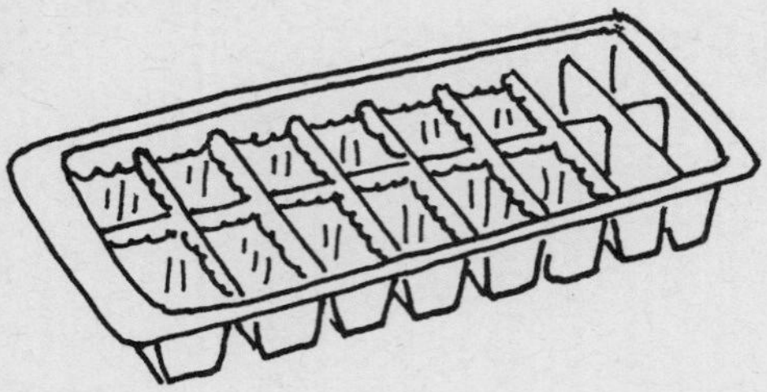

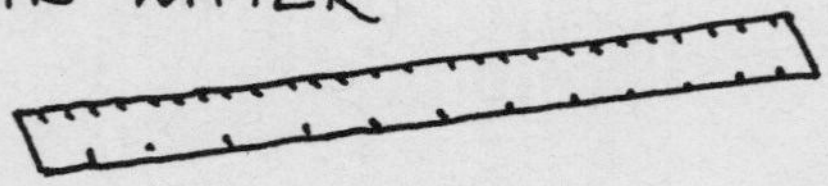

3. Secret Note

Prepare the Materials:

Cut the tagboard with the indented message from the crime scene into four pieces. Each piece should include a complete line from the indented letter pressed into it. Number the backs of the sections 1-4. The top section should be numbered "1," the second, "2" etc.

Set out these materials at the station:

1. The four tagboard sections
2. The four copies of the "Handwriting Samples" that you prepared.
3. Four small mirrors, preferably with stands (clay works as a make-shift stand)
4. Two plastic "eggs" of Silly Putty
5. Secret Note signs

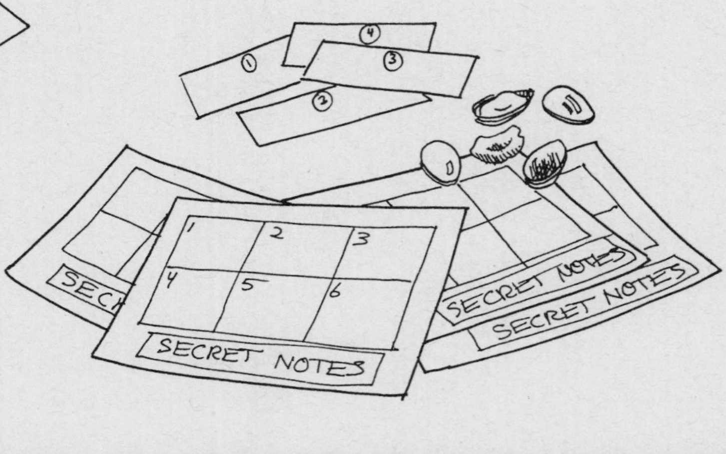

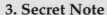

4. Powders (If possible, set this station up near a sink.)

Prepare the materials:

1. Gather the test trays, the five labeled cups previously prepared, and the iodine dropper bottles.
2. Before laying down the plastic sheet (made from the large plastic garbage bag as described in "Before the Day of the Activity") dribble a small amount of water onto the table surface. The plastic will adhere to the wet table.

Set out these materials at the station:

1. 1 sponge
2. paper towels
3. 1/8 teaspoon (a popsicle stick or wooden stirrer could also be used)
4. test trays
5. cups of different powders
6. dropper bottles of iodine
7. Powders signs

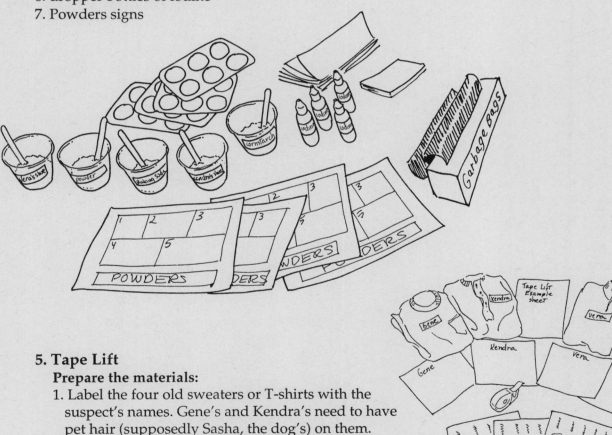

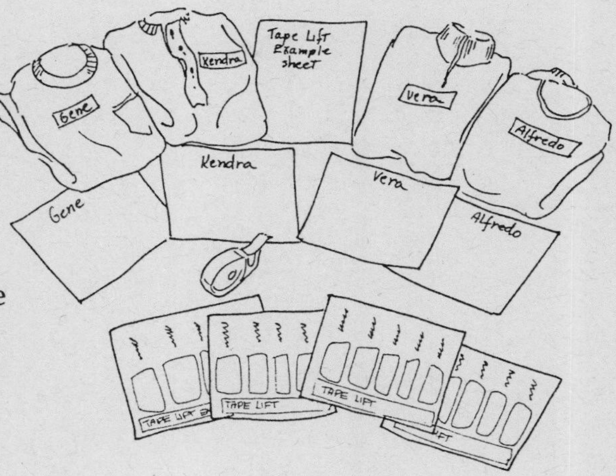

5. Tape Lift

Prepare the materials:

1. Label the four old sweaters or T-shirts with the suspect's names. Gene's and Kendra's need to have pet hair (supposedly Sasha, the dog's) on them.
2. Label the four white sheets of paper with the suspects' names.

Set out these materials at the station:

1. one roll of transparent adhesive tape
2. sweaters with paper next to them
3. tape lift example sheet
4. tape lift signs

Introduce the Stations

1. Explain to the students that today they will conduct five more chemical and physical tests on the evidence found at the scene of the crime.

2. If necessary, review the procedure they used in Session 3 (students work with partners to do tests; partners share data sheets, etc.).

3. Point out each station, and give a brief tie-in with the mystery. Again, read the signs and demonstrate the procedures at each station without actually doing the test or giving away any results.

   1. **DNA Testing:** A comb with human hair in it was found near the body. Whose hair is it? Show the class a "DNA Fingerprint" sheet, and explain that DNA is found in the cells of living things, and is in the cells in the roots of hair. Each human being's DNA is different from every other person's, except for identical twins, so it's similar to a fingerprint. Explain that the procedure they will be doing at this station is similar to what other scientists do when they compare real DNA samples. They will be able to tell whose hair was in the comb at the crime scene by matching the bands in the DNA. (See "Behind the Scenes," page 233 for more information.)

   2. **Melted Ice Cube Test:** A puddle of melted ice cubes was found at the scene of the crime. Was something added to the ice cube water? Check the pH and find out if it's different from regular tap water.

   3. **Secret Note:** Someone wrote a note on a piece of paper at the scene of the crime. Although the paper is gone, use Silly Putty to try to read the impression left on the cardboard. Tell the students that this is a real crime lab technique. Caution them not to play with the putty. Mention that taking an imprint of a whole phrase at once is too difficult, and that they should do just one word at a time.

Don't worry if some students can read the secret note without using the silly putty. It's fine for them to decipher the note in any way they can, just as real crime lab scientists would do.

   4. **Powders:** Tell your students that it has been discovered that the blood at the crime scene is fake! It is red food coloring mixed with a **white powder**. Remember that we found an unidentified white powder on both Vera's and Kendra's shoes. Test to see what powder was used to lead us astray, and what powder was found on Vera's and Kendra's shoes. Is it the same kind of powder?

Note: Sometimes students watch the first drop of iodine *just* as it lands on the powder, and they conclude that it stays yellow. Explain that they are to watch the **powder,** not the iodine, to see if it turns yellow or black/purplish when mixed with iodine.

5. **Tape Lift:** Use tape to find out what kinds of threads, hairs or plants are on the suspects' clothing. Caution the students to use just one piece of tape for each piece of clothing, so there will be evidence left for other students to test. Explain that real crime lab scientists often have only **one** hair or blade of grass as a clue. In this activity, students will each get to lift off just a little bit of the evidence.

Crime Lab Testing and Recording Results

1. Remind the students that when they finish their first station, they may go to any other available station they like, until they have completed all of them. Remind them not to run, and to go to uncrowded stations.

2. Say that in between stations, or if they finish early, they may return to the Crime Scene Map and Clue Board to attempt to piece together the evidence.

3. When they understand what they are to do, hand out data sheets and pencils, and assign the partners to their first stations.

4. Allow student teams to perform their tests. Circulate as needed to assist.

Pooling Class Data

1. Pool the class data at the Crime Scene Map and the Clue Board as in Session 3.

2. Collect data sheets so that students will have them for the next session.

3. Point out to the students that they've now examined the crime scene, conducted scientific tests on the evidence, and had a chance to discuss many ideas and possibilities about the crime and what might have happened. In the next session, based on their data, they will attempt to solve the mystery!

HUMAN HAIR

DOG HAIR

THREAD

WOOL YARN

GRASS

TAPE LIFT EXAMPLES

DNA "Fingerprints"

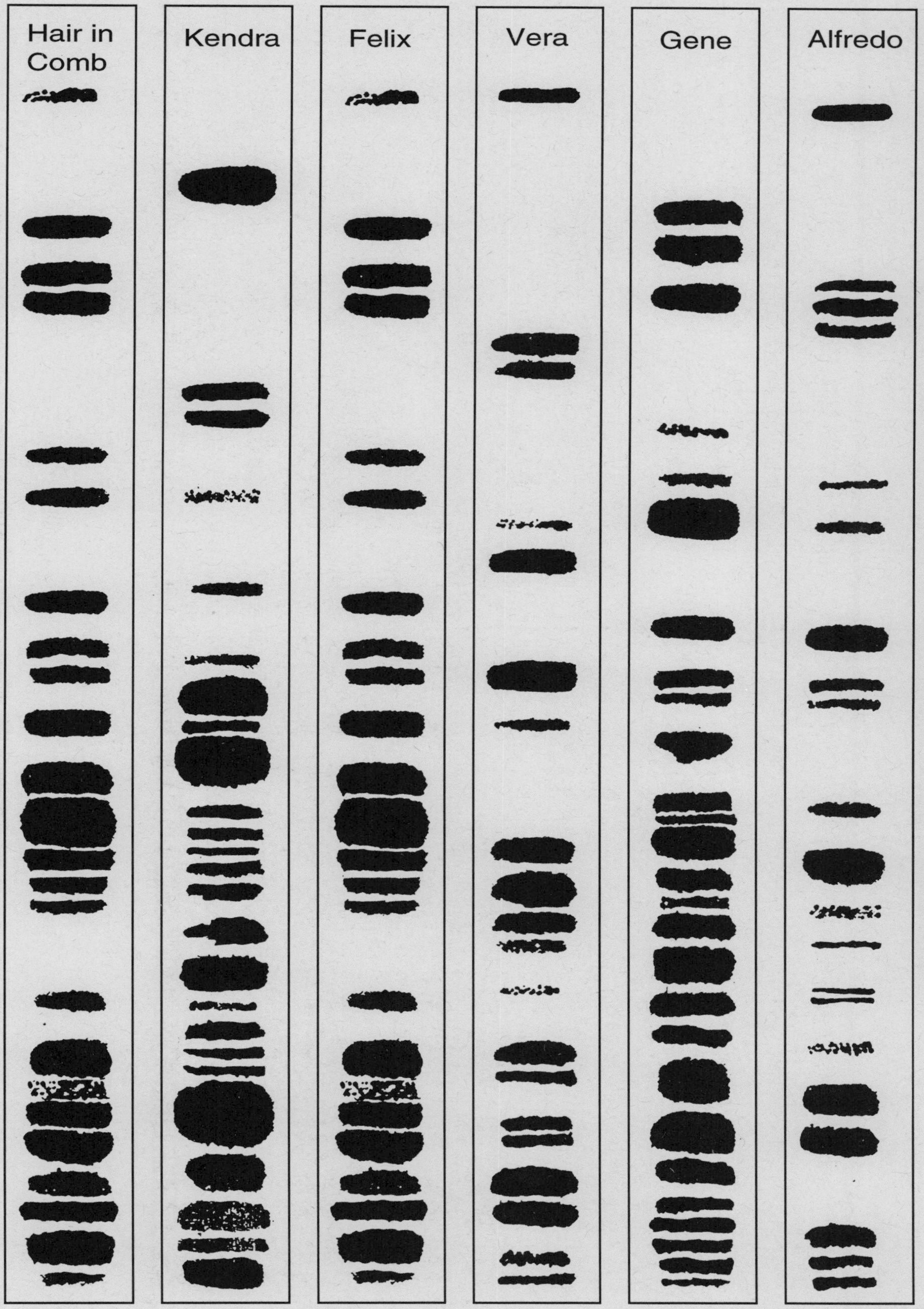

DNA "Fingerprinting" STATION SIGN

1 Every cell has DNA in it. Your DNA, like your fingerprints, is different from everyone else's.

2 If we find hair at the scene of a crime, we may find cells in hair roots.

3 Does the DNA pattern from the hair on the comb match the DNA pattern of any of the suspects or the victim? Circle the name on your data sheet.

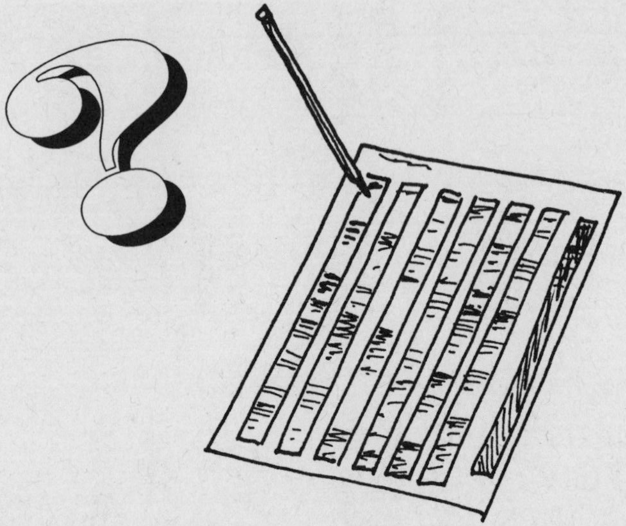

1 Measure and tear off a piece of pH paper 2 centimeters long.

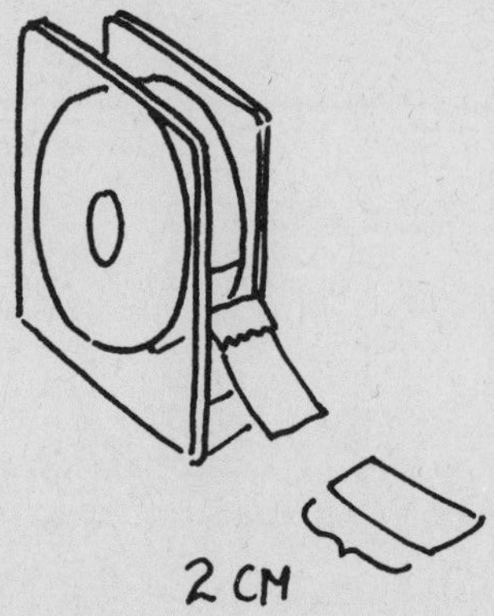

2 Dip the pH paper in the cup of tap water.

3 Compare the color of your wet pH paper with the colors on the pH chart.

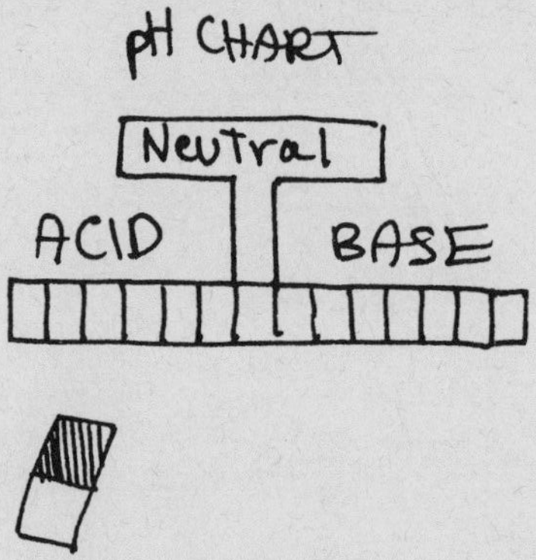

4 Write down on your data sheet the pH number, and if it is ACID, NEUTRAL or BASE.

5 Throw away the used pH paper in the garbage can.

6 Do the same with the ice cube liquid.

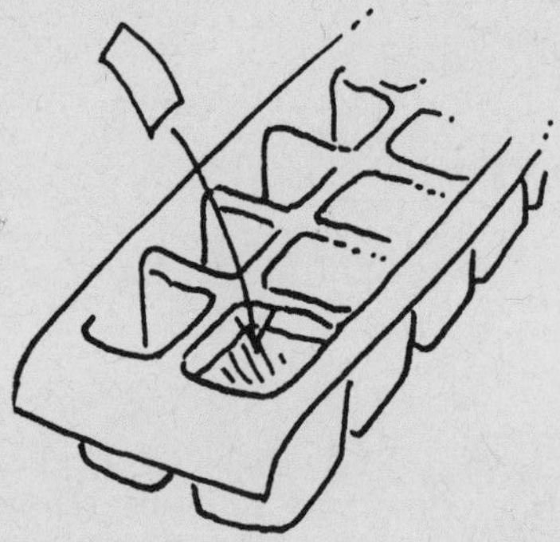

7 Write down the pH number on your data sheet, and if it is ACID, NEUTRAL or BASE.

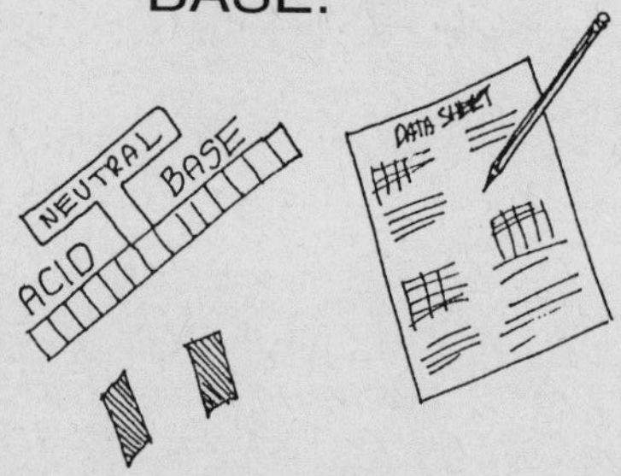

Melted ICE CUBE TEST

STATION SIGN

SECRET NOTE STATION SIGN

1 Get a piece of cardboard and a ball of silly putty that are not being used.

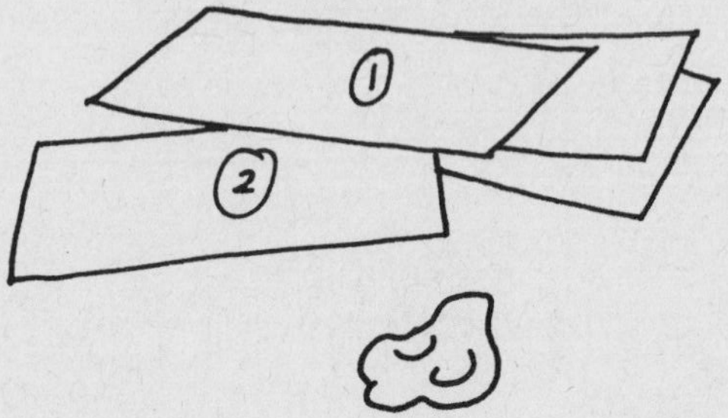

2 There is writing pressed into the cardboard. Look at and feel the cardboard to find the first word.

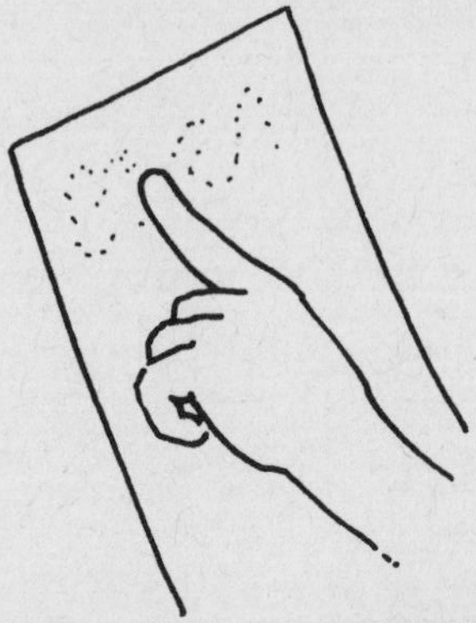

3 Flatten your silly putty onto the first word. Press hard.

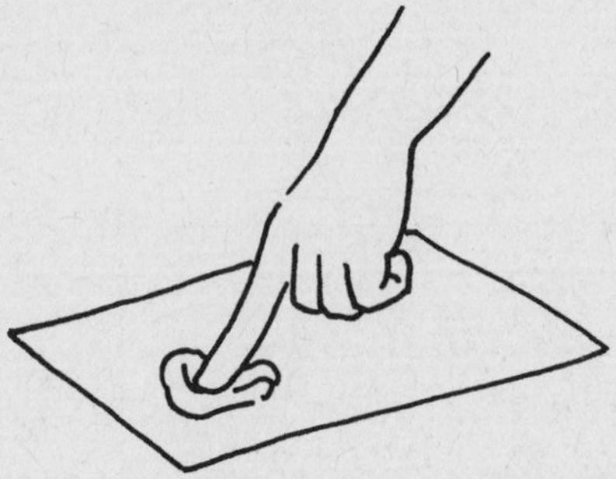

4 Hold up the silly putty to a mirror. Read the word and write it down.

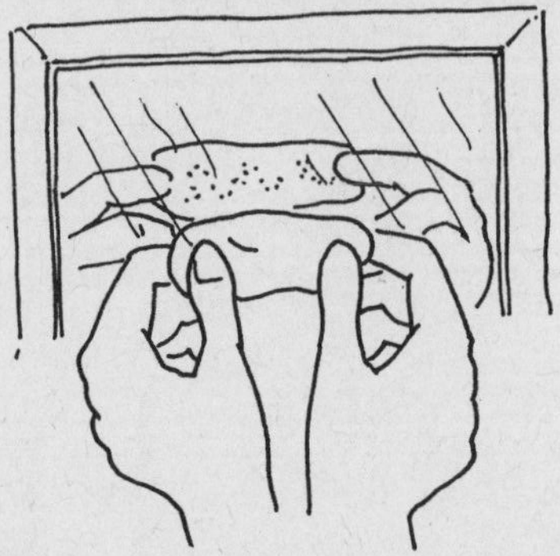

5 Do the same for the whole message.

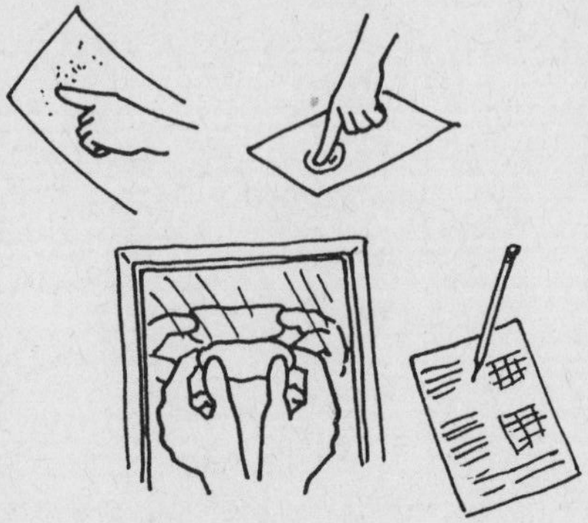

6 After carefully looking at the handwriting and comparing it with the handwriting samples, who do you think wrote this note? Write it down on your data sheet.

7 Leave the silly putty and cardboard at the station.

1 Put 1 tiny spoonful of "blood powder" into the first compartment.

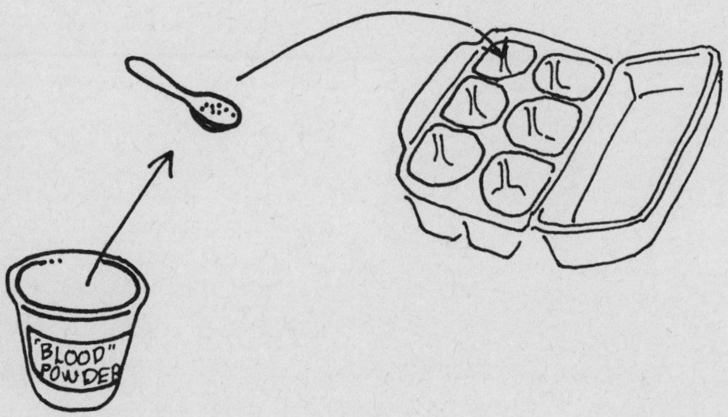

2 Add 2 drops of iodine, and observe the color. Write it on your data sheet.

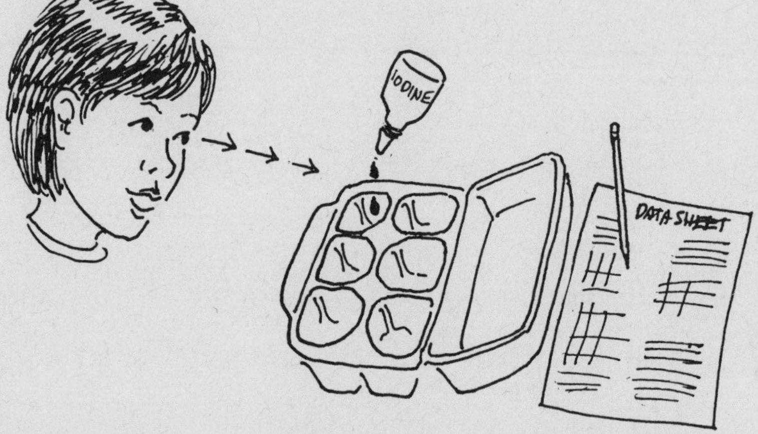

3 Do the same with the other powders, one at a time.

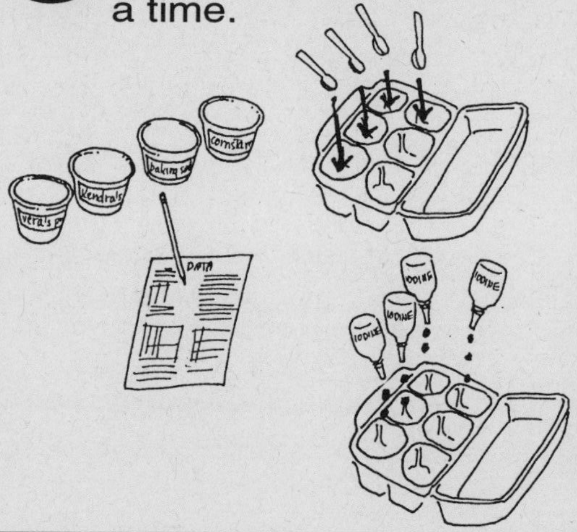

4 Circle all those that turned the same color - they are the same powder. Write on your data sheet what powder you think they are.

5 Rinse out your reaction tray with water and a sponge, and leave it CLEAN for the next group.

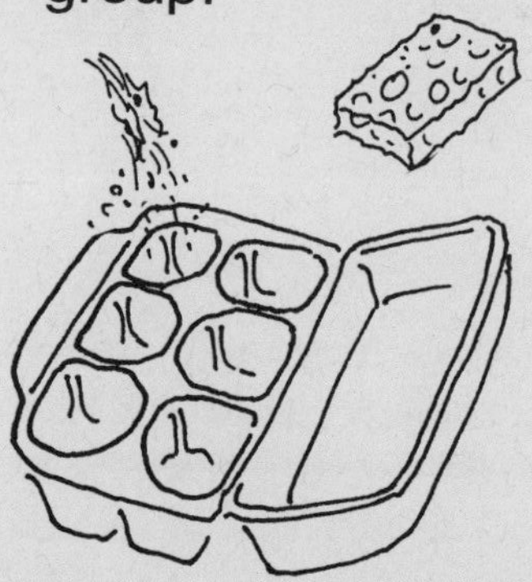

POWDERS STATION SIGN

TAPE LIFT STATION SIGN

1 Take one short piece of tape, and touch the sticky side on one spot of the suspect's sweater or shirt.

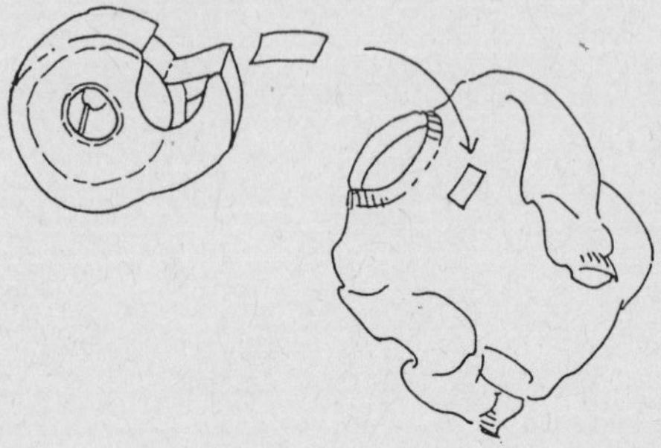

2 Stick your piece of tape onto the paper.

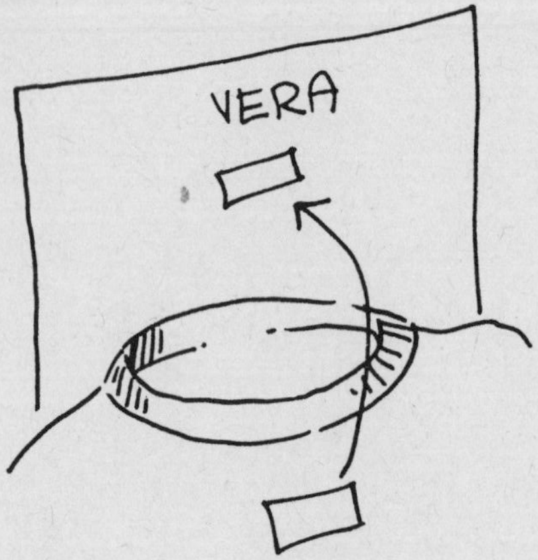

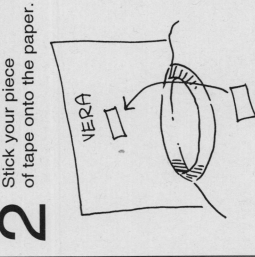

3 Look at the other pieces of tape on the paper to see what was found on the suspect's clothing. Compare it to the tape lift examples to see what it is.

4 Write down what you can identify from the suspect's clothes on your data sheet.

5 Do the same with the other suspects' clothing.

HANDWRITING SAMPLES

VERA CRUISE

Hello, My name is Vera

ALFREDO FETTUCINE

Hello My Name is Alfredo

KENDRA GOODE

FELIX NAVIDAD

Hello, my name is Felix

GENE POULE

Hello, my name is Gene Poule

STUDENT OF THE WEEK
Monitors

Session 5: Solving the Mystery

Overview

In this session, your students attempt to take into account all the evidence— and the results of their tests—to solve the mystery. Depending upon the ability level of your students and your own preferences, there are many options for this last session. We have provided five options for solving the mystery. Each of these options is outlined below, first briefly, then in more detail.

For older students, keep in mind the distinction between evidence and inference that has been a part of the Festival thus far. You may want to ask questions that help students further recognize this distinction. In this way, you can assist students to understand the difference between, on the one hand, what they observed at the crime scene and obtained from their tests and, on the other hand, the inferences and conclusions they draw about how the events may have happened and "who-done-it." Over the course of the Festival, and during this final session, trying to solve the mystery can help students improve their ability to distinguish evidence from inference, to make logical inferences based on plausible evidence, to evaluate whether or not various inferences are more or less plausible, and to draw conclusions.

You may also want to emphasize other important lessons, for example, pointing out that both science and crime detection work require extremely careful observation and collection of data and evidence. In fact, the processes of science and crime detection have much in common. Forensic science brings science and detective work together, and its many scientific tests can have very useful and revealing results in the solution of a crime. See the "Behind the Scenes" section on page 233 for more on forensic science and the science behind the Mystery Festival crime lab tests.

What You Need

- ❒ Student data sheets for the Felix mystery, "Who Done It?" (master on page 195)
- ❒ The Crime Scene map (from previous sessions)
- ❒ Clue Board (from previous sessions)

Depending on the option you choose you may also need:

- ❒ pencils and paper
- ❒ a chalkboard and chalk

Getting Ready

Choose one of the following mystery-solving activities which you feel is appropriate to your class' interest and skill levels, as well as your time frame. Following are summaries of the four options.

Options for Solving the Mystery

On pages 189-194, you will find more detailed suggestions for presenting each of the options below.

Option #1: Draw a Picture
Students draw a picture to show what happened at the beach house that day. This could be a single, large picture or a series of pictures (comic book narrative form) with captions describing the events depicted.

Option #2: Write Your Own Story
Using the "WHO DONE IT" worksheet, students focus on who they believe may have committed the crime, then write their own version of the crime story. See pages 196-197 for some examples of thoughtful and exciting versions done by other students.

Option #3: Courtroom Simulation
Students are selected to role-play the various suspects on the witness stand. All others in the class play the role of prosecutor. Suspects answer questions and defend themselves. As a jury, the class votes on the suspect(s) they believe to be guilty.

Option #4: Class Vote
Students vote as a class to decide "who done it." This of course can be done in combination with any of the options above.

Option # 5: Names on the Board
Students take turns writing their names on the board under the name of the suspect they believe to be guilty. As they do so, they are each given the opportunity to verbally explain their reasoning.

Solving the Mystery

1. Explain to the class that they will now have the chance to try to figure out what happened to Felix.

2. Pass out the "WHO DONE IT?" worksheet (on page 195) to individual students, pairs, or groups, depending on how you'd like your students to work.

3. When they have completed the worksheet, introduce and explain whichever option or options you've decided on for your class. Remind them that no one knows what actually happened, so no one can tell them that their story is wrong. Encourage them to take into account all the evidence they observed at the crime scene, along with the results of the many crime lab tests they've conducted as crime lab scientists, as well as their charts and discussions.

Option #1: Draw a Picture
Have students draw a picture of what they think happened, based on the evidence. Perhaps a comic strip "novel" would be well-suited to including all the events.

Option #2: Write Your Own Story
1. Offer one of the three writing challenges below, or give students a chance to choose one of the three. Many teachers who presented these activities during the testing process had students write their own stories, and some sent us student writing samples from the point of view of the culprit (as outlined in "A Suspect Talks" below).

The Detective's Report: Write from the point of view of the detective who investigated the case, explaining what probably happened, and, using the "WHO DONE IT?" worksheet, backing up conclusions with "hard evidence." This story could be entitled: "The Case of the Missing Millionaire" or students can come up with titles of their own.

In the Local News: Have students write out their version of what happened as a story in the newspaper, or an in-depth report on the evening news. Again make sure they include the information from their "WHO DONE IT?" worksheets. Remind them that responsible journalists report only hard evidence as fact, and are careful to distinguish the facts and direct evidence from people's opinions, guesses, and allegations. For example, in writing about the murder suspect, they should be sure to use the word "alleged"

*Assigning the detective report or news report will give students an opportunity to practice making the distinction between **evidence** and **inference** in their writing. In contrast, the "Suspect Talks" option allows students to be creative and write as though their inferences are true—not only about what may have happened but also the motivations involved. Of course, even when writing very creatively, students should seek to take into account the evidence that they have uncovered during the Mystery Festival.*

until after there has been a conviction by a jury, and they should qualify their other conclusions as appropriate, depending on the evidence.

A Suspect Talks: Write from the point of view of one of the suspects, maybe even the murderer! Again, students should use the information from their "WHO DONE IT?" worksheet. Encourage them to make inferences about what may have happened and the motivations involved. They could write in a style or "voice" that sounds like the character who is "talking." Encourage them to be creative, and to include surprise "twists."

2. Once the writing assignment has been completed, have volunteers read their stories out loud to the class, or post them for the other students to read. After the stories have been read, you may choose to have your students vote as a group to decide on an outcome (see Option #4, Class Vote).

You may want to mention to your students that one of the important principles of real-life jurisprudence is that a person is considered "innocent until proven guilty." This is why words like "suspect" and "alleged" are used in press reports of crimes and trials. The "burden of proof" falls on the prosecution to prove "beyond a reasonable doubt" that the person on trial committed the crime. It is up to the jury to decide just how much evidence is needed to prove guilt—a process quite parallel to what students go through in Mystery Festival as they weigh the evidence against each suspect. The principle of "innocent until proven guilty" is far from universal; there are countries where the legal burden of proof falls on the accused rather than the accuser.

Option #3: Courtroom Simulation

The following scenario is described in some detail as one way to present a courtroom simulation in class. Some teachers have set up the courtroom simulation in other ways, also with excellent results and involvement. On page 194 we include the comments of one teacher on how he presented the courtroom simulation. You know the experience and abilities of your class best, so feel free to adjust the following suggestions as appropriate.

Judge = teacher
Suspects = four or more verbally adept students
Prosecutor/jury = all the other students

1. Ask for four student volunteers to play the four suspects: Alfredo, Kendra, Vera, and Gene. These should be students who are comfortable with thinking creatively on their feet, and expressing themselves verbally.

2. Tell your "volunteer suspects" that they are each in charge of defending themselves **as their characters,** *without* "breaking down" and confessing. They must do their best to explain away any evidence that seems to point to them. Remind them that they must also stick to the evidence and statements provided.

Note: One way of taking some of the "heat" off these brave students is to have two students work as a pair to represent each character. Another way of alleviating the pressure is to use a "tag-team option." If a suspect gets stuck, and can't explain something, she may say, "tag." Any member of the class may then volunteer to switch with her, taking over where she left off.

3. Prepare large name tags that can be easily transferred to another student. (One teacher brought in hats for the different suspects to wear.)

Suspects and Prosecutors Prepare

1. Have the students representing the suspects carefully re-read the Clue Board, including the character statement and information about them.

2. Tell the "suspects" to go through the chart, making note of all the evidence that appears to point to them. It is their job to prove their innocence by explaining away this incriminating evidence with their own version of the story.

3. Let the students playing the suspects know that if they are asked a question that their character would not know the answer to, they should answer, "I don't know," rather than making something up. Circulate and help "suspects" with their stories as necessary.

4. Tell the rest of the class that their job is to together play the role of prosecutors. Explain to them that the prosecutors' job is to make each suspect look guilty by asking challenging questions that the suspects cannot easily explain away or evade. (In the unlikely event that your students don't point it out themselves, you could note that some of the statements conflict with each other.)

5. Instruct your "prosecutors" to write down challenging questions, either in groups or individually, to be directed toward each of the characters.

Court Is In Session

1. When your class is ready, call court into session.

2. Call up the first "suspect" to tell her version of the story. Take questions from the prosecuters one at a time, for whichever suspect is on the stand.

You may want to simplify this activity by first allowing the students to vote on which of the character(s) they wish to put on trial, instead of trying all four.

3. The suspect does her best to explain her story as convincingly as possible, while answering the questions directed at her by the class. The judge endeavors to keep everything under control, and protects the feelings of the students playing the suspects by keeping the class from "badgering the witness." The judge also interjects clarifying questions, and helps to keep the students from wandering off on irrelevant tangents.

4. Each of the remaining suspects is called up in the same way.

5. At the end of the court session, tell your students (who are now the jury) to vote on who they think is guilty. Before they vote, elicit ideas from the students about what happens at the end of real courtroom cases, and, as needed, explain these possibilities:

Guilty : The jury agrees, and convicts one or more of the suspects.
Not Guilty: The jury decides there is not enough evidence to convict anyone.
Hung Jury : The jury cannot agree and a mistrial is declared.

Note: It's important to stress beforehand that any of these outcomes is a success, because the goal of simulating a realistic and complex crime-solving situation has been achieved, and everyone has gained experience in evaluating evidence.

Option #4: Class Vote

1. Tell the students to decide which character(s) they believe committed the crime.

2. Have your students vote on who they think is guilty. To enliven the proceedings, you may want to have five students stand up front to represent the five characters: Alfredo, Kendra, Vera, Gene, and Felix. (Felix's name is included in case any students decide that he committed suicide or is still alive.)

3. Before voting, emphasize "thinking for yourself," and ask for ideas from the students about what happens at the end of real courtroom cases, and, as needed, explain these possibilities:

Guilty : The jury agrees, and convicts one or more of the suspects.
Not Guilty: The jury decides there is not enough evidence to convict anyone.
Hung Jury : The jury cannot agree and a mistrial is declared.

Note: It's important to stress beforehand that any of these outcomes is a success, because the goal of simulating a realistic and complex crime-solving situation has been achieved, and everyone has gained experience in evaluating evidence.

Option #5: Put Your Name on the Line (30–60 minutes)
1. Write the five character names on the board: Alfredo, Kendra, Vera, Gene and Felix, with space left blank under each. (Felix's name is included in case any students decide that he committed suicide or is still alive.)

2. Allow each student an opportunity to write her name on the board under the name of the character who she thinks did it. Don't require, but do encourage students to share with the group why they chose that particular suspect as the guilty one, and to briefly describe what they think happened. You may also choose to include a category for undecided.

Note: You may want to simplify this activity by first allowing the students to decide on one or two characters they wish to vote on, instead of voting on all four.

One teacher told us he conducted the court scene much as described in this guide, with some variations. "I had one student be a defense lawyer and help answer questions the suspects hadn't anticipated. The other students were prosecuting attorneys. Each suspect made his or her own statement and was asked questions. The questions could only address known information and evidence. As judge I could throw out a question or prevent a lawyer from questioning or doubting an answer of a suspect. I could also rule "asked and answered" if a question had been asked before, and the questioner would have to choose a new question. As judge I also found students asking questions that were speculative, which I stated did not address the evidence... In general, this session was wonderful. The students listened attentively and presented possible scenarios. The questions were insightful and they were visibly pleased when they asked a question that surprised a suspect."

Your Name ______________________________

"WHO DONE IT?"

1• Do you think Felix died, and, if so, how?

2• Do you think someone murdered Felix, and, if so, who?

3• What evidence makes you think so?

4• When do you think the suspect did it?

5• Why do you think the suspect did it?

6• What evidence makes it look like somebody else did it?

7• If you don't think the others are guilty,
can you explain how that evidence got there?

The following are just a few excerpts from many imaginative examples of student writing already generated by the Mystery Festival. These outstanding examples were selected by several trial test teachers, and are mostly by fifth and sixth graders (one from fourth grade) all of whom investigated the Felix mystery. Other student writing appears on page 252 and on pages 256 and 257. Send us more!

HER EYES WERE DANGEROUSLY GREEN...

I made myself comfortable in my reclining chair. Nobody really loved Felix Navidad. But I did. I knew it was my job to look after him. I was the one who took his body...Kendra Goode had always made me nervous. When she was 17 her parents had a treacherous divorce. She was always scampering around making trouble. Her eyes were dangerously green making me nervous all the more. When Gene introduced her to Felix her eyes glimmered of evil like she had seen him before...

IN HER QUIVERING HANDS...

Vera's third step was to swiftly get back to the house to poison Felix's cup. She had secretly hidden a miniature box of baking soda in one of the big oak cupboards. She went to that same dark oak cupboard and quickly grabbed the box of baking soda. Once the box was in her quivering hands she gingerly crept onto the patio where Felix was sitting all by himself. She sat down near the cup Felix had just taken a sip from...

A VERY ODD MAN INDEED...

Felix Navidad was a very odd man indeed. His parents had just died and left Felix a huge amount of money in their will. He had very few friends, and the ones he did have weren't too fond of him. The four friends he invited to his party only came because they knew they might get some money. Well, you can't buy back your parents or friendship, and Felix probably realized he had nothing to live for, so he committed suicide by poisoning himself. However, in the meanwhile, he also wanted to ruin their lives by making his suicide look like a murder. It probably took him a week or two to think of and plant all the false evidence...

THE NEXT MORNING...

Hello, my name is Kendra Goode. I'm here to tell you about the murder of a friend of mine. Actually, he's not really a close friend, but so long as I'm in his will, who cares?

Two mornings before the murder I got a phone call from my banker saying that I was in pretty bad financial trouble. After thinking for a while, I called my best friend, Vera Cruise. When I told her my plan she agreed that we'd discuss it at dinner.

Two days later, that morning, at about 10 A.M., I sneaked over to Felix's house and put the powder Vera had given me in his ice cube tray and set out his glass. Accidentally, I spilled some on my shoe. After taking a shower, I heard Alfredo yell. I looked out the window and smiled as I saw Felix laying dead and Alfredo leaning over him. I grabbed a Diet Coke and ran out the door.

Later the police came out and studied the scene of the crime. As I started to leave, Vera edged over to me and whispered, "I'll tell. You know I will." Of course, I spent two hours worrying about it. Finally, at 11 P.M., I sneaked into the morgue and stole Felix. Then I destroyed all the evidence.

The next morning,Vera didn't wake up.

A MAD SCIENTIST...

Vera Cruise was a disturbed young woman. When she was only 9 years old, her parents had died in a horrible car accident. Since then she went crazy. She wanted to make innocent people pay for her parents' death... No one knew she was crazy. No one knew she was a mad scientist...She was going to kill him, steal the will, and make it so that she inherited a greater amount than the rest of them... Vera was in the kitchen preparing the concoction that she was going to murder Felix with. As she was mixing it, Kendra walked in and scared her. She dropped the powder and it scattered all over the floor. As Kendra bent down to help her pick it up, she asked what it was. Vera just replied, "a science experiment." ... When the police arrived they found a number of interesting pieces of evidence. One was an indentation of a note that Vera had planted. The note was signed by Vera but the writing had been forged by Vera to look like Kendra's handwriting. The police noticed this and automatically suspected Kendra. Vera thought this was great...The police closed the case after three weeks of investigating. Vera became the proud holder of 75,000 dollars. She packed her bags after this and left the country. She was never heard from again.

JUST AN AVERAGE GUY...

My parents' death left me with a very large inheritance. I became very rich. I decided to throw a party at my small beach house. I didn't have many friends at all. The people that I invited really weren't my friends but I liked them a lot. I'm just an average guy, but for some odd reason people don't like me. I was very sad and needed a friend badly. Kendra had just gotten through laying out on the beach. Vera, Alfredo, and Gene had not arrived yet. Before Kendra got in the shower, she gave me a glass of Coca-Cola. I turned on the Ranger game and drank my Coke and then...

ARF, MY NAME IS SASHA...

Arf, my name is Sasha. I faithfully follow my owner, Gene Poule. He's my best friend. One of his other so called friends, Felix Navidad, invited us over. I had been put outside like I always am, but someone let me in. I don't know who it was because I was rendered blind in a freak ping-pong accident, but anyway, I went in and heard the bathroom door shutting, but I couldn't tell if one or two people went in. I went out to the patio where I smelled something funny. I stepped on something, it turned out to be Felix lying dead on the floor. I smelled a Coke, so I walked over and tried to take a drink. After that, I walked back to Felix and tried to give him mouth-to-mouth re-dogitation. When that didn't work I barked. My master, Gene, came in. I jumped up on him, and he moved around a little. After that he yelled for the others and they came, and here we are wondering who dun-it.

DEAR JOURNAL...

I have the best friends in the world. I can always trust them. Alfredo just went to the restroom. I am sipping my Coke thinking of the joys of life like my friends.

I must be getting sick. My stomach is hurting. I feel terrible. I wonder what could have made me so sick? I want to get Alfredo but I can't get up. I'm too sick.

Felix Navid...

Going Further

There are many great ways to extend the experiences your students have gained in *Mystery Festival*. We welcome your suggestions! Here are a few of our ideas.

1. Have your students act out their agreed-upon version of the story. If your class was unable to decide between two or more options, divide up the class and have each group act out one version. You may choose to have your students stick to the facts, or you may want to give them the creative license to elaborate upon and embellish the story. The class could present their drama(s) to other classes.

2. Consider having groups of students work together to make graphs and/or other charts to represent the data they collected. Class graphs of the results on many of the tests could be made, as could a bar graph showing the proportions by which a suspect or suspects were chosen as the guilty party.

3. Have students make up their own mysteries. Depending on grade level and experience working together, students could work in groups to come up with plots and then write them down or present them dramatically to the class.

4. Consider numerous other writing challenges: have students amplify one scene from the Felix mystery, with their own dialogue and description; have students write the "Felix" story from the point of view of one of the characters; put themselves "in" the story as a professional detective; or write a tense courtroom drama in which the "murderer" is brought to justice, "Perry-Mason-style." You and your students are sure to come up with many other writing ideas, either based on the mysteries in this guide, or on original stories.

5. A more ambitious class project for older students might involve the teacher working with the class to create an entirely new Mystery Festival scenario, perhaps using some of the same crime lab stations and tests, and/or adding some different ones.

6. Work with other teachers and classes to put on an all-school large group Mystery Festival for a school open house or other community event. (For more information about putting on a large group festival, see pages 247–252.)

7. To celebrate their completion of *Mystery Festival*, students could come to class dressed as a famous fictional detective or mystery character of their choice. In costume, they could visit other classes and tell them about the *Mystery Festival*.

8. Take the class on a field trip to a local crime lab, or invite a police detective, forensic scientist, or person in a related occupation to come to class, make a brief presentation, and answer student questions about their work. Ask the crime lab scientist(s) to talk about the scientific basis of their work and to comment as appropriate for the class level on the way that the distinction between evidence and inference is involved in what they do.

9. Have your class conduct an interview with you, the teacher, for an article they would write that would describe you, such as a feature article in a newspaper or magazine. After they write their articles, you could discuss with the class whether their article stuck to the facts or made any unwarranted assumptions or unfair inferences about a subject you know very well—yourself!

10. Students could do research on famous scientific discoveries and write or report on the ways in which the scientific progress toward the discovery could be compared to solving a mystery. They could also select and read a well-known mystery book, and analyze how much science, mathematics, and experimenting is involved in the story.

11. Reading mystery stories or other young people's literature that stimulates logical thinking processes and problem solving skills can extend the learning of this unit and connects nicely to mathematics, language arts, social studies, and many other curriculum areas. Please see "Literature Connections" on pages 241–246.

Dear Parents,

Your child's class will soon begin a unit called Mystery Festival, in which the students will act as crime lab scientists to help solve an imaginary mystery. In an effort to discover which fictional suspect (or suspects) may have committed a "crime" at Felix's beach house, the class will examine a large variety of clues and do tests on evidence, while learning important science skills and concepts. This program was developed by the Great Explorations in Math and Science (GEMS) program at the Lawrence Hall of Science and tested in classrooms nationwide.

There are many materials that we need for this highly motivating unit, so we are asking for your help. Please see if you have any of the following items to donate, or if you know of others who do. Any items crossed out have already been gathered. We will need the materials by __________________.

Thank you very much!

- 1 paintbrush (any kind)
- 1 paint container (a plate or cup is fine)
- 16 or more clear plastic cups (flexible, wide-mouthed 9-oz cups)
- 2 one-gallon ziplock plastic bags
- 2 empty cola cans
- 1 can of cola, any kind
- 1 ice cube tray
- 1 wastebasket
- 1 chocolate candy wrapper
- 1 white cotton towel
- 1 comb with several strands of human hair
- 1 roll white paper towels
- 1 box baking soda
- 1 box cornstarch
- 1 ounce red food coloring
- 1/2 ounce green food coloring
- about 6 feet of white cotton yarn (no synthetic yarns, please)
- about six feet of colored cotton yarn
- about six feet of colored wool yarn (preferably "woolly" looking)
- 1 "broken" alarm clock (needs to be able to be set at a certain time)
- about 40 feet of string or rope to barricade the "crime scene" (or yellow plastic barrier tape)
- 1 roll of string (at least 60 feet) for dividing the crime scene into sections
- 5 colognes or perfumes, as different from each other as possible (samples from department stores, your bathroom cabinet, magazines etc. Having one of the colognes in its original container would be helpful.)
- several packages of 3x5 inch cards or "post-it" notes
- 1 guitar pick
- 1 pair of sunglasses
- 1 clip-on earring
- 1 small container Krazy Glue ™
- 1 pair plastic gloves
- 2 brown felt water-base markers of the same brand
- 4 rolls of clear tape
- 2 small, plastic dropper bottles
- 2 rolls of Universal pH paper (with color chart)
- 6 empty film canisters with lids (preferably plastic)
- 1 package aluminum foil
- 2 votive candles
- 1 book of matches (for teacher to carry)
- At least 4 pairs of goggles (swimming, snorkeling, ski or safety goggles)
- 4 pairs of metal tweezers, tongs, or equivalent
- 4 small mirrors, preferably with stands
- 4 "eggs" of Silly Putty™
- 4 or more test trays (white styrofoam egg cartons, white plastic paint trays, or white ice cube trays)
- 3 large plastic trash bags
- 2 sponges
- Four 1/8 teaspoons (or four 1/4 teaspoons)
- 4 small dropper bottles
- 1/2 ounce of iodine (strong or mild tincture of iodine; teacher dilutes before student use.)
- 4 old sweaters or T-shirts
- pet hair (about 30 strands—dog or cat hair is fine)
- small amounts of human hair, grass, threads

Preparation Checklists & Summary Outlines

(for the Felix mystery)

▶ Felix Session 1: Scene of the Crime

Getting Ready Before the Day of the Activity:

___ 1. Decide where the crime scene will be.

___ 2. Make one copy of each of the 21 footprint pages and 8 copies of the suspect footprint sheet.

___ 3. Prepare the "Suspect Fingerprint" sheet.

___ 4. Put fingerprints on Alfredo and Felix's cups and label the cups.

___ 5. Make the "Brown Stain" paper towels.

___ 6. Make the secret note.

___ 7. Cut the cotton threads.

___ 8. Prepare the white towel with initials, a rip, and cologne.

___ 9. Make fake blood.

___ 10. Prepare Crime Scene Map.

Getting Ready On the Day of the Activity:

___ 1. Spread out butcher paper and rope off crime scene.

___ 2. Draw body outline.

___ 3. Tape the 21 footprint pages to butcher paper as on diagram.

___ 4. Add some fake blood according to diagram.

___ 5. Put the white towel in the wastebasket, along with a candy wrapper and (optional) Gene's empty cologne bottle.

___ 6. Mix baking soda and water. Fill all but 4 compartments of ice cube tray with baking soda solution.

___ 7. Put cola in cups with fingerprints and add baking soda to Felix's cola.

___ 8. Set the alarm clock for 2:57 PM.

___ 9. Place all clues on the crime scene according to the diagram:

- wastebasket
- ice cube tray
- two cola cups
- two empty cola cans
- comb with hair
- paper towel with brown stain
- cotton yarn
- secret note on cardboard
- paintbrush
- paint container

optional clues:

- guitar pick
- sunglasses
- tempera paint
- carpet tacks
- clip-on earring

___ 10. Use string to divide crime scene into 8 sections. Number sections and label with 3 x 5 cards or "post-its."

___ 11. Put up paper for Crime Scene Map, draw lines to make 8 sections.

___ 12. Have handy: pencils, paper, index cards, marking pens, masking tape and eight "Suspect Footprint" Sheets.

___ 13. Decide on student teams.

Introducing the Challenge

1. Gather the class *away* from the crime scene. Say that today they will observe the scene of a "made-up" crime, and that in the next few days they will be crime lab scientists, working to solve the mystery of "who done it."

2. Remind the students to keep an open mind.

A First Look at the Scene of the Crime

1. Tell the students to spend five minutes carefully observing the scene, staying behind the barrier.

2. After five minutes, gather the class away from the scene and ask for observations. List them on the chalkboard and discuss.

Examining the Crime Scene

1. Hold up one object from the crime scene and ask for descriptions. Help students understand the difference between *evidence* and *inference*. Say that they should record only what they observe directly (evidence).

2. Explain that each team will examine one of the eight sections. Explain the procedure for drawing and recording the evidence.

3. Introduce the Suspect Footprints sheet, and ask students to use them to identify footprints they find on the scene.

4. Pour cola out of the cups on the scene into the extra cups labeled, "Felix's Cola" and "Alfredo's Cola." Set aside. Put the empty cups with fingerprints into ziplock bags and return them to the scene.

5. Show students how to label their index cards, and how to place them on the Crime Scene Map

6. Assign each team to a section of the crime scene. Distribute drawing paper, pencils, index cards and Suspect Footprints sheets and have them begin.

▶ Felix Session 2: The Story

Getting Ready Before the Day of the Activity:

1. Make one copy of each suspect's picture.
2. Prepare Clue Board
3. Have Krazy Glue and cups with fingerprints handy.

Introducing the Session

1. Hand out post-it notes to the 8 groups. Have them write the names of the evidence in their section, on each "post-it."

Present The Scenario

1. Read the information about Felix and the suspects in the case.

Present the Suspects and their Statements

1. Have 4 students read the suspects' statements from the Clue Board. Have another volunteer summarize each statement.

2. Read the extra information at the bottom of each statement.

3. Point out that they will need to decide which evidence is important, and that there is no "right answer."

Discussing and Classifying the Clues

1. Have each group of students report their findings from the previous sessions and allow the class to discuss.

2. Put each clue into the column where the majority think it should go. If unsure about a clue, put it in the "Can't Decide" column.

3. As they classify each clue, ask them if it is 1) hard evidence, 2) shaky evidence, or 3) unimportant.

4. Make an identifying mark next to all the clues the class thinks are "hard evidence."

Develop the Fingerprints

1. Hold up each of the two ziplock bags with the empty cups with fingerprints. Add three or four drops of Krazy Glue to each. Seal the bag.

2. Explain that the Krazy Glue gas will adhere to the oils on the fingerprints and make them appear white, and easier to see.

3. Say that they will get to examine the fingerprints and do crime lab tests on other evidence in the next two class sessions.

▶ Felix Session 3: Crime Lab Stations

Getting Ready Before the Day of the Activity:

___ 1. Make four copies of each station sign.

___ 2. Copy data sheets, one for every pair of students.

___ 3. Arrange for volunteer help if necessary.

___ 4. Decide how many "brown stain" stations you will set up.

___ 5. **Prepare the Brown Stain Station:**

- Cut up the "brown stain" paper towels from Session 1 and put into a cup.
- Cut up some blank paper towels and put into a cup.
- Fill dropper bottle with brown food coloring and label it.

___ 6. **Prepare Cola Station:**

- Label pH color chart and make extras if needed (or make a large one for the class).

___ 7. **Prepare Smell Station:**

- Label five containers and their lids with the five names.
- Put a different cologne in each (Be sure that Gene's cologne is the same as the scent on the white towel).

___ 8. **Prepare Threads Station:**

- Tear off aluminum foil sheets.
- Cut each type of yarn into 25 two-inch pieces.
- Label and fill 3 cups with Mystery Thread, Cotton Thread and Wool Thread.

Getting Ready On the Day of the Activity:

___ 1. **Brown Stain Station**

Prepare the Materials:

- Gather previously prepared paper strips, blank paper towels, dropper bottle, with cups.
- Pour water into cups.

Set out:

- brown stain strips in cup
- blank strips in cup
- roll of clear tape
- Five pencils
- the brown pen
- dropper bottle of "brown candy" food coloring
- four cups with a half-inch of water
- Brown Stain Station signs

___ 2. **Cola Test Station**

Prepare the Materials:

- Gather two clear plastic cups labeled "Alfredo's Cola" and "Felix's Cola" and refill if necessary (make sure Felix's has baking soda).
- Put cola into a third cup and label it "Regular Cola."

Set Out:

- three labeled cups of cola
- roll of pH paper and pH color chart(s)
- metric ruler
- wastebasket
- Cola Test Station signs

___ 3. **Fingerprints Station**

Set Out:

- Alfredo's and Felix's cups with Krazy Glue® finger-prints.
- Suspect Fingerprint sheet
- Fingerprints Station signs

___ 4. **Smells Station**

Prepare the Materials:

- Gather the smell containers you prepared.

Set Out:
- white towel from Session 1
- five containers with scents
- Smell Station signs

___ 5. **Threads Station**

Prepare the Materials:
- Gather the yarn containers you prepared.

Set Out:
- three yarn samples in labeled cups
- two votive candles on foil sheets
- one to four pairs safety goggles
- two pairs tweezers
- matches (away from students)
- Threads Station signs

Introducing the Stations

1. Explain that students will work in pairs and do tests on the evidence found at the scene of the crime.

2. Hold up each station sign and demonstrate the procedure without actually doing the test.

3. Explain how each station test ties in with the mystery.

Crime Lab Testing and Recording Results

1. Show how to record results on the data sheet.

2. Explain that after the first station, they can go to stations in any order. Remind them not to run, and to choose uncrowded stations.

3. Say that if they have extra time, they may return to the Crime Scene Map and Clue Board to review the evidence.

4. Hand out data sheets and pencils and assign teams to their first stations. Circulate as needed to assist.

Pooling Class Data on the Crime Scene Map

1. Gather students with their partners near the Crime Scene Map. Give them a few minutes to discuss their data.

2. Ask a volunteer for results from each station. Ask who agrees or disagrees. Find out the results of those who disagree.

3. Ask why people may have come up with different results. Say that scientists also often disagree, and decide how to record the class results on the 3x5 cards on Crime Scene Map.

Putting Test Results on the Clue Board

1. Ask the students if the new evidence points to any suspect, and record this on the Clue Board.

2. Ask why some evidence may be important, and other clues not significant.

3. Explain that in the next session they'll do five more tests on the evidence, and their ideas about the case may still change.

▶ Felix Session 4: Crime Lab Stations

Getting Ready Before the Day of the Activity:

___ 1. Make 4 copies of each station sign.

___ 2. Make 4 copies of "DNA Fingerprints" sheet.

___ 3. Prepare "Suspect Handwriting Samples" sheet.

___ 4. Make "Tape Lift Examples" sheet.

___ 5. Arrange for volunteer help if necessary.

___ 6. Have student data sheets from Session 3 ready.

___ 7. Decide how many Powders stations you will set up.

___ 8. **Prepare Powders Station:**

- Cut egg cartons into test trays.
- Label and fill five cups with powders.
- Fill four dropper bottles with iodine.

___ 9. **Prepare Tape Lift Station:**

- Label 4 sweaters or t-shirts with suspect names.
- Tape your samples to the "Tape Lift Examples" sheet

Getting Ready On the Day of the Activity:

___ 1. **DNA Station**

Set Out:

- "DNA Fingerprints" sheet
- DNA Station sign

___ 2. **Melted Ice Cube Test**

Prepare the Materials:

- Fill and label cup of regular water.
- Gather pH paper and charts from cola station.

Set Out:

- roll of pH paper and pH color chart(s)
- metric ruler
- ice cube tray with baking soda solution from Session 1
- labeled cup of regular water
- Melted Ice Cube Test Station signs

___ 3. **Secret Note Station**

Prepare the Materials:

- cut up and number the secret note written on tagboard from Session 1.

Set Out:

- tagboard secret note pieces
- four mirrors with stands
- two Silly Putty eggs
- four "Handwriting Samples" sheets
- Secret Note Station signs

___ 4. **Powders Station**

Prepare the Materials:

- Gather test trays, powders and iodine.

Set Out:

- sponge or paper towels
- 5 1/8 teaspoons or popsicle sticks
- four egg carton test trays
- five labeled cups of powders
- four dropper bottles of iodine
- Powders Station signs

___ 5. **Tape Lift Station**

Prepare the Materials:

- Gather suspect sweaters and "Tape Lift Examples" sheet.
- Put pet hair on Gene's and Kendra's sweaters
- Label sheets of paper with suspect names.

Set Out:

- roll of clear tape
- four sweaters in with paper next to them
- "Tape Lift Examples" sheet
- Tape Lift Station signs

Introducing the Stations

1. Review the procedure for station activities, if necessary.

2. Read the sign for each station and demonstrate the procedures.

3. Give a brief tie-in with the mystery for each station test.

Crime Lab Testing and Recording Results

1. Remind students that they can go to any uncrowded station when they have completed the first one.

2. Say that if they finish early they may return to the Crime Scene Map or the Clue Board.

3. Hand out data sheets and assign partners to their first stations. Circulate as needed to assist.

Pooling Class Data

1. Pool the data at the Crime Scene Map and the Clue Board as in Session 3.

2. Collect data sheets and save for the next session.

3. Say that now they have all the evidence, and, in the next session, they will attempt to solve the mystery.

▶ Felix Session 5: Solving the Mystery

Getting Ready

Choose one or more of the options for solving the mystery:

- Draw a picture
- Write your own story
- Courtroom simulation
- Class vote
- Names on the board

Solving the Mystery

1. Pass out the "Who Done It?" sheet to each student.

2. When they have completed the sheet, choose from the options described (or invent your own) to provide students a chance to come up with their solutions to the mystery and an opportunity to make inferences and draw conclusions from their findings.

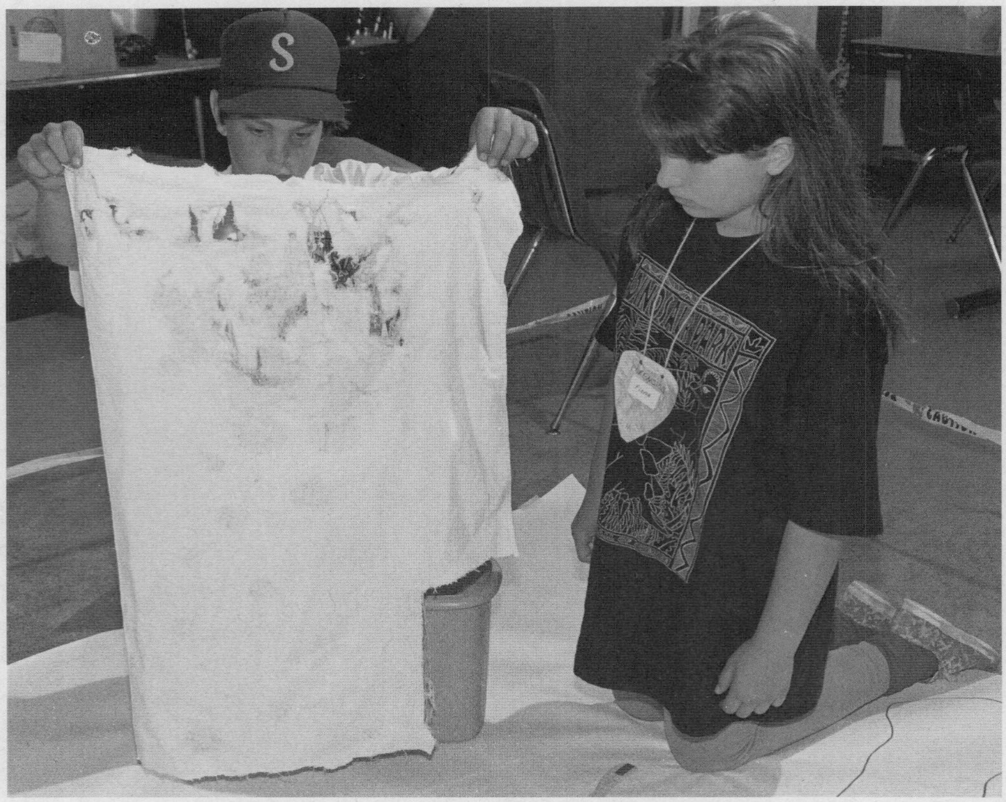

1

2

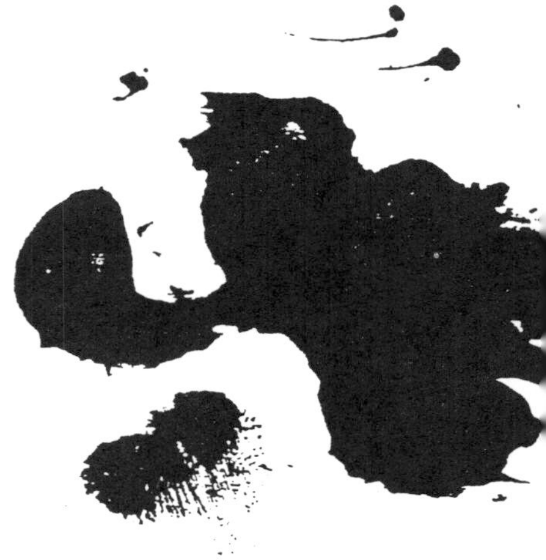

3

4

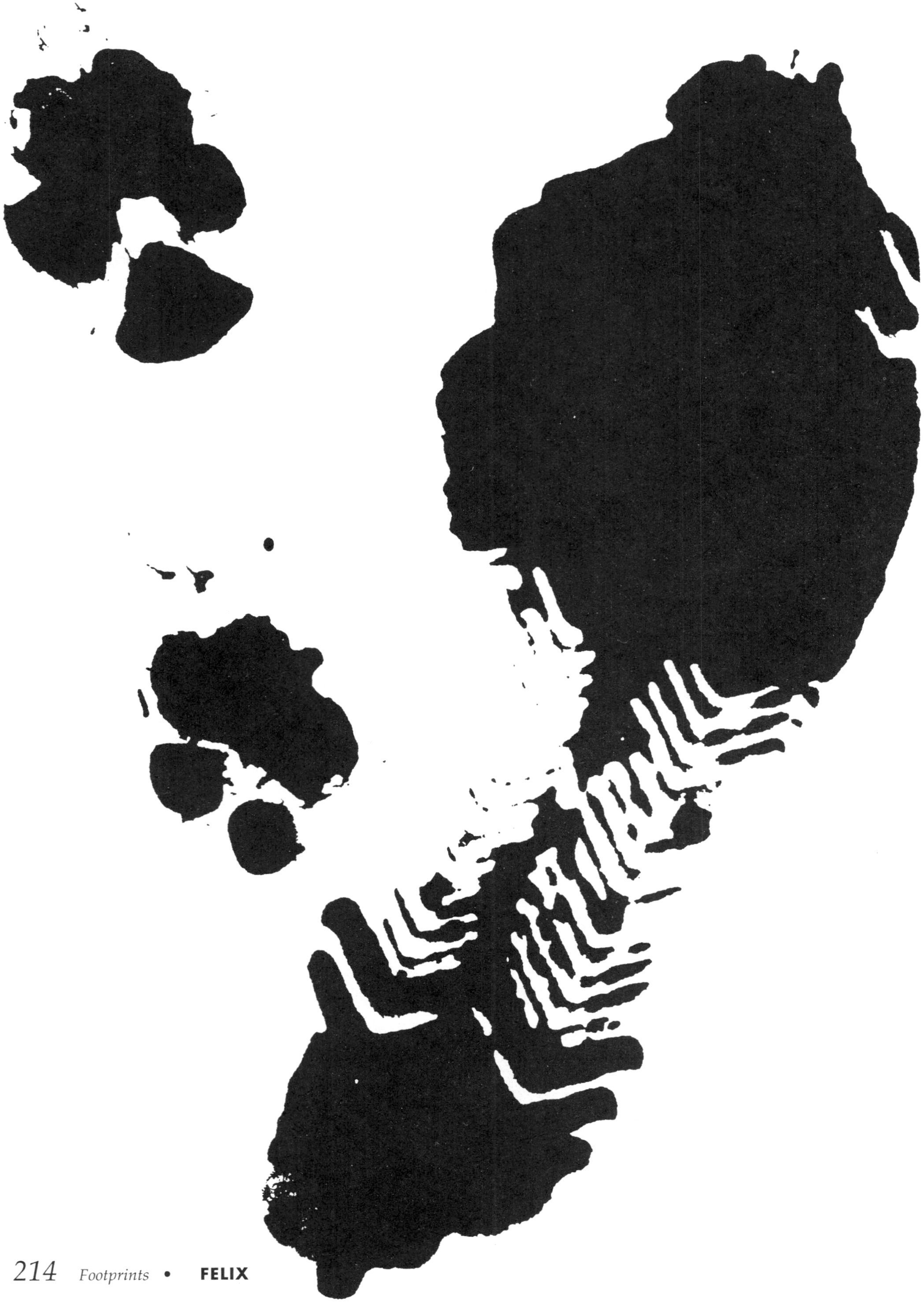

5

6

7

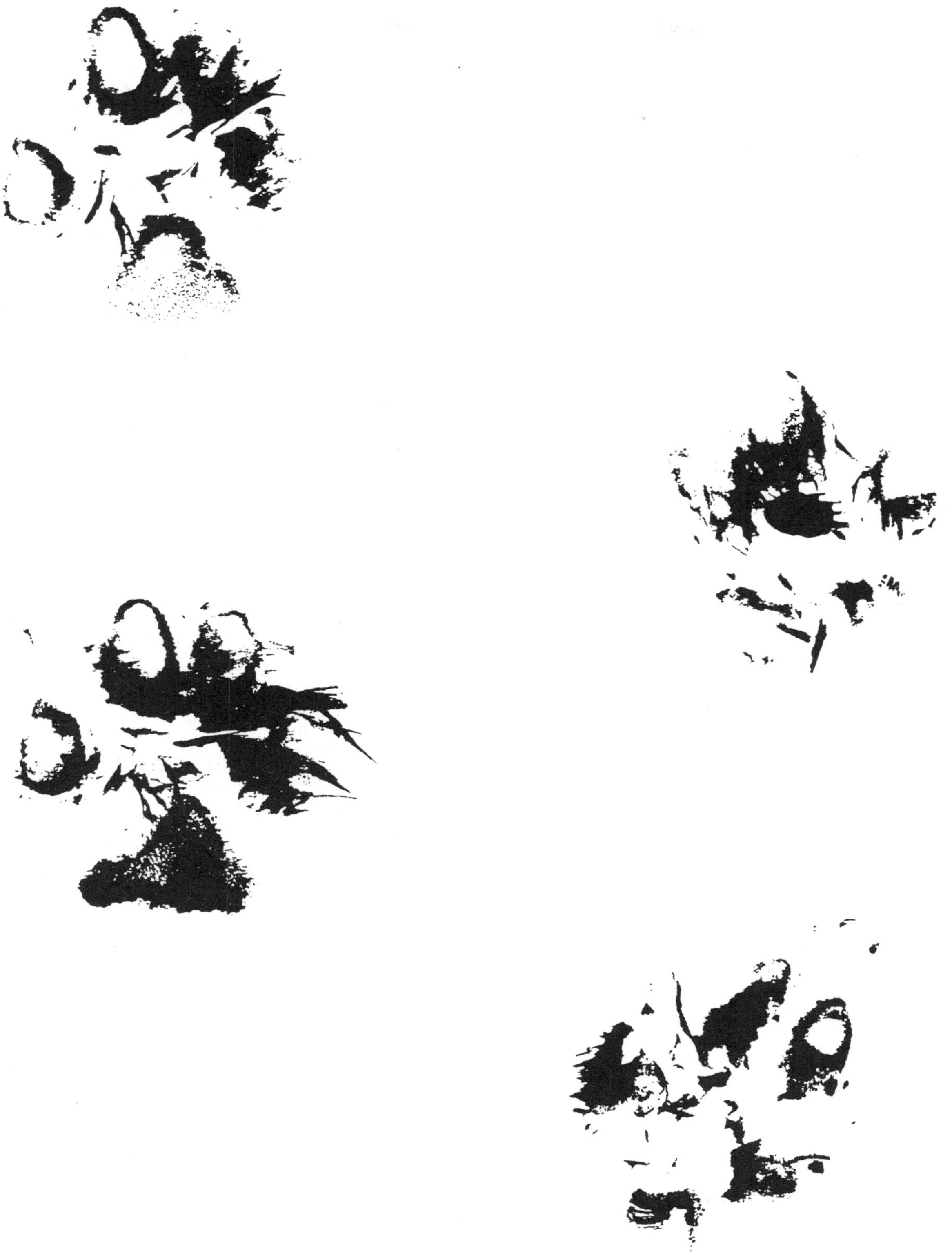

8

9

10

12

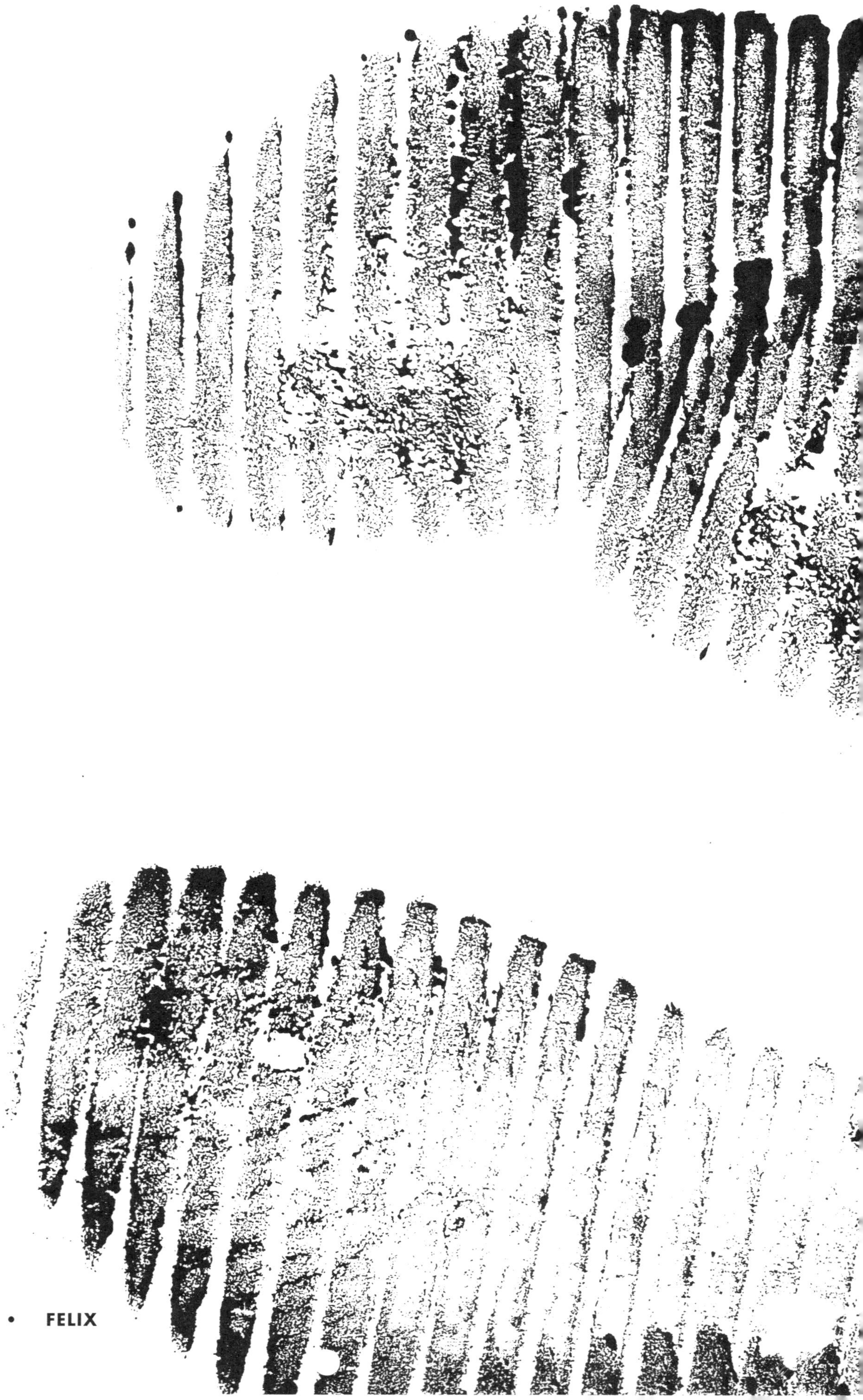

13

14

16

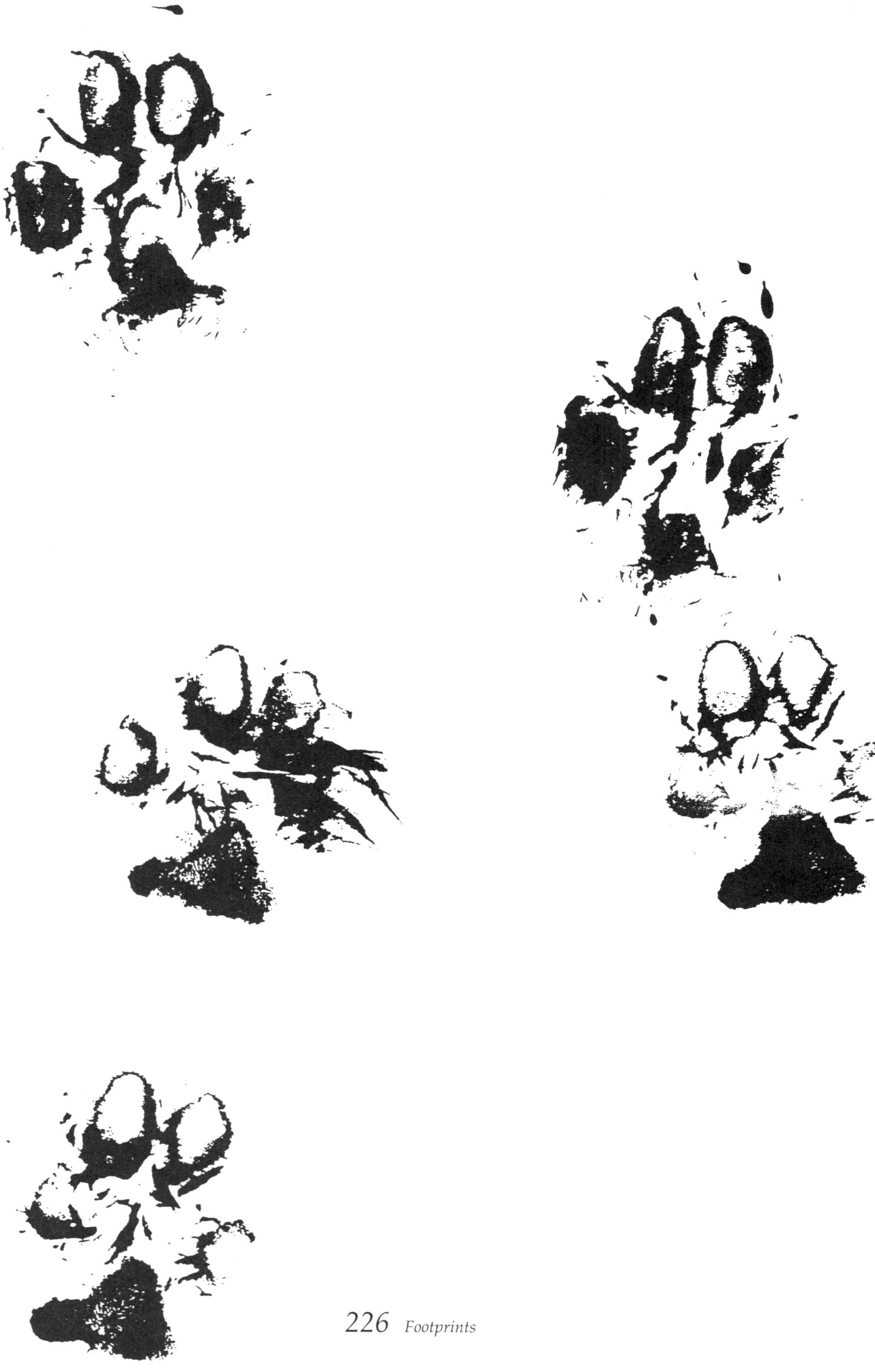

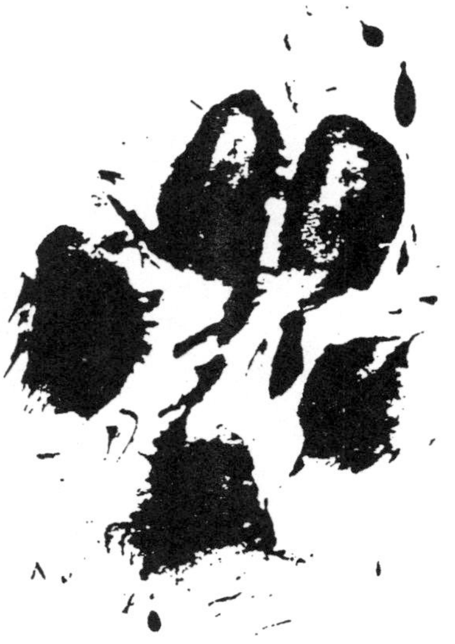

18

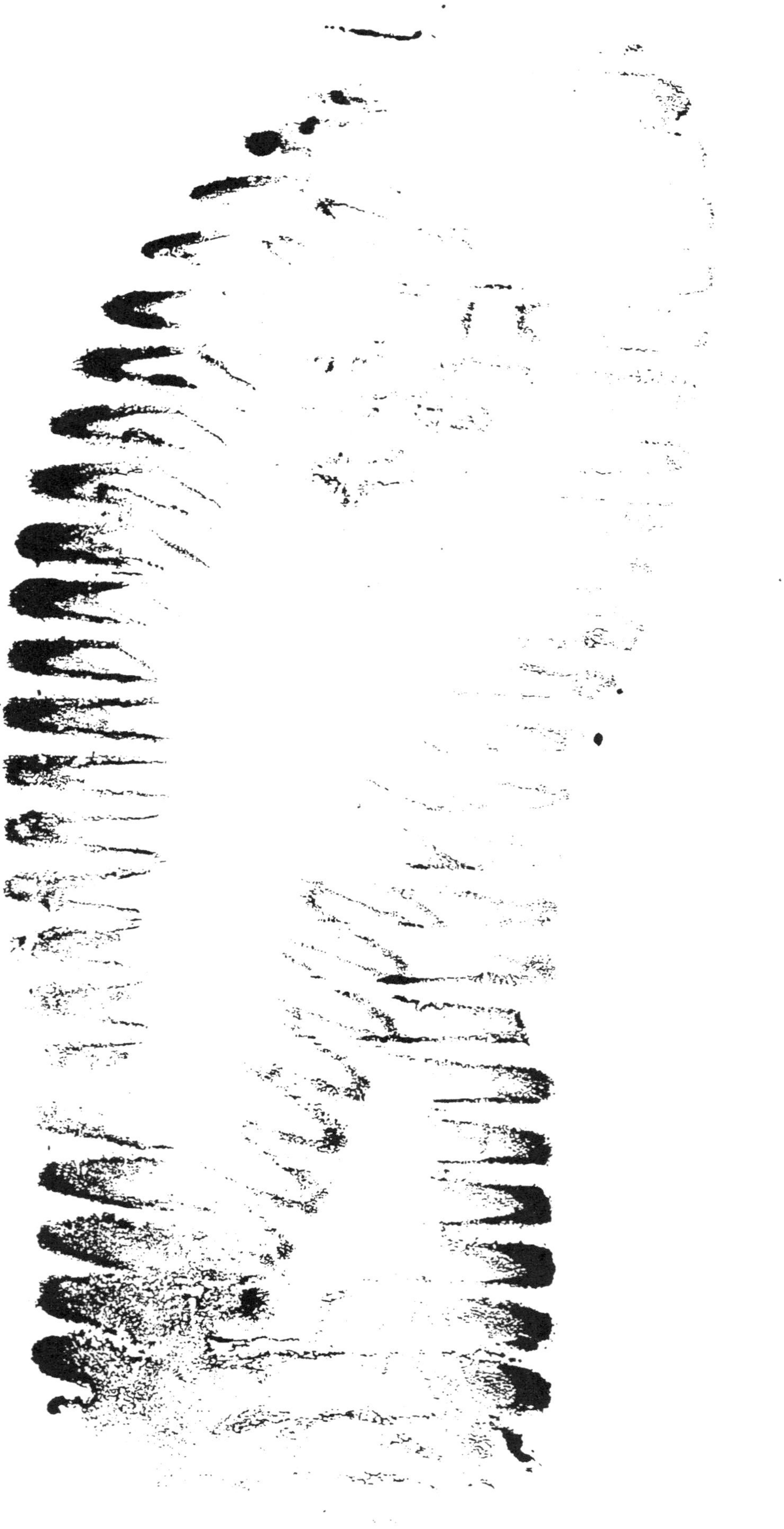

19

20

21

Paint brush?
DATA SHEET

Behind the Scenes

This section is *not* meant to be read out loud to students. It is intended as further scientific background for the interested teacher, and may assist you in answering student questions and helping consider student investigations and extensions of this unit. None of this information is necessary to present the *Mystery Festival* program. If you are using the *Mystery Festival* as an introduction to a larger science unit, or to help explain how science is used in different careers, this background may also be helpful. The first section concerns forensic science in general, followed by brief background on many of the crime lab stations.

Forensic Science and Scientists

The word *"forensic"* means having to do with a court of law, or suitable for a law court. A forensic scientist's work does relate eventually to the courtroom, although much of the actual scientific testing may take place in a police laboratory or at the actual scene of a crime or accident.

A ***criminalist*** is anyone who uses science to analyze, compare, and interpret physical evidence for use in court. This is not to be mistaken with a criminologist, a social scientist who studies why people commit crimes and how to prevent them from doing so. The differences between a forensic scientist and a criminalist are subtle, and the terms are often interchangeable. To avoid confusion, the term forensic scientist is used in this guide.

Because forensics involves so many disciplines, forensic scientists are often "renaissance men and women," although the current trend is toward specialization. Forensic scientists often enter an investigation at the very beginning, directing or performing the actual search for clues. All evidence, from the tiniest scrap of paper to the largest piece of a car or building must be found, photographed and collected to be studied in the lab. Although this job can be very difficult, due to weather, traffic or other adverse conditions, it is critical that this search be exacting. No amount of clever lab work can make up for evidence not found, or other careless fieldwork.

Back in the lab, each item must be studied to not only identify it, but also to compare it to others to see if they came from the same source. Forensic scientists must also try to figure out how it got there and how it relates to other circumstances. In studying and testing evidence, a forensic scientist also attempts to use techniques, such as light microscopy and energy dispersive x-ray analysis, which do not destroy the sample.

In an article entitled *Chemistry in the Crime Lab: A Forensic What?* John deHaan, a criminalist/physical chemist with the laboratory of the Bureau of Alcohol, Tobacco, and Firearms of the U.S. Treasury Department states: "The heart of forensic science is not only to identify a substance, but to compare it to others to establish common origin, recreate its transfer, or determine its relation to other circumstances. Considerable effort is made to preserve as much of the original sample as possible, while extracting the most information."

Interestingly, the careful examination methods, comparisons and reconstructive clues used by modern forensic scientists are not that different from those described by Conan Doyle in his Sherlock Holmes stories. It is also said that the Holmes stories helped inspire Edmond Locard to establish the first forensic science laboratory, in France 1910.

There are many different disciplines within forensic science: forensic pathologists who conduct scientific tests to determine how or when people died; forensic dentists who identify people by their teeth or bitemarks; biologists; toxicologists; fingerprint analysts; document experts; forensic chemists and many others. Specialists from other fields, while they may not be located in the crime lab, can also play highly significant consultant roles in forensic science, including anthropology, psychiatry, psychology, and engineering.

Forensic scientists utilize multidisciplinary methods, including chemical, biological, and instrumental techniques, ranging from much use of microscopes with various contrast and flourescence techniques to infra-red and ultraviolet spectrophotometers, gas chromatographs, liquid chromatography, x-ray fluorescence, emission spectrography, and much else. Sub-specialties have developed, including forensic scientists who specialize in analysis of paint, soil, hair, fibers, firearms, and blood. Scientific advances in forensic serology (blood chemistry) have been striking: new research into biochemical blood factors and components now allows a blood stain left at the scene of the crime to help pinpoint and narrow down that person's identity much more closely than before. Other physiological fluids can also be much more carefully analyzed and individualized with modern techniques. Firearm, drug, and document analysis are important components of the forensic scientists' work. The branch of forensic science called "trace chemistry" deals with fibers, hair, paint, glass, impressions of shoes, tires, clothing, carpets, explosive residues, arson-related flammable liquids, tool mark analysis—seeking to analyze the "traces" left on the scene and from this evidence and its comparison to other samples seek to derive inferences about what might have happened and who might have done it. Significantly, a forensic scientist is the only witness in a criminal trial who may actually offer an opinion (based on evidence and logical inference) given his or her classification as an expert witness.

In his excellent book, *Beyond the Crime Lab,* (see note for full reference) Jon Zonderman summarizes the work of forensic scientists in the following clear manner: "The basic principle in examining physical evidence is rather simple. Whenever a person leaves a place, he or she both takes something away from that place and leaves something at that place. It is the role of the forensic scientist and criminalist to examine what is left at the scene and hypothesize where it might have come from and who might have brought it there. Forensic scientific investigators are responsible for (1) identifying the bit of evidence, (2) comparing it with other similar substances and with substances known to be those of the victim or suspect, (3) individualizing the questioned substance as best as possible, and (4) using all these bits of evidence to help reconstruct the circumstances of the incident being investigated." This is in fact what your students do as detectives and forensic scientists in *Mystery Festival*.

One recommended adult reference book is Criminalistics: An Introduction to Forensic Science by Richard Saferstein (4th edition), Prentice Hall, 1990. There is also an accompanying lab manual. Another good reference is Beyond the Crime Lab: The New Science of Investigation by Jon Zonderman, Wiley Science Editions, John Wiley & Sons, Inc., New York, 1990.

Station-by-Station Background

Brown Stain—Chromatography

A ***pigment*** is a chemical that makes something look a certain color. The brown color of a brown felt pen is a ***mixture*** of different colored pigments, which, when combined, appear brown. Brown food coloring or another brand of brown felt pen may be made up of a different combination of pigments, which also appear brown.

When a piece of paper is dipped in water, the water gradually moves up the paper, as it is absorbed. As the water moves through a water soluble brown stain, it dissolves the pigment or pigments in the stain. Depending on the size, shape and weight of pigment, it may be carried along by the water quite a way up the paper or it may be carried a short distance. When a substance/stain is made of a mixture of pigments (as is the case with these stains) each pigment will be carried up the paper in a different way, resulting in different bands of color, with each color representing a different pigment. This "rainbow streak" up the paper is called a ***chromatogram***. We can recognize a mystery stain by comparing its chromatogram to that of the streak of brown pen and that of brown food coloring. ***Chromatography*** is also featured in the GEMS guide *Crime Lab Chemistry*.

Cola Test and Melted Ice Cube Test

In both these tests, students are testing the pH of a substance in an effort to determine more about how the "crime" may have occurred. In so doing, they are also gaining experience with testing a substance to see how ***acidic*** or ***basic*** it is, or whether it is classified as ***neutral***. Measuring this aspect of a substance and learning how pH affects the behavior of a substance and its relation to other chemicals is an important component of chemistry.

Chemicals dissolved in water can be categorized into three groups: acids, bases, and neutrals. Acids taste sour (although very acidic acids should never be tasted!) and will dissolve metal. Lemon juice, vinegar, stomach acid, and battery acid are all examples of common acids. Bases feel slippery (although bases of high basicity should not be touched!). Soap, toothpaste, baking soda, ammonia, and lye are examples of common bases. Both very acidic acids and bases of high basicity are harmful to human tissue, especially the eyes. Although some acids and bases are classified as **"strong"** and some as **"weak"** in standard chemistry terminology, these are extremely misleading terms, because the ***concentration*** of an acid or base is a key factor, meaning that a so-called "weak" acid in high concentration can be extremely dangerous, just as damaging as a so-called "strong" acid.

The ***pH scale*** is a logarithmic numbering system used to quantify how acidic or basic a substance is. The pH scale runs from 0 to 14, with the middle number, 7, representing neutral. Numbers less than 7 quantify acids; the lower the pH number, the "more acidic" the acid. Numbers above 7 quantify bases; the higher the number, the "more basic" the base. When a base is added to an acid, the pH number of the resulting solution rises, or comes closer to a neutral value. In this way a solution can be neutralized. *(Be sure to see the GEMS guides Of Cabbages and Chemistry and/or Acid Rain for more hands-on activities and understandings, as well as more background, on acids and bases.)*

Fingerprints on Cups

Using Krazy Glue ® to find fingerprints is a relatively new crime-solving technique that was discovered by accident, or by "serendipity." The manufacturers of this product kept noticing distinct white fingerprints on the inside of their plastic packaging. Police now use the technique to find hidden prints at crime scenes.

In its liquid form, Krazy Glue is made up of many small molecules called monomers. When fingers touch the surface of a plastic or glass cup, they leave oil and water fingerprints, which are difficult to see. Krazy Glue is made up of a chemical called cyano acrylate, which quickly turns into a gas at room temperature. When we put a drop of Krazy Glue inside a sealed container with the cup, this gas spreads throughout the container, but stays relatively concentrated, since it cannot escape. When this gas comes in contact with the oil and water fingerprints on the cup, it turns into a solid white plastic. The small molecules called monomers now have been joined to form chains of long repeating molecules called polymers which make up the solid plastic.

Fingerprints in General

Fingerprints form the basis for the most reliable system of identification in use today. Every person has a unique pattern of ridges on his or her fingertips. While hair color, appearance, weight, and height change over time, fingerprints stay virtually the same throughout a person's lifetime. Fingerprints have been recorded for thousands of years by people all over the world. It has only been in the last century, however, that an organized system of fingerprinting has been used in crime detection. An early "literature connection" to fingerprinting. published just two years after *Fingerprints*, Francis Galton's extremely influential scientific classification book, is Mark Twain's *The Tragedy of Pudd'n'head Wilson*, in which a lawyer's hobby of collecting fingerprints acquits two of his friends of murder.

Sometimes fingerprints are left at the scene of a crime. Police compare these prints to the fingerprints of each suspect to see if they match. There are, however, many other uses. For example, a child of unknown identity can be fingerprinted and those prints compared to the fingerprints of all missing children. High security workplaces including some banks, military bases, and government buildings have computers that check the fingerprints of employees at the entrance to the building.

In addition to fingerprints, detectives and forensic scientists collect and compare hair samples, blood type, voice prints, handwriting, DNA, and other descriptive characteristics of human beings. While some of these forms of evidence are legally valid, none are as conclusive as the positive identification of fingerprints.

The GEMS guide *Fingerprinting* provides "fingers-on" activities in fingerprint classification along with more general background on fingerprinting and how it is used in forensic science.

Smell

Gas molecules enter our noses as we inhale and are taken into the nasal cavity. What we smell is our perception of whichever gas molecules have been inhaled. On the roof of the nasal cavity, these gas molecules encounter millions of extensions of nerve endings, bathed in mucus. These nerve extensions are located on two small brownish patches of specialized cells on each side of the roof of the nasal cavity. Each patch contains about 50 million receptor neurons! Each receptor cell ends in a tuft of six to eight olfactory cilia and smaller undulating parts of the cell membrane called microvilli. These tiny threads sway like sea grasses in the currents of our nasal passages. The membrane surfaces of the cilia and microvilli have receptor sites for the inhaled gas molecules.

Through a process not yet fully understood, the bombardment of these receptor sites by the gas molecules is turned into an electrical signal (receptor potential) that, if strong enough, triggers an electrical response (propagated action potential) that is transferred on to the olfactory bulbs.

Touch the spot between your eyebrows. Behind where you are touching are two little bulbs about the size of large grains of rice. These are the olfactory bulbs, which receive the signals from the olfactory nerves. Scientists think that a great deal of selective processing of information related to our perception of the gas molecules (our sense of smell) takes place in the olfactory bulbs themselves. From the bulbs, these signals continue onward to the brain, reaching parts of the upper brain stem and cerebral cortex.

The olfactory, or first cranial nerve, is the farthest forward and shortest of all our cranial nerves. Classified as one of our most "primitive" senses, the sense of smell is associated with some of our most important instinctual activities, including eating, pre-mating behavior, and procreation. Using our olfactory equipment we can distinguish about 10,000 different smells.

Threads (Felix Mystery)

Burning is an example of an oxidation reaction. When thread burns, oxygen from the air combines with carbon and hydrogen in the thread to make carbon dioxide and water gas. Energy in the form of heat and light is also released. The soot, ash and smoke are carbon that did not oxidize, or burn. Depending on the molecular make-up of a substance and contact with oxygen, some will burn/oxidize more efficiently, and some less efficiently. These factors affect the flame, smoke and ash, making them appear different.

Mystery Crystals

Different molecules bond together in different ways, depending on their atomic make up. Atoms with a negative charge tend to be attracted to atoms with a positive charge. Two negatives or two positives tend to repel each other. In a given solid chemical, the molecules may bond and line up in regular arrangements forming straight edges and flat surfaces as a part of a crystalline pattern. In different chemicals, the molecules bond and line up in different patterns, making crystals of different shapes. Chemical solids without a regular shape don't form crystals and are called amorphous.

Secret Note

Silly Putty™ is a polymer also known as polydimethyldichlorosilane (wow!). A polymer is a long chain of many simple molecules bonded together. These simple molecules are called monomers. Polymers may be human-made (e.g., plastic or silly putty) or natural (e.g., wood). Yes, real forensic scientists actually do use this same silly putty technique to help solve crimes.

Powders

Starch is a long chain of repeating simple sugar molecules bonded together to form what is known as a polymer. When iodine is added to a starch, a chemical reaction takes place. In this chemical reaction, the long chain of sugar molecules that make up starch is slowly broken down into separate simple sugar molecules. When iodine is *first* added and the chains are just beginning to break down, the simple sugars react with the iodine to form a compound whose color is black/blue/purple. As the chains continue to break down into smaller pieces, the color gradually turns to red. When it turns colorless, the starch chains have completely broken down, leaving only simple sugars. See the special note on page 170 concerning iodine and safety issues.

Tape Lift

Forensic scientists actually do use adhesive tape to help solve crimes, just as you students do in *Mystery Festival*. In an actual forensic study, however, scientists would also use microscopes to, for example, compare the hairs found with those from a variety of individuals/animals.

DNA "Fingerprinting"

DNA stands for ***deoxyribonucleic acid,*** which is found in the cells of nearly every living thing, and in many viruses. It is essentially an instruction manual for how to make an individual, down to the last detail. Each of us carries a unique genetic pattern in our DNA; each human being's DNA is different from every other individual's (except for identical twins, triplets etc.). If skin, semen, root hairs, or other DNA-containing substances are found at the scene of a crime, the DNA can be compared with that of suspects to identify the culprit. Just as importantly, evidence derived from DNA found at the scene can sometimes prove that someone did NOT commit a crime, or provide other important information about what happened to the victim or how the crime took place. Because of this, **the scientific process called "DNA fingerprinting" has been described by some as the most important breakthrough in crime solving since fingerprinting.**

Genetic or ***DNA "fingerprinting"*** has received increasing attention as laboratory techniques for analysis of DNA become more sophisticated, reliable, and widespread. The use of the term "fingerprinting" is of course not meant literally. DNA "fingerprinting" has been accepted as evidence in some courtrooms and other legal situations, although not yet universally—reliability and standardization of testing procedures remain issues. There are also concerns that the DNA of members of smaller ethnic and religious groups who have tended to intermarry are much more similar and difficult to distinguish and individualize than that of the general population.

To make a DNA "fingerprint," enzymes are added to a sample of DNA. These particular enzymes are used because they cut DNA at specific places, called "restriction sites." The chopped-up DNA is then forced up through a gel, using the attractive power of an electrical current. This separates the pieces of DNA according to size. The gel is porous, with "holes" in it, so the smaller pieces of DNA go through more easily than larger ones. When an investigator shines a special light through the gel, the pieces of DNA light up and look like bands of different widths at various places in the gel. The DNA charts of the "suspects" that the students compare in the "Felix" mystery are approximations of these bands. The number and widths of the bands that are made by certain known sections of the suspect's DNA are compared to the DNA found at the scene of the crime.

Human DNA is arranged in 46 long threads known as ***chromosomes***. DNA contains the genetic instructions that allow an organism to create a multitude of ***proteins***. There are about 50,000 proteins found in cells for every part and special function of the human body. The protein keratin, for example, is a major part of cells that become hair; the protein melanin is a major part of cells that protect and color skin; actin and myosin are proteins that help muscles move. Each "recipe" for a specific protein is called a ***gene***. DNA contains the genetic information and biochemical instructions to make these and all the other needed proteins, and thus to specify and create in complex detail—to spell out—the genetic characteristics of a new organism—be it plant, panther, or famous detective! Although DNA as a biochemical entity was first described and named in 1869, it was not until the 1950s that scientists Alfred Hershey and Martha Chase identified DNA as the hereditary material. Soon after, James D. Watson, Francis Crick, and Maurice Wilkins discovered the *"**double-helix**"* shape or spiraling biochemical structure of DNA.

There is an excellent article on "Genetic Fingerprinting" by Pauline Lowrie and Susan Wells in New Scientist magazine, Number 52, November 16, 1991. The article explains what a DNA fingerprint is, and how it is recorded as patterns in a gel (somewhat similar to the chromatography techniques in the GEMS guide Crime Lab Chemistry). The article also explains the use of DNA fingerprinting in the identification of rapists, other legal and medical applications, and discusses reliability controversies. New Scientist carried another article, in the March 31, 1990 issue, entitled "Is DNA Fingerprinting Ready for the Courts?" Older students could do a research project on this subject, using current newspaper and magazine articles, to help the class keep up with new scientific and legal developments in this rapidly-changing field.

■■■

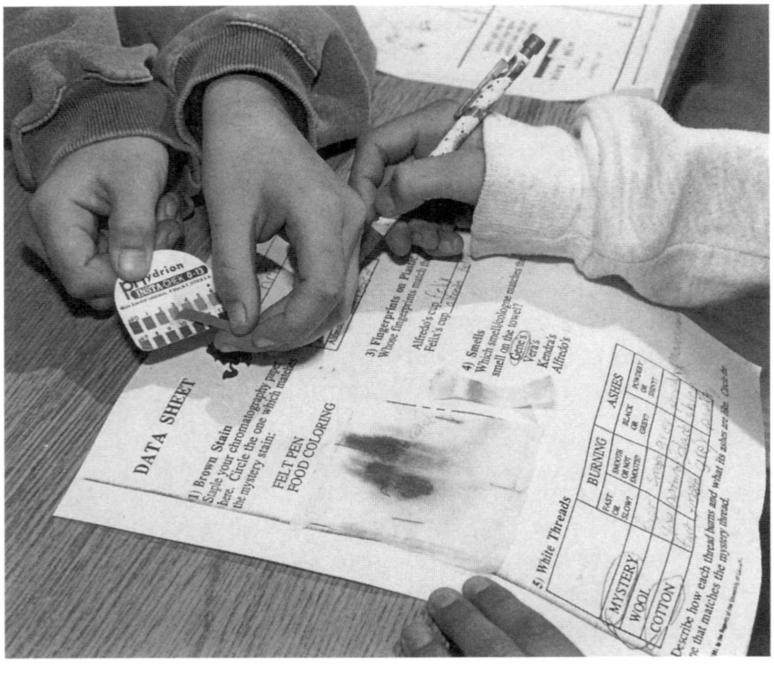

Literature Connections

Naturally, the books listed on the next pages are mysteries of one kind or another. While some are simple and others more complex, they all share in the collection of evidence or clues, and use analysis to make inferences or conclusions. The distinction between evidence and inference is emphasized in the *Mystery Festival* unit and comes alive through its application to a diverse collection of mysterious situations. Some teachers also make use of newspaper articles with their students to explore the evidence/inference distinction further, using articles that describe a crime (usually unsolved), the evidence, and some possible inferences.

There are of course numerous books that focus on solving mysteries. Many of them can make wonderful connections to science and math activities. The process of science and mathematics is, after all, parallel to that of detection and making inferences to solve a problem.

You and your students no doubt have your own favorite mystery stories/books and authors. There are a number of well-known series, such as those involving the Boxcar Children, Encyclopedia Brown, Einstein Anderson, Two-Minute Mysteries, and even the Nancy Drew and Hardy Boys mysteries. Teachers who tested these activities also suggested, among many nominations: Nate the Great books by Marjorie Weinman Sharmat; the Piggins series by Jane Yolen; and the Miss Mallard series by Robert Quackenbush. There are also many new books that combine environmental awareness and respect for diverse cultures with a compelling mystery plot. We would especially welcome hearing about those mysteries that include details of scientific tests and evaluation of evidence similar to those in *Mystery Festival.*

You may also want to refer to the GEMS literature handbook, *Once Upon A GEMS Guide: Connecting Young People's Literature to Great Explorations in Math and Science*, for literature listings under the GEMS guides *Fingerprinting* and *Crime Lab Chemistry*, and for the mathematics strands of Logic and Pattern. For more advanced students, there are many excellent mysteries written for the adult audience that include detailed discussion of evidence and inference, the process of elimination and other logical reasoning processes, and the importance of forensic science and scientists. We have included a few of these here, but there are many more!

Age-appropriate non-fiction books that focus on how famous cases were solved scientifically, or tell more about the work of forensic scientists would also make good accompaniments to this unit. Such accounts would be particularly apt if they involved one or more of the scientific tests that students conduct in *Mystery Festival*, if they delve deeper into subjects like DNA "fingerprinting," and/or especially if they demonstrate how interwoven science and solving mysteries really are. Students could be asked to write the story of a great scientific discovery in typical mystery-story style. The classic book *Microbe Hunters* by Paul de Kruif is as exciting as any fictional mystery, as is *The Double Helix* by James D. Watson, recounting the putting together of puzzle pieces in the search for the structure of DNA.

Both the GEMS literature handbook and this teacher's guide will be revised in future years, and we very much welcome your suggestions for stimulating literature connections to *Mystery Festival.*

Cam Jensen and the Mystery of the Gold Coins
by David A. Adler; illustrated by Susanna Natti
Viking Press, New York. 1982
Dell Publishing, New York. 1984
Grades: 3–5

Cam Jensen uses her photographic memory to solve a theft of two gold coins. Cam and her friend Eric carry around their 5th grade science projects throughout the book and the final scenes take place at the school science fair. (Other titles in the series include *Cam Jensen and the Mystery at the Monkey House* and *Cam Jensen and the Mystery of the Dinosaur Bones* in which she notices that three bones are missing from a museum's mounted dinosaur.)

Chip Rogers: Computer Whiz
by Seymour Simon; illustrated by Steve Miller
William Morrow, New York. 1984
Out of print
Grades: 4–8

Two youngsters, a boy and a girl, solve a gem theft from a science museum by using a computer to classify clues. A computer is also used to weigh variables in choosing a basketball team. Although some details about programming the computer may be a little dated, this is still a good book revolving directly around sorting out evidence, deciding whether or not a crime has been committed, solving it, and demonstrating the role computers can play in human endeavors. By the author of the Einstein Anderson series.

The Eleventh Hour
by Graeme Base
Harry N. Abrams, Publishers, New York. 1988
Grades: 3–8

This uniquely illustrated picture book is about an elephant's eleventh birthday party with other animals as guests. In addition to being an illustrative and poetic *tour de force*, this book is a compelling mystery, and a great connection to *Mystery Festival*. We learn that one of the animals has managed to gobble up the special birthday banquet. All eleven animals are suspects, and the solution is said to be contained in the many layers of clues provided throughout the book. The end of the book is sealed so you can't find out who did it until you think you have it solved!

From the Mixed-Up Files of Mrs. Basil E. Frankweiler
written and illustrated by E.L. Konigsburg
Atheneum, New York. 1967
Dell Publishing, New York. 1977
Grades: 5–8

Twelve-year-old Claudia and her younger brother run away from home to live in the Metropolitan Museum of Art and stumble upon a mystery involving a statue attributed to Michelangelo. This book is a classic, and has been recommended to GEMS by many teachers. Because the detecting techniques used include fingerprinting and chromatography it is a particularly apt connection to *Crime Lab Chemistry* and *Fingerprinting*.

The Great Adventures of Sherlock Holmes
by Arthur Conan Doyle
Viking Penguin, New York. 1990
Grades: 6–Adult

These classic short stories are masterly examples of deduction. Many of the puzzling cases are solved by Holmes in his chemistry lab as he analyzes fingerprints, inks, tobaccos, mud, etc. to solve the crime and catch the criminal. As noted in "Behind the Scenes" inspiration for the first real crime lab is said to have come from these very stories. Various collections of these stories are available from many different publishers and in many editions and make a great connection to *Mystery Festival*.

Let's Go Dinosaur Tracking
by Miriam Schlein; illustrated by Kate Duke
HarperCollins, New York. 1991
Grades: 2–5

The many different types of tracks dinosaurs left behind and what these giant steps reveal is explored. Was the creature running ... chasing a lizard ... browsing on its hind legs for leaves ... traveling in pairs or in a pack ... walking underwater? At the end of the book, you can measure your stride and compare the difference when walking slowly, walking fast, and running. The process involved in attempting to draw conclusions about an animal's behavior or movement patterns from its tracks is similar to the way inferences are drawn from evidence in the GEMS mystery-solving activities. You could discuss with your students how they would weigh the evidence and consider the suspects if, for example, muddy shoeprints of a suspect had also been found at the scene of the crime.

The Missing 'Gator of Gumbo Limbo: An Ecological Mystery
by Jean C. George
HarperCollins, New York. 1992
Grades: 4-7

Sixth-grader Liza K and her mother live in a tent in the Florida Everglades. Liza becomes a nature detective while searching for Dajun, a giant alligator who plays a part in a waterhole's oxygen-algae cycle, and is marked for extinction by local officials. She is motivated to study the delicate ecological balance by her desire to keep her outdoor environment beautiful. This "ecological mystery" combines precise scientific information and important environmental concerns with excellent characterization, a strong female role model, and an exciting, complex plot. For older students, this book connects their detective work in *Mystery Festival* to the real world needs of environmental protection.

Motel of the Mysteries
by David Macaulay
Houghton Mifflin Co., Boston. 1979
Grades: 6-Adult

Presupposing that all knowledge of our present culture has been lost, an amateur archaeologist of the future discovers clues to the lost civilization of "Usa" from a supposed tomb, Room #26 at the Motel of the Mysteries, which protected by a sacred seal ("Do Not Disturb" sign). This book is an elaborate and logically constructed train of inferences based on partial evidence, within a pseudo-archaeological context. Reading this book, whose conclusions they know to be askew, can encourage students to maintain a healthy and irreverent skepticism about their own and other's inferences and conclusions, while providing insight into the intricacies and pitfalls of the reasoning involved. This book can help deepen the practical experiences students have gained in distinguishing evidence from inference. It also helps demonstrate, in a humorous and effective way, the connection between detective work and t he science of archaeology.

The Mystery of the Stranger in the Barn
by True Kelley
Dodd, Mead, & Co., New York. 1986
Grades: K–4

A discarded hat and disappearing objects seem to prove that a mysterious stranger is hiding out in the barn, but no one ever sees anyone. A good opportunity to contrast evidence and inference.

The One Hundredth Thing About Caroline
by Lois Lowry
Houghton Mifflin, Boston. 1983
Dell Publishing, New York. 1991
Grades: 5–9

Fast-moving and often humorous book about 11-year-old Caroline, an aspiring paleontologist, and her friend Stacy's attempts to conduct investigations. Caroline becomes convinced that a neighbor has ominous plans to "eliminate" the children and Stacy speculates about the private life of a famous neighbor. Due to hasty misinterpretations of real evidence, both prove to be wildly wrong in their inferences. Gathering evidence, weighing it, and deciding what makes sense are good accompanying themes. A somewhat inaccurate portrayal of "color blindness" is a minor flaw.

The Real Thief
by William Steig
Farrar, Straus & Giroux, New York. 1973
Grades: 4-8

King Basil and Gawain, devoted Chief Guard, are the only two in the kingdom who have keys to the Royal Treasury. When rubies, gold ducats, and finally the world-famous Kalikak diamond disappear, Gawain is brought to trial for the thefts. But is he the real thief? As the mystery unfolds, it becomes clear that it is important to investigate fully before making judgments or drawing conclusions.

Susannah and the Blue House Mystery
by Patricia Elmore
E.P. Dutton, New York. 1980
Scholastic, New York. 1990
Grades: 5–7

Susannah (an amateur herpetologist) and Lucy have formed a detective agency. They check into the death of a kindly old antique dealer who lived in the mysterious "Blue House." They attempt to piece together clues in hopes of finding the treasure they think he has left to one of them. The detectives evaluate evidence, work together to solve problems, and prevent a camouflaged theft from taking place.

Susannah and the Poison Green Halloween
by Patricia Elmore
E.P. Dutton, New York. 1982
Scholastic., New York. 1990
Grades: 5–7

Susannah and her friends try to figure out who put the poison in their Halloween candy when they trick-or-treated at the Eucalyptus Arms apartments. Tricky clues, changing main suspects, and some medical chemistry make this an excellent choice, with lots of inference and mystery. (There is also mention of a field trip to the Lawrence Hall of Science!)

The Tattooed Potato and Other Clues
by Ellen Raskin
E.P. Dutton, New York. 1975
Penguin Books, New York. 1989
Grades: 6-9

Answering an advertisement for a portrait painter's assistant in New York City involves a 17-year-old in several mysteries and their ultimate solution, such as the "Case of the Face on the Five Dollar Bill" where the smudged thumbprint of the counterfeiter is a clue.

The Westing Game
by Ellen Raskin
E.P. Dutton, New York. 1978
Avon, New York. 1984
Grades: 6-10

The mysterious death of an eccentric millionaire brings together an unlikely assortment of 16 beneficiaries. According to instructions contained in his will, they are divided into eight pairs and given a set of clues to solve his murder and thus claim the inheritance. Newbery award winner.

Who Really Killed Cock Robin?
by Jean Craighead George
HarperCollins, New York. 1991
Grades: 3–7

A compelling ecological mystery examines the importance of keeping nature in balance, and provides an inspiring account of a young environmental hero who becomes a scientific detective.

Whose Footprints?
by Masayuki Yabuuchi
Philomel Books, New York. 1983
Grades: K–4

A good guessing game for younger students that depicts the footprints of a duck, cat, bear, horse, hippopotamus, and goat.

YOU ARE THE JUDGE —YOU ARE THE JURY

If your students became intensely involved in evaluating evidence and determining possible guilt in *Mystery Festival*, we recommend the *Be the Judge • Be the Jury*™ book series by award-winning children's author Doreen Rappaport, as an excellent extension to these GEMS activities. The books in this series describe famous court cases, simplified for young people. In the beginning of each book the different roles and procedures of a courtroom trial are clearly and simply defined. The reader becomes the jury, to whom first the prosecution, then the defense, present their evidence and witnesses. After closing statements, the instructions of the judge to the jury are included. As the reader, you are then expected to come up with your own verdict, so you can't help but feel drawn in and become very actively involved in the trial. At the end of the book, the actual verdict of the trial is revealed, with historical perspective. The following books are currently available: The Lizzie Borden Trial, The Sacco-Vanzetti Trial, The Alger Hiss Trial, and Tinker vs. Des Moines: Student Rights on Trial. We recommend these books for the way they strongly involve young readers in the important process of evaluating evidence and drawing inferences, as well as for their historical and social interest. The author is quoted as saying she wrote the series "because I was on a jury once and found out how hard and scary and important it was deciding the fate of another human being." The series is published by Harper Collins Children's Books, A Division of Harper Collins Publishers, 10 East 53rd Street, New York NY 10022.

Large Group Festival Notes

In this guide, we have included listings of materials needed for presenting large group versions of both the Mr. Bear and Felix mysteries. These listings begin on page 250. In future editions of this guide, we intend to publish more detailed instructions for the presentation of a Large Group Mystery Festival. If you are interested in presenting a large group festival and would like to receive more information, please contact "Felix" at the GEMS project. Your comments on this information will help us further refine the Large Group instructions for inclusion in the next edition of this guide!

The original Lawrence Hall of Science Mystery Festival program was designed as an outreach program to be taken to different schools and serve an entire school in a day, with each session accommodating up to 150 students. In this teacher's guide we have adapted this program to enable a teacher or team of teachers to put on the program with just her own class or classes, at classroom learning stations. In the classroom version, students have the advantage of being able to spend five sessions studying details of the crime, and can develop their thinking and problem-solving skills over time. The set-up and materials acquisition can be daunting for an individual teacher, and for this and many other reasons, some schools may prefer to plan and present a large group version, which is also highly suitable for after-school programs, community centers and group gatherings. Although the time allotted is much shorter in the large group version, it has the advantage of being able to reach an entire school in one or two days, generating more whole-school excitement. In addition, preparation can be shared with even more other teachers, or even taken on by industrious parent volunteers. The following information is for those who wish to do the large group version with their school.

In the large group version, the crime lab stations (plus the crime scene) are set up at tables in a multipurpose-type room, or in smaller rooms adjacent to each other. As the students enter, they sit down on the floor surrounding the crime scene, and listen to an introduction given by the Mystery Festival leader. After hearing about the suspects, scenario, and festival procedure, the students are sent to the learning stations to do tests on the "evidence." Each station is monitored by an adult volunteer, who makes sure students understand the procedures, and that the station activity flows well. (*Please note*: The Mystery Festival that Lawrence Hall of Science takes to schools actually has 12 stations. The additional two, "Hidden Prints" and "Invisible Inks" make use of silver nitrate and phenolphthalein solutions and involve more preparation. Although they are both interesting, neither of these two stations is critical to solving the mystery. The ten stations described in this teacher's guide already provide plenty of activity, complexity, scientific/technical knowledge, as well as revealing clues and results.)

At the end of the Festival, the students take their data with them back to their classrooms where they attempt to solve the crime in a format selected by their teacher. If the festival is being used on a parent/child night, or some other setting where they cannot reassemble in class groups, you can make take-home sheets for students to state their ideas about the solution to the mystery.

Do you n**eed to collect two completely different sets of materials if your school wants to run both the older and younger mystery programs?** The two mysteries were designed so that many of the materials and stations involved are shared by both, with minimal modifications. While some schools are able to switch between the two mysteries in one day, other schools offer one mystery on one day, then switch to the other the next day. **The large group materials listings for both mysteries which follow these notes should be helpful in your preparation.**

How many stations are enough? To make sure students don't have to spend too much time waiting in line, and that they get enough adult volunteer help, you should set up at least one station (including the crime scene) for every 12 students for the "Felix" mystery, or one for every eight students at the "Mr. Bear" mystery. By setting up two of some stations, such as two "Brown Stain" stations and two "Powders" stations, you can accommodate more students.

Getting Help

The key to conducting a successful Large Group Mystery Festival is having enough stations, and an adult volunteer at every station. It's also a good idea to enlist a couple of extra volunteers per session, in case you have "no-shows." **Do not consider running the large group Mystery Festival without volunteers.** Volunteers are especially important with younger students, and it's generally agreed that the more adults present, the better. You'll be surprised how easy it is to get adult volunteers to come (a Mystery Festival is far more appealing than carpooling). It has been our experience that adult volunteers enjoy the experience of Mystery Festival nearly as much as the children! In fact, we have had schools tell us that after one of our festivals they were deluged with volunteers for other activities.

If most of the parents in your school community work, and you are having a hard time obtaining a team of volunteers, you could: 1) Invite grandparents; 2) Contact a local branch of the American Association of Retired People; 3) Set up two tables of the same activity next to each other, so that one adult can monitor both tables; 4) Enlist *mature* high school students; 5) Allow a few stations to run without volunteers. (Although we strongly recommend against this latter option, the following stations are the easiest to allow to run without a volunteer, if absolutely necessary: **Mr. Bear**: Threads, Smells, Secret Note; **Felix**: Smells, DNA, Fingerprints on Cups); 6) Use teacher aides. We strongly recommend against the use of teachers, however, since they will be leading the follow-up afterward. Your classroom teachers need an understanding of the overall mystery, and will benefit greatly from the opportunity to observe their students and perform or witness the tests at **all** the stations.

To help you enlist the help of volunteers, we have included a sample letter to volunteers. It is extremely important to stress to volunteers that the students **need to do their own tests and make their own discoveries, and that their role as volunteers is to help create the conditions for that student discovery to happen.**

(Sample Letter to Volunteers)

Dear Mystery Festival Volunteer:

We're delighted that you will be available to help out at the Mystery Festival. *The Mystery Festival program was developed at the Lawrence Hall of Science at the University of California at Berkeley, and has been a huge success in schools all around the country The volunteers who have participated deserve a lot of the credit! The students who attend are intrigued by the mystery and it's fun to watch the gears turn in their heads as they use critical thinking skills and deductive reasoning to try to solve the made-up crime. Most of the students' time in the festival will be spent performing hands-on experiments at each forensic test station. After the festival they will use their data back in their classrooms to attempt to "solve the crime."*

What to expect at the Mystery Festival: *You'll see a room full of activity stations, surrounding a central "crime scene." When the students enter, they will all sit on the floor for an introduction to the "crime" by the Mystery Festival leader. During the introduction they will hear about the suspects, situation, and general festival procedures. After the introduction they will work in pairs, going to as many stations as they have time for before the festival ends. Each station involves some type of forensic test which will help to solve the crime later on. Students use thread tests, fingerprint comparisons, chromatography, pH tests, and powder tests, to name a few stations. Each station has procedure signs and equipment/materials to perform the test.*

What your role is at the Mystery Festival: *You will be in charge of one of the forensic stations. Your role will be to make sure that the students who come to your station understand what the challenge is, and get a chance to participate and* ***make their own discoveries and conclusions****. You'll quickly become an expert as you help dozens of youngsters—your suggestions, hints, and encouragement to students will be invaluable.*

How you can prepare for the Mystery Festival: We will meet 15–30 minutes before the festival for a brief orientation meeting and for you to have time to try out the experiment at your station.

If you will be assisting during the entire Mystery Festival: *Between sessions, neaten up at your station—and don't forget to take a break when appropriate—you might want to bring a snack for yourself. Let the Mystery Festival leader know if you are having problems with the equipment or with one of the activities. You may get tired of being at the same station all day—find someone who would like to trade stations with you, show each other "the ropes," and go ahead and trade. At the end of the day we ask that volunteers spend 10–15 minutes helping us clean up and pack each station.*

If you will be assisting during just one session: *Neaten the station before you leave. If you meet the volunteer for the next session, pass on some advice. If something did not work smoothly, let the Mystery Festival leader know.*

Thank you in advance for your participation, and prepare to have a lot of fun!

Mr. Bear Mystery: Large Group Festival

• Shopping & Gathering List •

(for a group of about 100 students).

See page 97 for a sample letter asking parents to contribute materials.

- ❒ 7 identical stuffed teddy bears
- ❒ 4 other varied stuffed animals
- ❒ a long piece of string or rope to barricade the crime scene (~ 50 feet)
- ❒ ~ 20 inches of colored wool yarn
- ❒ ~ 20 inches of white cotton yarn
- ❒ ~ 20 inches of colored cotton yarn
- ❒ ~100 pencils
- ❒ 2 brown felt water-base markers of the same brand
- ❒ 1 large felt marker
- ❒ 2 packages of white paper towels
- ❒ ~36 feet. butcher paper or a white drop cloth at least 9 feet x 12 feet
- ❒ 11 sheets of 30" x 20" paper
- ❒ 30 sheets of 8 1/2" x 11" white paper
- ❒ 2 rolls of pH paper (the exact brand is not important)
- ❒ 1 roll of masking tape
- ❒ 1 pair of scissors
- ❒ 6 rolls of transparent tape
- ❒ 22 clear plastic cups
- ❒ 8 empty film canisters
- ❒ 3 ice cube trays
- ❒ 8 white test trays (Styrofoam egg cartons cut in half work well. If these are not available, use white plastic paint trays from an art store or white ice cube trays.)
- ❒ 8 small dropper bottles (empty medicine dropper bottles, saline fluid bottles or similar small bottles are fine)
- ❒ 2 empty cola cans
- ❒ 1 full can of cola
- ❒ ~8 oz. of baking soda
- ❒ ~32 oz. of corn starch
- ❒ 1/2 teaspoon of salt
- ❒ 1 1/2 teaspoons of sugar
- ❒ ~8 oz. of iodine
- ❒ 1 oz. of red food coloring
- ❒ 1/2 oz. of green food coloring
- ❒ stir stick
- ❒ 1/4 teaspoon
- ❒ 8 1/8 teaspoons (or use 1/4 teaspoons & have students estimate half)
- ❒ 1 paintbrush (any kind)
- ❒ 1 paint container (a plate or cup is fine)
- ❒ 2 colognes or perfumes, as distinctive as possible. (get samples from department stores, your bathroom cabinet, magazines etc.)
- ❒ 4 small mirrors, preferably with stands (clay works as a make-shift stand)
- ❒ 3 large plastic trash bags
- ❒ 2 sponges
- ❒ ~ 90 strands of pet hair (cat or dog hair is fine)
- ❒ ~ 1 tablespoon of grass
- ❒ 1 apron
- ❒ 2 dishtubs

Pages to be copied from this guide:

- ❒ Clue Board illustrations (pages 39-48)
- ❒ 8 copies of the "Suspect Fingerprints" sheet (page 63)
- ❒ 8 copies of the "Cup Fingerprints" sheet (page 62)
- ❒ 16 copies of the "Mr. Bear Footprints" sheet (page 31)
- ❒ 8 copies of each of the station signs (pages 66-70, 178-185)
- ❒ for every two students: 1 copy of the "Mr. Bear Mystery Data Sheet"

Felix Mystery - Large Group Festival

• Shopping & Gathering List •

(for a group of about 100 students)

See page 200 for a sample letter asking parents to contribute materials.

- ❒ ~10 feet of white cotton yarn
- ❒ ~10 feet of colored cotton yarn
- ❒ ~10 feet of colored wool yarn
- ❒ a long piece of string or rope to barricade the crime scene (~65 feet)
- ❒ ~36 ft. of butcher paper or a white drop cloth at least 9 ft. x 12 ft.
- ❒ 11 sheets of 20" x 30" paper
- ❒ 4 rolls of pH paper with charts (the exact brand is not important)
- ❒ 2 packages of white paper towels
- ❒ 3 pieces of 8 1/2" x 11" tag board (the backing of note pads work fine)
- ❒ ~100 pencils
- ❒ 2 brown felt water-base markers of the same brand
- ❒ 1 large felt marker
- ❒ 1 permanant marker (for labeling)
- ❒ 1 pair of scissors
- ❒ 1 roll of masking tape
- ❒ 8 rolls of transparent tape
- ❒ 4 metric rulers
- ❒ 40 clear plastic cups
- ❒ 4 one gallon size zip lock bags
- ❒ 10 dropper bottles (empty medicine dropper bottles, saline fluid bottles orsimilar small bottles are fine)
- ❒ 8 white test trays ("styrofoam" egg cartons cut in half work well, if these are not available, use white plastic paint trays from an art store or white ice cube trays.)
- ❒ 8 empty film canisters
- ❒ 1 full can of cola
- ❒ 2 empty cola cans
- ❒ ~32 oz. of baking soda
- ❒ ~32 oz. of corn starch
- ❒ ~8 oz. of iodine
- ❒ 10 1/8 teaspoons (or use a 1/4 teaspoon and have students estimate half)
- ❒ 1 oz. of red food coloring
- ❒ 1/2 oz. of green food coloring
- ❒ 1 paintbrush
- ❒ 1 empty paint container (plate or cup is fine)
- ❒ 3 ice cube trays
- ❒ 3 wastebaskets
- ❒ 1 chocolate candy wrapper
- ❒ 3 identical white cotton towels (any size)
- ❒ 1 comb with several strands of human hair
- ❒ 1 "broken" alarm clock
- ❒ 4 colognes or perfumes, as distinctive as possible (get samples from department stores, bathroom cabinet, magazines etc.).
- ❒ 1 small container of Krazy Glue®
- ❒ 4 sheets of aluminum foil~12" x 16"
- ❒ 8 votive candles
- ❒ 1 box of matches
- ❒ At least 8 pairs of goggles (16 pairs would be ideal, swimming, snorkeling, ski or safety goggles are all fine)
- ❒ 8 pairs of metal tweezers, tongs or equivalent
- ❒ 8 small mirrors, preferably with stands (clay works as a make-shift stand)
- ❒ 4 "eggs" of Silly Putty™
- ❒ 4 old sweaters or t-shirts
- ❒ ~ 90 strands of pet hair (cat or dog hair is fine)
- ❒ small amounts of human hair, grass, threads
- ❒ 3 large plastic trash bags
- ❒ 2 sponges
- ❒ 2 dishtubs
- ❒ 1 apron (plastic is ideal)

The following items are optional, but may be used to spice up the crime scene:

- ❒ 1 guitar pick
- ❒ 1 pair of sunglasses
- ❒ 1 clip-on earring
- ❒ spilled carpet tacks

continued ▶

Pages to be copied from this guide:

- ❒ pictures of suspects (pages 141–144))
- ❒ 8 copies of the "DNA Fingerprints" sheet (page 178)
- ❒ 8 copies of the "Suspect Fingerprints" sheet (page 130)
- ❒ 8 copies of the "Suspect Handwriting Samples" sheet (page 185)
- ❒ 8 copies of the "Tape lift Examples" sheet (page 184)
- ❒ 16 copies of the "Suspect Footprints" sheet (page 129)
- ❒ for every two students: 1 copy of the "Felix Mystery Data Sheet"
- ❒ 8 copies of each station sign (pages 160-164, 178-185)

THE PLAN WORKED UNTIL. . .
Alfredo and Kendra sneak up on Felix and
cover his mouth with her towel drenched
with Gene's cologne . . . All the materials
they gathered earlier are carefully placed
on the patio. They have fiendishly planned
this day ever since they found out they
were in Felix's will . . . Their plan was clever
yet baffling . . . Alfredo's and Kendra's plan
worked until the case was handed over to
Mr. Fenner's first four class!

Assessment Suggestions

Selected Student Outcomes

1. Students improve their ability to make careful observations.
2. Students are able to compare known samples to unknown clues.
3. Students improve their ability to distinguish evidence from inference, make logical inferences based on partial evidence, and evaluate whether various inferences are plausible or implausible.
4. Students improve their ability to draw conclusions.
5. Students demonstrate an increased understanding of how scientific methods are used to solve crimes.

Built-In Assessment Activities

Active Observers. In the introductory "A Note About Pre-Teaching," several activities are suggested to encourage your students to be active observers. These activities (Sharp Eyes, Find the Change, and Composite Drawing) challenge students to notice small changes. If used as a pre- and post-unit assessment, they will provide students with an opportunity to hone their observation skills and offer teachers an opportunity to see students' observation skills in action. (Outcome 1)

Footprint Activities. A number of footprint activities appear in "A Note About Pre-Teaching." Find that Print and Footprint Concentration offer opportunities to observe students as they match known and unknown clues (footprints). Footprint Mysteries and Student Footprint Mysteries enable the teacher to observe students as they draw conclusions based on evidence. All of these activities can be used before and/or after the unit. (Outcomes 2, 4)

Solving the Mystery: Session 5, Solving the Mystery, offers the teacher three options to have students evaluate their findings and attempt to solve the mystery. To assess students' abilities to think logically and distinguish evidence from inference, listen carefully to the reasons they use to support their conclusions. If no written work is involved, teachers may need to interview students to discern the reasons why they believe a particular suspect is guilty. (Outcomes 3, 4)

Additional Assessment Ideas

Newspaper Article: The teacher reads aloud a scenario about a possible arson. With a written version of the scenario, the students are asked to identify the unfair inferences made in a newspaper article about the situation and then to rewrite the article to better reflect the facts and avoid unfair inferences. (Outcome 2)

Science In Action: Invite local detectives, criminalists, or forensic experts to visit your classroom. Have students prepare questions to find out how these investigators use scientific techniques (for example, fingerprinting, chromatography, DNA analysis, etc.) to solve crimes. Students can then write a summary of what they learned through the interview. (Outcome 5)

Note: *Insights and Outcomes: Assessments for Great Explorations in Math and Science,* the GEMS assessment handbook, includes a classroom case study featuring the newspaper article assessment idea, as well as many other assessment strategies that could be adapted for *Mystery Festival.* The handbook is available from GEMS and includes selected student outcomes for the entire GEMS series.

GARY AMBROSE / Los Angeles Times

Student sleuths Rebecca Box, left, and Jessica MacDonald wear goggles while burning thread in "murder" investigation.

This Course Is Murder

School Sleuths Use Elementary Deductions to Learn 'Who Killed Mr. Felix?'

By LILY ENG
TIMES STAFF WRITER

HUNTINGTON BEACH—It's a murder dying to be solved: There's an outline of a dead body on the patio of a luxurious beach house. Somewhere around it are a couple of fingerprints, as well as a few thread fragments and strands of hair. And four people have a motive to kill the extremely rich victim.

It's up to the most resourceful and up-to-date medical examiner in the room to solve the murder. But it won't be Quincy in this case.

Instead, a slew of pint-size medical examiners from the Ocean View School District are ready to martial their classroom science and chemistry to settle the case of "Who Killed Mr. Felix?"

The students have just an hour to find the clues, analyze them at 14 makeshift laboratory stations and draw their conclusions, Sherlock Holmes style.

"Mr. Felix is no longer with us, and it's up to you to find out who killed him," visiting science coordinator Kevin Beals told the sixth- and seventh-graders from Spring View and Harbour View elementary schools who assembled Tuesday at the beach house (in truth, the auditorium of Spring View).

The premise of the science lesson is elementary: Youngsters have to check fingerprints, analyze threads and dismiss the red herrings that pop up at the scene of the crime. They don't have the help of Mr. Felix's body. That was stolen as soon as it got to the morgue. But the students do have their classroom science skills to put to good use.

Beals, who works for an educational foundation at UC Berkeley, created the learning game with the assistance of real forensic specialists as part of an educational program to

Please see SLEUTHS, B7

SLEUTHS: Case of Murder Tests Students' Skills

GARY AMBROSE / Los Angeles Times

Elementary school students examine clues at sealed "murder" scene, including outline of victim's body.

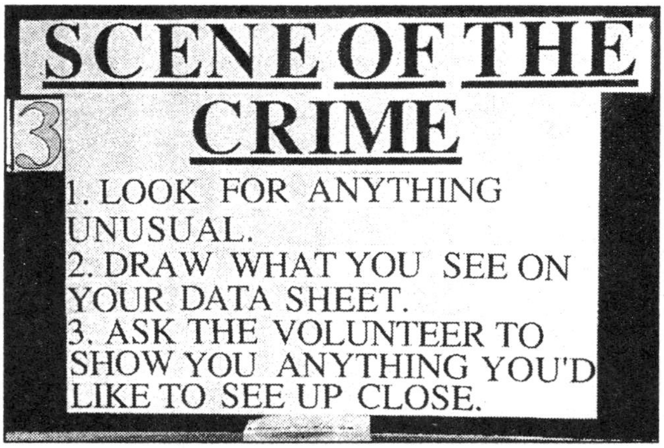
SCENE OF THE CRIME
13
1. LOOK FOR ANYTHING UNUSUAL.
2. DRAW WHAT YOU SEE ON YOUR DATA SHEET.
3. ASK THE VOLUNTEER TO SHOW YOU ANYTHING YOU'D LIKE TO SEE UP CLOSE.

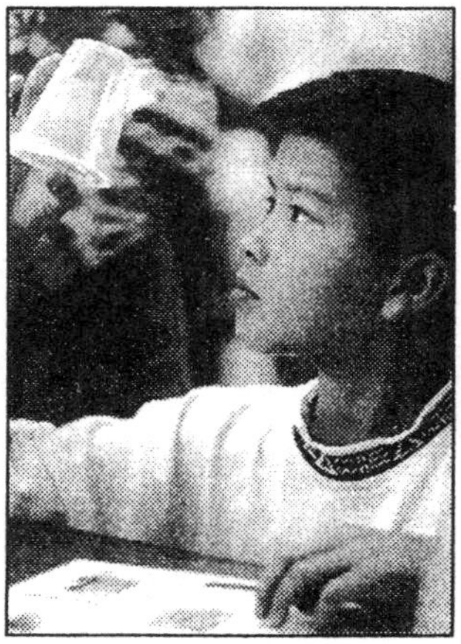

Sign at 13th of 14 stations, left, offers hints to likes of medical examiner Hoang Nguyen, checking a print.

Continued from B1

stimulate children's interest in science. The traveling program encourages youngsters to use their natural curiosity to solve mysteries. As a bonus, the student sleuths learn the latest crime techniques.

For example, scientists have found that gas emitted from Crazy Glue can lift fingerprints from certain surfaces, and the young sleuths were using the device to lift fingerprints from a glass.

As murders go, this one was a curious incident: Mr. Felix was a rich fellow who was extremely disliked. He was remodeling his beach house over the weekend with the help of four friends, all of whom are named in his will.

After Felix is killed, his best friends are the prime suspects.

They are: Vera Cruise, a chemist who likes brown M&Ms and white wool sweaters; Alfredo Fettuccine, a computer programmer who carries a brown felt pen in his pocket; Kendra Goode, an artist who has white powder stuck on her sneaker; and Gene Poule, a car mechanic, who is always followed by his faithful dog, Sasha.

All have a fondness for strong cologne and prefer sneakers and sandals to shoes.

According to the scenario, it is Alfredo who finds Felix sprawled on the floor of his patio. The two had chugged down some Cokes before Alfredo went to the restroom. When he returned, Felix was dead. At the scene of the crime are footprints, empty Coke cans, strands of hair and other pieces of evidence.

After a brief introduction to the murder scene, the game was on.

"It was Gene, the auto mechanic, definitely," surmised Brianna Bowden, 12, who inspected the murder scene with her crime-solving partner, Lori Seely, also 12. They pointed to paw prints near the body's outline.

"You see, Gene has a dog and you know he must have been around if the dog's prints are here," explained Brianna, who admits that she watches reruns of Alfred Hitchcock.

"Right," interjected Lori, who is partial to "Father Dowling Mysteries." "We also found sandal prints. Gene wore sandals."

It was Gene, definitely. But wait. What about the seemingly blank piece of paper that turned out to have a note written in invisible ink? It also was found near Felix's body.

And how to explain the fingerprints found on the Coke cans? Don't they point to another suspect?

"It was Kendra, the artist, definitely," declared students Cory Calcagno and Omar Qureshi, both 11.

"There's paint and a brush near the body. Kendra's an artist. It's got to be her," Cory said.

"Wrong," countered Lori after 30 more minutes of sleuthing.

"It's a conspiracy," whispered Lori in her best Oliver Stone impersonation. "Two of them plotted together to kill the guy."

So what do their teachers think?

"We have no idea," said George Fotinakes and John Keiter, who will help piece the murder and its perpetrator together in their upcoming science lessons. "It's a great mystery."

Beals is the only one who knows who the killer really is. And he won't tell anybody—even when he or she begs.

"Why take away all the fun?" Beals said. "They'll never know everything in a crime. That's part of the challenge of science."

KENDRA: SOMETHING IN ME SNAPPED . . .

When Felix announced that he was having a housewarming party, I didn't think much about it. But since everyone else was going, I decided to go. When we arrived at the house, I saw what kind of money Felix had. And when he told us we were all equally placed in the will, something in me snapped. I wanted that money now. I had to kill Felix. A shower helps me think, so I took one hoping for an idea on how to kill Felix. I was saying some ideas to myself and as I opened the door I saw Alfredo standing there with his ear pressed to the door. I realized he'd heard every word I said. I pulled him into the bathroom and told him my plan to kill Felix. To my surprise he agreed to help me right away. He said he was just having a drink with Felix. When I walked outside I saw Gene's shoes. This gave me the idea to frame both Vera and Gene, to put Alfredo and me in the clear. I grabbed the first thing I saw, Gene's cologne from the counter, and went downstairsto "talk" to Felix. I walked onto the patio and saw Felix ligh dozing in a chair. I spilled the cologne onto the floor and mopped it up with an old towel. I dumped half the bottle into the glass and shook Felix awake. Still groggy from sleep he took it gratefully and guzzled it down. Then Alfredo, being the klutz he is, knocked over a can of paint. That gave me the idea to make Gene's shoes lead a path away from the crime scene. Then that stupid dog followed the smell on the shoes and tracked through the paint too. I checked Felix's pulse and figured he was dead. By then it was 3:00. Alfredo had the dumb idea to use the fake blood he had left over from drama camp last summer ... Before we left for the hospital I wrote a fake note to Martha (who is Felix's old girlfriend and Vera's close friend) and signed it from Vera ... At the hospital the police told us about how an autopsy could tell them how Felix died. At that time, I started crying and excused myself and went to the bathroom, then down to the morgue. I ripped off the identification tag and put a fake one on. Then I stashed it in an empty locker. What a hard way to earn some bucks.

Notes